TEXAS
SPORTS

**JACK AND DORIS
SMOTHERS SERIES IN
TEXAS HISTORY, LIFE,
AND CULTURE,**
NUMBER FORTY-SIX

CHAD S.
CONINE

TEXAS
SPORTS

Unforgettable
Stories for Every
Day of the Year

UNIVERSITY OF
TEXAS PRESS

Austin

Publication of this work was made possible
in part by support from the J. E. Smothers Sr.
Memorial Foundation and the National
Endowment for the Humanities.

Requests for permission to reproduce material from
this work should be sent to:
    Permissions
    University of Texas Press
    P.O. Box 7819
    Austin, TX 78713–7819
    utpress.utexas.edu/rp-form

♾ The paper used in this book meets the minimum
requirements of ANSI/NISO Z39.48–1992 (R1997)
(Permanence of Paper).

Library of Congress Cataloging-in-Publication Data

Names: Conine, Chad S. (Samuel), 1977–, author.
Title: Texas sports : unforgettable stories for every day
    of the year / Chad S. Conine.
Description: First edition. | Austin : University of Texas
    Press, 2017. | Includes bibliographical references
    and index.
Identifiers: LCCN 2017009445
    ISBN 978-1-4773-1273-5 (cloth : alk. paper)
    ISBN 978-1-4773-1499-9 (library e-book)
    ISBN 978-1-4773-1500-2 (nonlibrary e-book)
Subjects: LCSH: Sports—Texas—History—20th century. |
    Sports—Texas—History—21st century.
Classification: LCC GV584.T4 C66 2017 | DDC
    796.09764—dc23
LC record available at https://lccn.loc.gov/2017009445

doi:10.7560/312735

To John and Shana Conine.
I'll call you after the game.

Contents

INTRODUCTION   1

January   4
February   24
March   42
April   62
May   82
June   104
July   124
August   142
September   162
October   180
November   200
December   220

SOURCES   243
ACKNOWLEDGMENTS   247
INDEX OF SPORTS   249
GENERAL INDEX   251

Introduction

I wrote most of this book in the first six months of 2016. It was interesting, at least to me, to see how the writing of it evolved. At first, with the whole calendar open and waiting to be filled, I would pick a subject—Earl Campbell or Hakeem Olajuwon or Sheryl Swoopes or Nolan Ryan or Jody Conradt—and find a few highlight-worthy days to write about that Texas sports personality. From this start, the research branched out into events like the Super Bowl or the Ryder Cup, but the process stayed basically the same and worked for a long time, for the first 250 entries or so. It served its purpose well and gave me a greater perspective on the pervasiveness of Texas and Texans in sport. When it came to the final hundred days to write, I took a break and traveled to St. Andrews, Scotland, to play golf and hang out in a pub I love, one, not coincidentally, owned by Texans (one native and one adopted).

While sitting in the pub one afternoon, I met a gentleman from Buffalo, New York. Like me, he had come to St. Andrews by himself to play golf and sit at the bar at the Dunvegan. We played golf late in the afternoon and then sat down for dinner. He was a former hockey player and current hockey coach, so I couldn't resist asking him about the 1999 Stanley Cup Finals. The Dallas Stars defeated the Buffalo Sabres in that series, grasping Lord Stanley's cup on a controversial triple-overtime goal by right wing Brett Hull (June 19, 1999). I expected him to react, but I was still thrown by his visceral, severe reply. His face went stone cold and he said, "We don't talk about that."

On my return trip to Texas, I stopped for a day in New York City. I turned on the television in my hotel room and found a Yankees versus Red Sox game in the early innings. The broadcasters were discussing pitcher David Price having signed a photograph commemorating Derek Jeter's 3,000th hit, which Price surrendered, and how it signaled a softening of the rivalry between hitters and pitchers. The broadcaster's first point of reference for the bygone days of vitriolic competition was, of course, the Nolan Ryan versus Robin Ventura brawl (August 4, 1993). That also happened to be the very first day I wrote about.

So there it was. Even on a trip intended as a mental break from writing this book about Texas sports, Texas sports proved inescapable.

As I reached the final days of writing, it became a challenge to identify subjects for specific days, something for April 18 or July 12 or May 14. I scoured old newspapers, hoping to find the right topic. I feared I would have to settle for events more ordinary than had become standard for the preceding 360-something days. But it ended with a testament to Texas sports when I landed on the spectacular high school track career of Nanceen Perry for the subject of the 366th day I wrote about (May 14, 1994).

I know some will argue that I picked the wrong subject for certain days. That kind of disagreement is inevitable, and I invite the debate. I didn't attempt to pick the grandest thing that ever happened on each day. I simply set out to show that Texas sports pack a punch 365 days a year—366 in leap years.

January

JANUARY 1, 1964

Southwest Conference champion and top-ranked Texas rolled to a 28–6 victory over second-ranked Navy, featuring Heisman Trophy winner Roger Staubach, in the Cotton Bowl Classic.

Longhorn quarterback Duke Carlisle tossed first-half touchdown passes of fifty-eight and sixty-three yards to wingback Phil Harris, and Carlisle ran nine yards for another score to boost Texas to a 21–0 lead by halftime.

Though Texas coach Darrell Royal famously eschewed the passing game—saying that only three things can happen when you pass, and two of them are bad—he turned to it to flog the Midshipmen. "We hadn't thrown that deep before," Royal explained in the Associated Press account of the game. "But they were crowding up on us and we had to throw deep."

The Longhorns' defense stymied Staubach and the Navy offense, which finally got on the scoreboard when Staubach ran two yards for a touchdown early in the fourth quarter.

Staubach passed for 228 yards, but it wasn't enough to overcome being thrown for -47 rushing yards by a relentless Texas defense. When asked after the contest which Texas players gave him the most trouble, Staubach had a colorful answer. "Well, they all had me down at one time or another and I didn't notice their numbers," Staubach said.

The Longhorns, already ranked first in the final polls of the season, completed a perfect 11–0 season to claim their first national championship.

JANUARY 2, 1978

Notre Dame, led by junior quarterback Joe Montana, snapped Texas's twelve-game winning streak and ruined the top-ranked Longhorns' bid for a national championship when the Fighting Irish seized a 38–10 victory over Texas in the Cotton Bowl.

Notre Dame running back Vagas Ferguson, the game's offensive most valuable player, ran for touchdowns of three and twenty-six yards and caught a seventeen-yard touchdown pass from Montana to help the Fighting Irish pull away from the Longhorns.

Texas was undone by six turnovers.

"Do you realize what six turnovers will do to your offense?" Longhorns coach Fred Akers asked reporters after the game. "We've had days like that when people turned the ball over to us and we took advantage. It was just one of those days. We had a bad one and Notre Dame had a good one."

By defeating Texas, and benefiting from losses by second-ranked Oklahoma in the Orange Bowl and fourth-ranked Michigan in the Rose Bowl, Notre Dame ascended from the number five ranking to national champion. The Fighting Irish leapfrogged third-ranked Alabama despite the Crimson Tide's 35–6 victory over Ohio State in the Sugar Bowl.

JANUARY 3, 1983

In a *Houston Post* column, sportswriter Thomas Bonk referred to the University of Houston men's basketball team as "Phi Slama Jama."

The nickname stuck and was upheld by Cougars players Clyde Drexler, Hakeem Olajuwon, Benny Anders, Reid Gettys, Michael Young, Larry Micheaux, Ricky Winslow, and others.

JANUARY 4, 2013

Heisman Trophy winner Johnny Manziel passed for 287 yards and two touchdowns and rushed for 229 yards and two more scores in leading Texas A&M to a 41–13 crushing of Oklahoma in the Cotton Bowl.

The Aggies led Oklahoma 14–13 at the half and then poured it on in the third and fourth quarters. Texas A&M scored twenty-seven unanswered points in the second half to cap its first season in the Southeastern Conference with a bowl-game victory over a team from its old league, the Big 12.

Texas A&M finished the season with an 11–2 record, the first time in fourteen seasons that the Aggies had reached double digits in wins. Neither that fact nor his contribution to it was lost on Manziel. "It's huge for this program, and for me especially, with the kind of woes A&M has had over the past decade or however long it's been since they had eleven wins," Manziel said in a postgame interview.

Manziel returned as Texas A&M's starting quarterback in the fall of 2013, but to less spectacular results. The Aggies finished 9–4 in Manziel's final college season before he left school for the NFL.

JANUARY 5, 2009

Texas quarterback Colt McCoy threw a dramatic twenty-six-yard touchdown pass to Quan Cosby with sixteen seconds left in the fourth quarter to lift the third-ranked Longhorns to a 24–21 victory over tenth-ranked Ohio State in the Fiesta Bowl in Glendale, Arizona.

On the final play of his college career, Cosby recognized a flaw in the Buckeyes' coverage of him. "I watched that defense and they only did it twice the whole game," Cosby said years later in an interview for the book *The Republic of Football*. "The other time, Colt threw it to a freshman. We had a nice little conversation on the sidelines. The next time it came up with twenty-three seconds left, I was like, 'Are y'all kidding me? Y'all are really going to run this again? All you got is a safety to tackle me?' I looked at Colt, he looked at me, we got a signal and boom."

McCoy exploited the Ohio State mistake, hitting Cosby in stride at the twenty-yard line. Cosby slipped a tackle from the safety, dashed toward the end zone, and dived in for the winning touchdown.

McCoy finished with 418 passing yards and two touchdowns, both to Cosby, who hauled in fourteen passes for 171 yards.

JANUARY 6, 2007

The Dallas Cowboys were poised to win their first playoff game in more than a decade. Cowboys quarterback Tony Romo completed a twelve-yard pass to Terrell Owens to the Seattle Seahawks' forty-six-yard line, and then Dallas running back Julius Jones burst up the middle for thirty-five yards to the Seahawks' eleven. Seattle led 21–20, but the Cowboys had a first down well within field-goal range with 3:03 remaining in the fourth quarter.

Romo completed a pass to tight end Jason Witten for six yards to the Seahawks' two-yard line, all but guaranteeing the Cowboys would take the lead with just over a minute left in the NFC wild card game at Qwest Field. All the Cowboys needed was a nineteen-yard field goal by kicker Martin Gramática to move in front and likely win the game.

But Romo, the holder on the field-goal attempt, fumbled the football as he was putting it in place for Gramática. Romo responded by picking up the ball and sprinting for the left corner of the end zone. But Seahawk safety Jordan Babineaux, a Port Arthur Lincoln High School alum, chased down Romo and tackled him at the line of scrimmage. That allowed the Seahawks to hold on to a 21–20 victory.

"I know how hard everyone in that locker room worked to get themselves in position to win that game today and for it to end like that, and for me to be the cause is very tough to swallow right now," Romo said as reporters surrounded him at his locker after the game. "I take responsibility for messing up at the end there. That's my fault. I cost the Dallas Cowboys a playoff win, and it's going to sit with me a long time."

It was Bill Parcells's last game as the Cowboys' head coach.

JANUARY 7, 2012

Houston running back Arian Foster raced forty-two yards for a score, wide receiver Andre Johnson hauled in a forty-yard touchdown pass, and defensive lineman J. J. Watt scored on a twenty-nine-yard pick-six (an interception run back for a touchdown) as the Texans notched their first playoff victory, 31–10 over the Cincinnati Bengals.

Houston finished the 2011 regular season with a 10–6 record and the AFC South championship. With that, the Texans earned their first playoff berth, an accomplishment almost a decade in the making, having joined the league in 2002. Houston kept forging ahead with the win over Cincinnati.

"This is something not just for me, but for the whole organization," said Johnson, whom the Texans selected with the third overall pick of the 2003 NFL draft. "It's a very special feeling. That's probably the most I've smiled in a long time."

The Baltimore Ravens defeated the Texans 20–13 in the next round of the playoffs.

JANUARY 8, 1921

Houston Heights and Cleburne slogged to a 0–0 tie in the first officially sponsored University Interscholastic League high school football state championship game, played on a rainy day at a muddy Clark Field in Austin.

JANUARY 9, 2010

JANUARY 10, 1982

Dallas quarterback Tony Romo passed for 244 yards, two touchdowns, and no interceptions as he led the Cowboys to their first playoff win in more than thirteen years, a 34–14 triumph over the Philadelphia Eagles in an NFC wild card game at Cowboys Stadium in Arlington. Cowboy running back Felix Jones sealed the win with a seventy-three-yard touchdown run midway through the third quarter that put Dallas ahead by twenty-seven points.

"It's just...rewarding," Romo said in a postgame press conference. "It makes me proud of the guys in there—fighting, grinding, staying committed to the approach. I'm happy for the guys, happy for (coach Wade Phillips), happy for (team owner Jerry Jones)."

Romo threw a one-yard touchdown pass to tight end John Phillips and a six-yarder to wide receiver Miles Austin during a stretch of five straight second-quarter scoring drives. After the Cowboys led 27–7 at halftime, Jones, who rushed for 148 yards on sixteen carries, broke loose for the longest postseason run in Cowboy history for a touchdown with 5:33 left in the third.

The Cowboys advanced to the divisional round of the playoffs, but fell to Minnesota.

On third down and three from the Dallas six-yard line, San Francisco 49ers quarterback Joe Montana scrambled and lofted a pass over the outstretched arms of Cowboy defensive linemen Ed "Too Tall" Jones and Larry Bethea. As the ball sailed high toward the end zone, 49ers wide receiver Dwight Clark jumped and reached high over his head to make "The Catch" over Cowboys defensive back Everson Walls. When Clark came down in the end zone with the touchdown reception, he and Montana had tied the NFC Championship game at 27 with fifty-one seconds left on Candlestick Park's scoreboard clock. Kicker Ray Wersching booted the extra point that lifted San Francisco to a 28–27 victory and the franchise's first Super Bowl appearance.

"We had pressure on Montana for three quarters," Jones said in a postgame interview. "But on that last drive we just couldn't get to him. He's got very quick feet and he can get rid of the ball quicker than any quarterback I've ever faced. He's a good one."

The 49ers' win kept Dallas coach Tom Landry from guiding the Cowboys to their sixth Super Bowl. It was the closest that Landry came to football's ultimate game for the rest of his career.

"We'll be kicking ourselves for months," Dallas defensive tackle Randy White said after the game. "We know we should have won this game."

JANUARY 11, 1997

Top-ranked college basketball powerhouse Kansas made its first foray into Texas during the Big 12 era, stomping Baylor 87–68 and improving its record to 16–0. Bear fans showed up for the occasion, selling out the Ferrell Center in Waco for the first time in its history, with a crowd of 10,475.

Forward Raef LaFrentz led Kansas with nineteen points and eleven rebounds. Baylor center Brian Skinner scored sixteen, but it was obvious to all that the Bears had a long way to go before they could compete with the Jayhawks.

"They were too big, too strong, too tall, too good, too good of shooters, too good of free-throw shooters, too good of defenders, and too good of passers," Baylor coach Harry Miller said in a postgame press conference.

Kansas won its first five road games in Texas in the Big 12 before losing to Texas Tech on February 13, 1999.

JANUARY 12, 2015

Ohio State defeated Oregon 42–20 in the inaugural College Football Playoff National Championship game, held at AT&T Stadium in Arlington.

JANUARY 13, 1974

JANUARY 14, 1996

Don Shula's Miami Dolphins crushed the Minnesota Vikings 24–7 in Super Bowl VIII in front of 71,882 at Rice Stadium in Houston.

Larry Csonka rushed for 145 yards and two touchdowns on thirty-three carries to lead Miami as it won the first Super Bowl played in Texas.

It would be thirty years before the Super Bowl returned to Texas: in 2004, it was again played in Houston, this time at Reliant Stadium.

Troy Aikman outdueled Green Bay Packer quarterback Brett Favre and led Dallas to a 38–27 victory in the NFC Championship game at Texas Stadium in Irving. Aikman passed for 255 yards and two touchdowns with no interceptions, and Favre hurled the ball for 307 yards, three TDs, and two picks.

Aikman hit wide receiver Michael Irvin for touchdowns of six and four yards in the first quarter as the Cowboys jumped to a 14–3 lead. In the second half, Aikman's best move was to turn and hand the ball to running back Emmitt Smith. The Dallas QB was well aware of that fact: "When Emmitt gets his legs going, he really drives us," Aikman told reporters following the win. "Some people think he turns it up in the playoffs, but I don't think it's possible for him to play harder than he does every week."

Smith finished the game with 150 rushing yards and three touchdowns. Irvin caught seven passes for 100 yards, boosting the Cowboys' record to 19–0 when both Smith and Irvin hit 100 yards.

JANUARY 15, 1978

The Dallas Cowboys' Doomsday Defense came up with four interceptions and four fumble recoveries, and sacked Denver Bronco quarterbacks four times, paving the way for the Cowboys' 27–10 victory in Super Bowl XII at the Superdome in New Orleans. Dallas defensive end Harvey Martin and linebacker Randy White combined for three sacks and were named the game's co-MVPs. "All those interceptions were caused by a very good pass rush," Cowboy coach Tom Landry said. "They've been that way all year and they were the ones who carried us when we needed it most."

Dallas rookie running back Tony Dorsett ran three yards for a touchdown in the first quarter to open the scoring. Cowboy quarterback Roger Staubach, who passed for 183 yards, threw a forty-five-yard touchdown pass to a diving Butch Johnson in the third quarter that gave Dallas a comfortable 20–3 lead. The Cowboys capped the scoring in the fourth quarter when fullback Robert Newhouse took a pitch while running left and then pulled up and tossed a twenty-nine-yard TD pass to wide receiver Golden Richards.

JANUARY 16, 1972

The Dallas Cowboys won their first Super Bowl, trouncing the Miami Dolphins 24–3 at Tulane Stadium in New Orleans, Louisiana.

Cowboys quarterback Roger Staubach earned the Super Bowl VI MVP award after passing for 119 yards and a pair of seven-yard touchdowns to Lance Alworth and Mike Ditka.

Dallas's Doomsday Defense held Dolphins running back Larry Csonka to 40 yards on nine attempts and intercepted Miami quarterback Bob Griese once while keeping the Dolphins from scoring a touchdown.

Going into the 1971–1972 season, the Cowboys had lost in Super Bowl V, been defeated in the playoffs by the Cleveland Browns in 1968 and 1969, and fallen in the NFL title games in 1966 and 1967. So Dallas's win over the Dolphins brought a huge sigh of relief along with the thrill of victory.

"I can't describe how we feel," Cowboy coach Tom Landry said in a postgame interview. "We fought so hard, had come so close so many times."

JANUARY 17, 1993

Dallas Cowboy coach Jimmy Johnson stood on a makeshift perch in the visiting locker room at Candlestick Park, showering his team with praise for its 30–20 victory over the San Francisco 49ers in the NFC Championship game.

The Cowboys' biggest stars shone brightly: Emmitt Smith ran for a touchdown and caught another from Troy Aikman. But Dallas's defense made the difference as James Washington and Ken Norton each intercepted 49er quarterback Steve Young, and Kevin Smith recovered a fumble for the Cowboys.

Johnson lauded his entire team for the effort and reminded the players that they had one game, the Super Bowl, left to play. Then he uttered the most famous words in the history of the Cowboys' organization: "And the only thing else I got to say is how 'bout them Cowboys!"

JANUARY 18, 1976

Pittsburgh Steeler quarterback Terry Bradshaw tossed a sixty-four-yard touchdown pass over the top of the Dallas defense to Lynn Swann, capping the Steelers' avalanche of points in the fourth quarter to win Super Bowl X 21–17 at the Orange Bowl in Miami.

Swann made a series of acrobatic catches as he hauled in seven passes for 124 yards and took home the game's MVP trophy. His Dallas counterpart, Drew Pearson, was not discouraged by the outcome, even though the Cowboys saw a fourth-quarter lead slip away. "We'll be back," Pearson said in a postgame interview. "You always say, 'Wait till next year,' but with the young guys we have on this team, we'll be back."

Pearson proved prophetic: Dallas won Super Bowl XII 27–10 over the Denver Broncos.

At least one Texan didn't have to wait to celebrate. North Texas State University and Temple Dunbar alum Joe Greene claimed the second of his four Super Bowl rings as a member of the Steelers' Steel Curtain defense.

JANUARY 19, 1937

Hubbard native Tris Speaker became the first Texan elected to the National Baseball Hall of Fame. The Hall had been established a year earlier when Babe Ruth, Ty Cobb, Honus Wagner, Christy Mathewson, and Walter Johnson were selected as the inaugural class. Speaker joined Morgan Bulkeley, Ban Johnson, Nap Lajoie, Connie Mack, John McGraw, George Wright, and Cy Young in the second class.

Speaker finished his twenty-two-year career with a Major League–record 792 doubles (still safe at the time of this writing, eighty-eight years after he retired) among his 3,514 hits. He drove in 1,531 runs and posted a .345 career batting average.

JANUARY 20, 1968

The Houston Cougars hosted the UCLA Bruins at the Astrodome in the first college basketball regular-season game broadcast nationally in prime time.

Guy Lewis's Cougars defeated John Wooden's Bruins 71–69. Elvin Hayes made a pair of free throws to break a 69–69 tie late in the game. Houston's victory snapped UCLA's forty-seven-game winning streak.

"Houston played a tremendous game," Wooden told the Associated Press. "We'll just have to start over again."

The game drew 52,693 fans to the first basketball game played at the Astrodome.

JANUARY 21, 2014

Texas forward Jonathan Holmes struggled with his shooting touch for most of the game against twenty-second-ranked Kansas State, but he was right on the money when it counted most. With 1.9 seconds left in the second half and the score tied at 64, Holmes caught an in-bounds pass from guard Isaiah Taylor in the right corner, behind the three-point line. Holmes turned and shot a fall-away jumper that hit nothing but net as the buzzer sounded and the backboard lights blazed, lifting the Longhorns to a 67–64 victory over the Wildcats.

Holmes's game-winning three-pointer gave him eight points on three-of-eight shooting in the game. But his big shot followed a trend for the red-hot Longhorns. Texas's win over Kansas State was its second in a streak of four straight victories over ranked opponents that culminated in an 81–69 win over sixth-ranked Kansas. That was the high point of the season for Texas, which finished tied for third in the Big 12 and exited the NCAA Tournament in the round of thirty-two.

JANUARY 22, 1973

In a heavyweight title bout fought in Kingston, Jamaica, Houston native George Foreman defeated Joe Frazier on a technical knockout in the second round, prompting broadcaster Howard Cosell to exclaim the nine most famous words in American sports television history: "Down goes Frazier! Down goes Frazier! Down goes Frazier!"

JANUARY 23, 2008

The Baylor Bears' basketball team, having earned a spot in the Associated Press top 25 for the first time in thirty-nine years, celebrated by surviving a quintuple-overtime thriller and claiming a 116–110 win over rival Texas A&M in College Station.

Baylor guard Curtis Jerrells scored thirty-six points and dished out eight assists, and forward Kevin Rogers had nineteen points and eighteen rebounds. That overshadowed the effort of Texas A&M forward Bryan Davis, who scored thirty points and grabbed fourteen rebounds.

"That just shows the ability, the dedication and the will of this team," Jerrells said during a postgame press conference. "If we put our minds to it, no matter what happens we're going to get it done."

The win showed the legitimacy of Baylor coach Scott Drew's rebuilt Bears. Drew took over an obliterated Baylor program that had been rocked by controversy in the summer of 2003 and subsequently banned from playing nonconference games during the 2005–2006 season. The NCAA placed Baylor on probation for lack of institutional control concerning infractions the basketball program had committed under coach Dave Bliss. The problems under Bliss were brought to light in the aftermath of the murder of Baylor basketball player Patrick Dennehy by teammate Carlton Dotson in June 2003.

The year 2008 marked a turnaround for Baylor on the court. The team earned its first NCAA tournament berth since 1988 and finished with a 21–11 record.

JANUARY 24, 2001

The Baylor women's basketball team drenched first-year head coach Kim Mulkey on her way into the locker room following the Lady Bears' 79–74 victory over seventh-ranked Iowa State at the Ferrell Center in Waco. Forward Danielle Crockrom scored twenty-five points and grabbed eleven rebounds to lead Baylor to its first win over a top 10 team in program history, thus earning Mulkey a cooler of ice water over her head in the wake of the win.

Baylor surged in front of the Cyclones by nineteen points in the first half, then held off an Iowa State charge over the final twenty minutes. The Lady Bears were coming off a last-place, 7–20 season, so the win over Iowa State marked a change.

"There were some leaders out there on the floor tonight that, instead of playing not to lose, they played to win the game from start to finish," Mulkey said.

Baylor finished 21–9 in the 2000–2001 campaign, an early sign of its eventual rise to become a superpower in women's college basketball. At the time, even Mulkey might not have realized the heights her team would achieve. "We want to be where Iowa State are someday," she said after the victory.

(PHOTO, OPPOSITE PAGE)
Baylor coach Kim Mulkey has led Baylor to a pair of national championships, in 2005 and 2012. Photo courtesy of Baylor University Photography.

JANUARY 25, 1986

Abilene native Billy Olson posted a new indoor pole vault world record, breaking his own previous record, when he cleared 19 feet, 4 inches on his first attempt at an invitational meet in Albuquerque, New Mexico.

Olson broke the world record in the event eleven times between January 1982, when he was a senior at Abilene Christian University, and August 1986. He and pole vault legend Sergey Bubka of Ukraine traded the record throughout the early and mid-1980s before Bubka began to dominate the sport in the late 1980s and early 1990s.

Olson set his final world record, 19 feet, 5½ inches, later in 1986. He made the 1988 Olympic team, but didn't medal. His best chances to win Olympic gold were wiped out by the US boycott of the Soviet Games in 1980 and a foot injury in 1984.

JANUARY 26, 1985

Texas Tech guard Bubba Jennings went thirteen for fifteen from the field and scored twenty-six points to lead the Red Raiders to a 64–63 upset victory over second-ranked SMU at Lubbock Municipal Coliseum. While Jennings filled the basket from all over the court, fellow Red Raider guard Tony Benford hit the ten-foot game-winning shot from the baseline with three seconds left in the second half.

The loss probably kept the Mustangs from reaching the top of the national rankings, since St. John's defeated top-ranked Georgetown on the same day.

"This definitely has to be one of the greatest victories since we've been here," Red Raider coach Gerald Myers said in a postgame interview. "But the importance of the game will be determined by how we use it down the line."

The Red Raiders built on the win to claim the Southwest Conference regular season and tournament championships.

JANUARY 27, 1984

The Rice Owls' men's basketball team snapped an eighteen-game losing streak against Arkansas by defeating the Razorbacks 65–62 at Autry Court in Houston. Rice had gone ten years and eight days without besting Arkansas before ending the slump in a big way by knocking off the sixteenth-ranked Hogs.

Arkansas led by eight early in the second half and appeared to be on its way to continuing its dominance of the Owls. But Rice put together a 12–0 run to take the lead and never trailed again. Tyrone Washington and Tony Barnett each scored fourteen points to pace Rice.

JANUARY 28, 1996

Dallas Cowboy cornerback and TCU alum Larry Brown claimed Super Bowl XXX MVP honors by intercepting two passes that set up a pair of Emmitt Smith touchdowns as the Cowboys defeated the Pittsburgh Steelers 27–17 at Sun Devil Stadium in Tempe, Arizona.

Cowboy quarterback Troy Aikman passed for 209 yards, including a three-yard touchdown to tight end Jay Novacek. Pittsburgh held Smith to 49 rushing yards on eighteen attempts. Meanwhile, Bam Morris, a Texas Tech alum and native of Cooper, Texas, led all rushers with seventy-three yards for Pittsburgh. But the difference in the game was Steeler quarterback Neil O'Donnell's two errant passes directly into the arms of Brown.

Dallas won its fifth Super Bowl in its eighth appearance in the NFL's ultimate game. But the victory marked the beginning of a record drought for the Cowboys, who have not returned to the Super Bowl in more than twenty years as of this writing.

JANUARY 29, 2009

San Antonio Spur guard Manu Ginobili enjoyed a perfect evening from the free-throw line, hitting all eighteen attempts and lifting the Spurs to a 114–104 victory over the Phoenix Suns in Phoenix, Arizona. Coming off the bench, Ginobili had a decent game from the field, hitting six of thirteen despite going zero for four from three-point range. But by being automatic from the free-throw line, Ginobili scored thirty, leading the Spurs. Ginobili's eighteen-for-eighteen effort from the stripe set a San Antonio record for free throws made in a game.

JANUARY 30, 1967

San Angelo native Nancy Richey hit a backhand down the sideline, past opponent Lesley Turner of Australia, and with that shot, Richey claimed the Australian Open, her first Grand Slam singles title.

Richey defeated Turner 6–1, 6–4 in the final to add the Australian championship to her trophy case, which already included doubles titles at the US Open (1965, 1966), Wimbledon (1966), and the Australian Open (1966). Richey won her second Grand Slam singles title at the French Open in 1967.

JANUARY 31, 1993

Dallas throttled the Buffalo Bills 52–17 in Super Bowl XXVII, played at the Rose Bowl in Pasadena, California, the Cowboys' first title in fifteen years.

Cowboys quarterback Troy Aikman threw two second-quarter touchdown passes to star wide receiver Michael Irvin, giving Dallas a 28–10 lead at halftime. Aikman added a forty-five-yard touchdown pass to Alvin Harper in the fourth quarter, and Waco native and Texas Tech alum Lin Elliott booted the extra point to help ice the victory.

"Early on, the whole team was a little up-tight," Aikman said. "I really had to talk myself into staying relaxed out there. This is the greatest feeling that I've ever had in my life and I wish every player could feel it."

Dallas had to wait only 364 days for its next Super Bowl. The team once again defeated the Bills, 30–13 this time, at the Georgia Dome in Atlanta. That marked the Bills' fourth straight Super Bowl defeat.

February

FEBRUARY 1, 2014

Baylor guard Odyssey Sims poured in forty-four points to lead the Lady Bears to an 87–73 victory over Texas at the Ferrell Center in Waco. Sims put up big numbers despite not being particularly hot from the field, making twelve of thirty-four field goals, including two of seven three-pointers. But she knocked down eighteen of twenty free throws and added seven assists, seven rebounds, and two steals.

It was the fourth time Sims had eclipsed forty points in her Baylor career, but the first time in a home game. "I think it probably means more to my fans," Sims said in a post-game press conference. "I'm pretty sure they witnessed forty points with (Brittney Griner), but it's pretty special. I'm glad they got to witness this victory."

Sims averaged a Baylor-record 28.5 points a game as a senior in 2014 and led the Lady Bears to the Elite Eight before they fell to Notre Dame.

FEBRUARY 2, 1949

Ben and Valerie Hogan were driving through West Texas on the way home to Fort Worth a day after Hogan lost a playoff to Houston's Jimmy Demaret in the Phoenix Open. On a foggy morning, a Greyhound bus crossed over the centerline and slammed head on into the Hogans' vehicle about twenty-nine miles east of Van Horn. Ben Hogan was driving, but thrust himself to his right at the last instant to protect Valerie in the passenger seat. The instinct to protect his wife likely saved Hogan's life as well. The steering wheel shot into the back seat of the car.

Hogan suffered multiple broken bones, including a fractured pelvis and a broken clavicle. Valerie Hogan walked away from the collision with only minor injuries, including a black eye. Hogan remained in the hospital for almost two months, and many questioned whether he would ever play competitive golf again.

In his stead, a trio of Texans—Demaret, Ralph Guldahl, and Lloyd Mangrum—were predicted to pick up the torch from Hogan.

But Hogan would return.

FEBRUARY 3, 2014

The University Interscholastic League released new district alignments, which included Class 6A for the first time.

The UIL designated the football classification of the smallest schools, formerly referred to as six-man, as 1A. That caused the large-school classification to bump up a digit to 6A. That move ended a thirty-five-year span during which the state's largest high school athletics classification was 5A.

UIL schools played under one classification and crowned one state champion in each sport from 1920 until 1948, when the organization expanded to award state championships in City, 1A, and 2A classifications in football, and City, 1A, 2A, and Class B in basketball.

FEBRUARY 4, 1989

Texas forward Clarissa Davis scored twenty-six points, including eighteen in the first half, as the Lady Longhorns made quick work of Baylor to win 88–50 in Waco. The win upped Texas's all-time winning streak in Southwest Conference regular-season games to ninety-six, and the Longhorns were well on their way to their seventh straight undefeated run through the SWC. Texas finished the 1988–1989 campaign with a 16–0 mark. Arkansas handed Texas a SWC loss in 1990, ending the Longhorns' winning streak at 109 games.

FEBRUARY 5, 1999

FEBRUARY 6, 2011

The NBA resumed play after a lockout wiped out the first three months of the season, allowing twenty-year-old center Dirk Nowitzki to make his debut in the NBA and as a Dallas Maverick.

Playing in the starting lineup with Steve Nash, Michael Finley, Shawn Bradley, and A. C. Green, Nowitzki played just sixteen minutes and scored two points with four assists against the SuperSonics in Seattle.

But Nowitzki and the Mavs soon found their footing. Dallas, which had gone 20–62 in the 1997–1998 season, won nineteen games in the strike-shortened 1999 campaign. Nowitzki's production more than doubled, to 17.5 points a game, in 1999–2000, beginning his and the Mavericks' ascent in the Western Conference.

Green Bay quarterback Aaron Rodgers threw three touchdown passes and Georgetown High School alum Mason Crosby kicked four extra points and a twenty-three-yard field goal as the Packers defeated the Pittsburgh Steelers 31–25 in Super Bowl XLV at Cowboys Stadium in Arlington.

It was the third Super Bowl played in Texas and the first in the Dallas–Fort Worth Metroplex.

FEBRUARY 7, 2010

Austin native and Westlake High School alum Drew Brees added a major bullet point to his Hall of Fame résumé by leading the New Orleans Saints to a 31–17 victory over the Indianapolis Colts in Super Bowl XLIV.

Brees, in his ninth NFL season, and his fourth with the Saints, had passed for more than 30,000 yards and 200 touchdowns before reaching his first Super Bowl. He made the most of it, passing for 288 yards and two touchdowns against the Colts to earn MVP honors in the Saints' first Super Bowl championship.

FEBRUARY 8, 1986

Dallas native Anthony "Spud" Webb twirled 360 degrees and threw down his second dunk in the NBA Slam Dunk Contest, to the delight of the hometown Reunion Arena crowd. That dunk seemed to create momentum for the five-foot, seven-inch Webb. His next dunks gained in flashiness and earned higher marks from the judges. Webb's two dunks in the final round each earned perfect scores of 50 as he surged ahead of his Atlanta Hawk teammate and defending dunk-contest champion Dominique Wilkins.

In the second round, Webb tossed the ball high in the air from the left wing and, right on schedule, caught it at its arc with his back to the basket and slammed home a reverse jam for his first 50. In the final round, the field was narrowed to Webb and Wilkins. Webb opened with another perfectly executed 360. Then, to finish off Wilkins, he bounced the ball hard off the court from the free-throw line, and as it caromed off the backboard, he rushed to meet it above the rim and finish the dunk. Moments after Wilkins threw down a two-handed windmill dunk, the Reunion Arena crowd chanted "Spud" until Wilkins's score of 48 was posted, signifying that Webb had won the contest.

"There was a lot of competition with great guys and my best friend here on the team,"

FEBRUARY 9, 2002

Webb told Bill Russell in a postcontest TV interview. "We just went out and showed the people what we could do."

The Wilmer-Hutchins graduate also acknowledged that he might have had an edge. "I was at home and I had the crowd behind me," Webb said. "(Wilkins is) a great person and it was great to have him with me in the championship."

Texas claimed its 1,400th victory in men's basketball as the Longhorns defeated Colorado 104–95 at the Frank Erwin Center in Austin. Texas guard T. J. Ford scored twenty-two points and dished out twelve assists to drive the Horns on the offensive end. Forward James Thomas added eighteen points and eleven rebounds, and guard Royal Ivey pitched in eighteen points.

The Longhorns, who began playing basketball in 1906, won their 1,500th game in 2006.

FEBRUARY 10, 1968

Houston Cougars' power forward Elvin Hayes scored fifty points and grabbed a school-record thirty-seven rebounds in the top-ranked Cougars' 107–56 victory over Centenary. Hayes's monster game began a phenomenal month in which he scored forty-nine or more points four times, including a school record sixty-two against Valparaiso on February 24, and grabbed twenty-seven or more rebounds in each of those games.

Hayes led Houston to the Final Four, but the Cougars lost to eventual national champion UCLA in the semifinals. Later that spring, the San Diego Rockets selected Hayes as the top overall pick in the NBA draft.

FEBRUARY 11, 2003

Fort Worth Dunbar boys' basketball coach Robert Hughes guided his Flying Wildcats to a 71–62 victory over Fort Worth Polytechnic in the regular-season finale at TCU's Daniel-Meyer Coliseum. With the win, Hughes reached 1,275 coaching victories, surpassing the national high school record previously held by Morgan Wootten of DeMatha Catholic High in Hyattsville, Maryland. The record-setting game brought a standing-room-only crowd to TCU's 7,200-seat basketball arena.

"Hot dog and hallelujah," Hughes said after the game. "I'm glad it's over with. I tried to play it off like it wasn't there. It really surprised me how much interest this has all generated."

But Hughes and the Wildcats weren't finished. Dunbar went on to defeat Beaumont Ozen 66–54 for the 2003 Class 4A state championship. Hughes, who was seventy-five when he posted the record-setting win, coached two more seasons and retired in 2005 with a career record of 1,333 wins, 264 losses, and 5 state championships.

FEBRUARY 12, 1989

FEBRUARY 13, 1920

Houston hosted a record-setting NBA All-Star Game as 44,735 fans showed up to see the West All-Stars defeat the East 143–134 at the Astrodome. It was the largest crowd to witness an NBA All-Star Game. The record stood until 2010, when AT&T Stadium in Arlington smashed it with a gargantuan crowd of 108,713.

Although Utah Jazz stars Karl Malone and John Stockton propelled the West team—Malone scored twenty-eight points, and Stockton served up seventeen assists—it was Laker center Kareem Abdul-Jabbar who gave it a fitting finish as he made the final basket with a skyhook.

Abdul-Jabbar was a late addition to the game, playing in place of the injured Magic Johnson. It was Abdul-Jabbar's nineteenth and final All-Star Game appearance.

Calvert native Andrew "Rube" Foster founded the Negro National League, which gave segregated black baseball autonomy through organization.

Foster thrived as a pitcher and manager of the independent Chicago American Giants from 1914 to 1919. But he saw how the white men who booked the team's venues and games controlled the destiny of black players. His stance was quoted in multiple biographies: "The wild, reckless scramble under the guise

(PHOTO, RIGHT)
Andrew "Rube" Foster established the Negro National League. Photo courtesy of Negro Leagues Baseball Museum, Inc.

of baseball is keeping us down and we will always be the underdog until we can successfully employ the methods that have brought success to the great powers that be in baseball of the present era: organization."

To that end, Foster arrived at a summit of African American team owners in February 1920 with documents to create the Negro National League. "To (Foster's) undying credit, let it be said that he has made the biggest sacrifice," journalist Ira Lewis wrote in a column in the *Competitor*, a national magazine. "For be it known that his position in the world of colored baseball was reasonably secure. Mr. Foster could have defied organization for many years. But, happily, he has seen the light—the light of wisdom and the spirit of service to the public."

Baylor center Brittney Griner led a charge in the final four minutes that lifted the top-ranked Lady Bears to a 67–58 victory over fifth-ranked Texas A&M at the Ferrell Center in Waco. Texas A&M had held a 54–50 lead with 4:33 remaining in the second half before Griner took over.

Griner, who finished with a game-high twenty-six points and eleven rebounds, scored nine points as Baylor used a 17–4 run at the end to surge to the win.

"There's an old saying in basketball, 'When the game is on the line, the right people better touch the ball,'" Baylor coach Kim Mulkey said in a postgame press conference. "We got the ball to Brittney and big things happened."

Baylor guard Odyssey Sims, who contributed twenty-two points and five assists, made a fast-break pass to Griner ahead of the Aggie defense, and Griner finished with a layup that boosted the Lady Bears into a lead they did not relinquish.

Baylor all but wrapped up the Big 12 championship with the win in front of a sellout crowd of 10,299 in its home arena. The Lady Bears defeated Texas A&M three times in 2011, including a 61–58 win in the Big 12 Tournament final. But the Aggies would get their revenge in March.

FEBRUARY 15, 2013

In his debut as Texas Tech's head baseball coach, Tim Tadlock started freshman Eric Gutierrez at first base in the Red Raiders' season opener versus Northern Illinois. Gutierrez went one for three with a run scored and an RBI in Texas Tech's 8–0 victory.

Gutierrez remained in the starting lineup for his entire four-year career at Texas Tech, a span that included 244 games and the Red Raiders' first two appearances in the College World Series. "Coach (Tadlock) gave me an opportunity. He believed in me," Gutierrez said following his final game in a Red Raider uniform at the 2016 CWS in Omaha, Nebraska. "And, I mean, it (second-round elimination) hurts. But I know this team's going to be back next year. It's going to be expected to be here every year competing for the national championship."

FEBRUARY 16, 1962

The expansion Houston Colt .45s began their first spring training in Apache Junction, Arizona. The Colt .45s and New York Mets joined the National League, bringing Major League Baseball to twenty teams. The Colt .45s finished eighth in the National League in their first season. Three years later, Houston moved into the Astrodome and changed its name to the Astros.

FEBRUARY 17, 1994

FEBRUARY 18, 1999

San Antonio Spur center David Robinson dominated the Detroit Pistons and achieved the ultrarare quadruple-double.

Robinson scored thirty-four points, grabbed ten rebounds, dished out ten assists, and blocked ten shots. San Antonio extended its winning streak to eleven games with a 115–96 victory over the Pistons.

The Admiral notched his tenth block with about five minutes left in the fourth quarter, and with it he posted the fifth quadruple-double in NBA history. He said in a postgame interview that he was acutely aware of where he stood, thanks to the team's stat crew and backup center Jack Haley. "How could I not know I was close with the bench and the stat crew?" Robinson said. "Every time I came to the bench, Jack would tell me how many more blocks I needed."

Robinson joined Hakeem Olajuwon, Alvin Robertson, and Nate Thurmond as the four players to register quadruple-doubles. Olajuwon did it twice in a one-month span for the Rockets in 1990, but Robinson had the distinction of scoring the most points in a quadruple-double game.

The New York Yankees traded pitchers David Wells and Graeme Lloyd and infielder Homer Bush to the Toronto Blue Jays in return for Roger Clemens, an alum of Spring Woods High School and the University of Texas.

Giving up Wells, who had pitched a perfect game for the Yankees in the previous May, showed how badly New York wanted Clemens, who had won the American League Cy Young Award in 1997 and 1998. But Clemens, speaking to the media on a telephone press conference call from his home in Houston, attempted to downplay the magnitude of the trade. "They are the champions," Clemens said. "I just want to slide in the side door and go to work with these guys and hopefully fit right in."

The trade allowed New York to pair the right-handed Rocket with lefty Andy Pettitte, from Deer Park High School and San Jacinto College, in an imposing pitching staff with Texas roots. Clemens won twenty-seven games and Pettitte won thirty-three over the next two seasons as the Yankees won back-to-back World Series titles.

FEBRUARY 19, 2003

Texas Tech women's basketball coach Marsha Sharp guided the Lady Raiders to a 59–48 victory over Oklahoma, notching her 500th coaching victory. "It has not been as big a factor for me as just winning games this year," Sharp said about the milestone in a postgame press conference. "At the same time, I don't want this to pass by without thinking about a lot of people who have been involved in this. I've told several people this week that this program is bigger than one person."

Forward Plenette Pierson scored twenty-three points and grabbed twelve rebounds in helping Texas Tech erase a nine-point deficit in the first half and overtake the Sooners. In the postgame presser, Lady Raider guard Natalie Ritchie made an emphatic point about Sharp's influence. "I have to speak for all the others, because coach Sharp is an extremely humble person," Ritchie said. "But from the beginning, she took this program and had a vision for it. She's done so many things for women's basketball. She's the reason a lot of us play, and it's an honor to play for her and an honor to be a part of this."

FEBRUARY 20, 1979

Vinnie "the Microwave" Johnson heated up in the first half and never cooled off as he scored a Baylor-record fifty points in leading the Bears to a 109–72 victory over TCU at the Heart O' Texas Coliseum in Waco. With several members of the Baylor squad suffering from injuries and the flu, Johnson played almost the entire game despite the fact that Baylor led by twenty-four points at halftime. He scored twenty-nine points in the second half to help keep the Bears far in front of the Horned Frogs.

Johnson's fifty-point output left him one point short of the Southwest Conference single-game scoring record, set by SMU's Gene Phillips against Texas in 1971.

FEBRUARY 21, 1896

FEBRUARY 22, 2008

British prizefighter Bob Fitzsimmons knocked out opponent Peter Maher of Ireland in the first round of a match held on a sandbar of the Rio Grande River near Langtry, Texas.

Langtry justice of the peace Judge Roy Bean helped organize, promote, and stage the fight, keeping out of the jurisdiction of the Texas Rangers by holding it just over the border, but not quite in Mexico.

Waco angler Alton Jones brought an opening-day catch of seventeen pounds, five ounces into the boat and onto the podium at the Bassmaster Classic on Lake Hartwell near Greenville, South Carolina. Jones's first-day catch put him in tenth place in the three-day tournament. He added a catch of eighteen pounds, eleven ounces on the second day to move into the lead. Jones's haul of thirteen pounds, seven ounces on the final day of competition gave him the win in professional fishing's premiere event.

"I always thought it would be fun to win a Classic, but I never dreamed it would be quite this much fun," Jones said in a post-tournament interview. "It's a little overwhelming and there's a lot of humility when I look at the names on those flags up around those rafters and I don't feel worthy. They're my heroes, so I'm humbled to be part of this."

Jones's first Bassmaster Classic title came with first-place prize money of $500,000.

FEBRUARY 23, 2001

FEBRUARY 24, 2007

Fort Bend Willowridge guard Daniel Ewing scored seventeen points, and backcourt mate T. J. Ford added eleven as the Eagles dismissed a Houston Bellaire team led by Emeka Okafor from the playoffs 56–42 at Houston's Don Coleman Coliseum.

Willowridge stayed on track to win its second straight Class 5A state championship. The Eagles defeated Bryan in the state final and finished the season with a 39–0 record and a second-place spot in the USA Today Super 25 boys' basketball rankings.

Texas women's basketball coach Jody Conradt led the Longhorns to one more victory from her perch on the Texas bench at the Frank Erwin Center. Conradt guided Texas to a 59–47 victory over Texas Tech in her final home game.

Conradt, a Goldthwaite native, retired two weeks later, having finished her coaching career with a 900–307 record. She took Texas to the 1986 national championship and two more Final Four appearances to go along with twelve regular-season conference titles. As the Longhorns' coach for thirty-one seasons, Conradt led the program from its final years in the Association for Intercollegiate Athletics for Women, into the Southwest Conference in the 1980s, and in the Big 12 in the 1990s and 2000s.

"The things that have changed—counting around the room, there are eleven media representatives here. If I could think back to when I first came here, if there were this many people in the stands, it meant someone's family was in town," Conradt said in a press conference announcing her retirement on March 12. "Things have changed and changed for the better, not just for the University of Texas but for women's athletics in general in terms of the credibility and visibility that women's basketball now has."

FEBRUARY 25, 2006

Texas softball pitcher Cat Osterman struck out seven University of Nevada–Las Vegas batters to become the NCAA career strikeout record holder. Osterman, who passed the previous mark of 1,773 strikeouts early in her senior season, finished her Longhorns career with 2,265 Ks.

In her Texas career, which finished at the 2006 Women's College World Series, Osterman won 136 games and struck out 2.04 batters per inning in 1,105⅔ innings pitched.

Pitcher Cat Osterman helped the Longhorns reach the Women's College World Series in 2003, 2005, and 2006. Photo courtesy of University of Texas Athletics.

FEBRUARY 26, 1989

FEBRUARY 27, 2010

Dallas Cowboy president Tex Schramm and the Cowboys' new owner, Jerry Jones, met Tom Landry at The Hills of Lakeway near Austin, where he was playing golf. Schramm and Jones informed Landry, the only coach in the franchise's history, that he would no longer be the Cowboys' head coach.

Jones bought the team from Bum Bright a day earlier for $140 million and wasted no time in making wholesale changes. Jones hired his old Arkansas teammate Jimmy Johnson to replace Landry. Schramm lasted a month before he too was fired and Jones seized control of the team president's duties.

Jones's action alienated many Cowboys fans, who viewed Landry as a fixture of the team's identity.

San Antonio native Justin Olsen and teammates Steven Holcomb, Curtis Tomasevicz, and Steve Mesler raced to the gold medal in the four-man bobsled at the Vancouver Olympics.

With Holcomb driving a sled nicknamed "Night Train," the US team completed four runs in 3:24.46, 0.38 of a second better than the silver-medalist German team. That gave the American team its first gold medal in the four-man bobsled in sixty-two years.

Olsen joined Todd Hays of Del Rio as the second Texan to win an Olympic bobsled medal; Hays was a member of the 2002 US team that took silver in the four-man sled at the Salt Lake City games.

FEBRUARY 28, 2007

FEBRUARY 29, 1984

Texas freshman forward Kevin Durant scored thirty points and pulled down sixteen rebounds in his final home game to help the Longhorns outlast rival Texas A&M 98–96 in double overtime at the Frank Erwin Center in Austin.

Durant and guard A. J. Abrams combined for Texas's ten points in the second overtime. Abrams hit a three-pointer and another jumper to start the period, then Durant made five of six free throws to finish off the Aggies.

Durant entered the 2007 NBA draft after one season with the Longhorns. The Seattle SuperSonics took him with the second overall pick.

Houston Cougars center Hakeem Olajuwon dominated Baylor as he led the Cougars to an 80–65 victory over the Bears at Hofheinz Pavilion in Houston. The Cougars improved to 15–0 in Southwest Conference play and clinched the conference championship with the win. Olajuwon made all nine shots he took from the field, scoring twenty-four points in all to go along with eighteen rebounds and six blocked shots.

Houston captains Michael Young and Olajuwon were playing their final home game for the Cougars. After claiming the SWC regular season and tournament titles, Houston advanced to the NCAA Tournament national championship game, falling to Georgetown 84–75. In June, the Houston Rockets selected Olajuwon with the first pick of the NBA draft, and Young was selected twenty-fourth overall by the Boston Celtics.

(PHOTO, OPPOSITE PAGE)
Hakeem "the Dream" Olajuwon played all but one year of his college and professional basketball career in Texas. He helped the Houston Cougars reach the NCAA Final Four every year from 1982 to 1984. He led the Houston Rockets to NBA titles in 1994 and 1995. Photo courtesy of University of Houston Athletics.

March

MARCH 1, 2006

Texas A&M guard Acie Law hit a three-pointer with one second left on the clock, giving the Aggies a 46–43 slugfest victory over rival Texas in College Station. The Aggies' win over the sixth-ranked Longhorns was key to earning their first NCAA Tournament appearance in nineteen seasons.

Law posted just eight points in the low-scoring affair, but he had the ball in his hands in the moment that counted the most. "Words can't describe the feeling when you beat a rival with so much at stake," Law said. "The Big 12 championship for them and a chance to get into the tournament for us. The game had a lot of meaning for both teams."

Texas A&M's NCAA Tournament berth in 2006 highlighted a phenomenal rebuilding job by second-year coach Billy Gillispie. When Gillispie took over as head coach, the Aggies were coming off a 0–16 record in Big 12 play in 2003–2004. Gillispie guided Texas A&M to a 21–10 season and the National Invitational Tournament in his first season and then got the Aggies back into March Madness with a 22–9 mark in 2006.

MARCH 2, 1991

The Panhandle and South Plains regions of West Texas flexed their girls' hoops muscles as Amarillo Tascosa won the Class 5A state title, Levelland won 4A, Tulia won 3A, Abernathy won 2A, and Nazareth claimed the 1A state championship.

Nazareth was the smallest in classification, but the Swiftettes boasted by far the grandest girls' basketball dynasty, winning their fourth consecutive state championship and a national-record twelfth in school history. Nazareth kept it going well into the twenty-first century as the Swiftettes won their twentieth girls' basketball state title in 2015.

MARCH 3, 1990

MARCH 4, 2009

The Duncanville Pantherettes claimed their third consecutive girls' basketball state championship with a 74–51 victory over Houston Yates in the Class 5A final. The win marked the pinnacle of Coach Sandra Meadows's twenty-four seasons at Duncanville, though it would be almost a year before the Pantherettes' remarkable run ended.

On March 1, 1991, Victoria defeated Duncanville 38–36 in the 5A semifinals, snapping the Pantherettes' 134-game winning streak.

Meadows, whose battle with cancer forced her to leave the Pantherette bench after the 1993 season, finished her coaching career with a record of 906–227. She led Duncanville to ten state-tournament appearances and four state championships. She was posthumously inducted into the Texas Sports Hall of Fame in 1998.

Hurst L. D. Bell alum Alan Voskuil exploded for thirty-five points as he led Texas Tech to an 84–65 upset victory over ninth-ranked Kansas. Voskuil hit nine of fourteen from three-point range and made six of six free throws on his way to his career night at the United Spirit Arena in Lubbock.

Texas Tech, which snapped a six-game losing streak, finished the 2008–2009 season with a 14–19 record and didn't advance to the postseason, while Kansas won the Big 12 and reached the Sweet Sixteen of the NCAA Tournament. But no one doubted which team was better on that particular night.

"(Voskuil) was by far the best player in the gym," Kansas coach Bill Self said. "Things just kind of fell together for (the Red Raiders) and they had a great game."

MARCH 5, 2016

Texas A&M clinched the Southeastern Conference men's basketball championship with a 76–67 victory over Vanderbilt at Reed Arena in College Station. It was the twentieth-ranked Aggies' first men's hoops regular-season conference title in thirty years, a period that spanned the last decade of the Southwest Conference and Texas A&M's tenure in the Big 12.

Aggies guard Jalen Jones scored seventeen points and grabbed eleven rebounds to lead the charge against Vanderbilt. He also summed up Texas A&M's emotions after cutting down the nets in the team's home gym. "I'm just at a loss for words," Jones said in a postgame press conference. "It's just overwhelming right now, all the adversity we faced during conference and all the hard work that we put in during the summer. To win the conference championship feels great, and we've got to continue to build on this and get other championships as well."

Texas A&M finished its SEC schedule 13–5, the same mark as Kentucky. But the Aggies defeated the Wildcats 79–77 in the teams' only regular-season contest.

MARCH 6, 2009

Houston Nimitz center Brittney Griner scored a state-tournament-record forty-four points, grabbed eighteen rebounds, and blocked eight shots in leading the Vikings to a 74–47 victory over Pflugerville in the Class 5A girls' basketball state semifinals at the Frank Erwin Center in Austin.

Nimitz guard Alicia Seay joined Griner in double-digit scoring with eleven points, helping the Vikings improve their record to 37–1.

Griner put the exclamation point on the win in the third quarter when she went up for a two-handed dunk, the first ever at the girls' state basketball tournament.

The next day, Mansfield Summit held Griner to twenty-two points as the Jaguars pulled off an upset, winning 52–43 and claiming the state title.

MARCH 7, 1991

Texas women's basketball's monumental, decade-long winning streak in the Southwest Conference Tournament came to an end as Texas Tech defeated the fourteenth-ranked Longhorns 63–61 in the semifinals. Jennifer Buck scored nineteen points to pace the Lady Raiders, and Krista Kirkland made three crucial free throws in the final thirty-one seconds to give Texas Tech its first victory over Texas in thirty-seven contests.

Texas won its first twenty-four SWC Tournament games, claiming the conference tournament title the first ten times it was played. The Longhorns' unusually rough postseason ended soon after as tenth-seeded Lamar upset seventh-seeded Texas in the opening round of the NCAA Tournament.

Arkansas defeated Texas Tech 60–51 in the SWC Tournament final.

MARCH 8, 1985

The twentieth-ranked SMU Mustangs edged Houston 84–72 in the opening round of the Southwest Conference men's basketball tournament at Reunion Arena in Dallas. The next day, Arkansas eliminated SMU from the tournament, and Texas Tech defeated Texas A&M to reach the tournament championship. The SWC regular-season champion Red Raiders defeated Arkansas in the final to earn the automatic bid to the NCAA Tournament.

That confluence of events helped the SWC land three teams—Texas Tech, SMU, and Arkansas—in the NCAA Tournament as the field expanded to sixty-four teams for the first time.

MARCH 9, 2002

Chris Bosh scored twenty-one points, grabbed eleven rebounds, and blocked seven shots to lead Dallas Lincoln High School to a 71–51 victory over Kendrick Perkins's Beaumont Ozen High School team in the Class 4A state championship game.

Perkins had a double-double of his own with twenty points and fourteen rebounds, but he couldn't carry the Panthers to their second straight state championship. Ozen had defeated San Antonio Lanier to win the state championship in 2001.

Lincoln entered the game ranked number 1 in the nation by *USA Today*, and Ozen held the number 7 spot. The clash attracted a sellout crowd of 16,995 to the Frank Erwin Center in Austin. By defeating Ozen, the Tigers finished the season in the number 1 spot, claiming a national high school basketball championship. "We were only talking about a national title joking around, but as the season went on it meant more to us," Bosh said in a postgame interview.

A little more than a year later, the Toronto Raptors selected Bosh with the fourth pick of the 2003 NBA draft following his freshman season at Georgia Tech. The Memphis Grizzlies chose Perkins with the twenty-seventh pick of the same draft after Perkins's senior season at Ozen.

MARCH 10, 2012

Baylor, already the Big 12 women's basketball regular-season champion, notched a meaningful three-game sweep of Texas A&M as the Lady Bears claimed a 73–50 victory in the Big 12 Tournament championship game in Kansas City, Missouri.

A year earlier, the Aggies had defeated Baylor in the NCAA Tournament regional final to steal a Final Four berth from the top-seeded Lady Bears.

But Baylor responded ferociously.

The Lady Bears began the 2011–2012 season ranked number 1 and proved their mettle with a victory over second-ranked Connecticut in December. Baylor was 34–0 by the time it completed its season sweep of Texas A&M at the Big 12 Tournament. But the Lady Bears had their attention focused on loftier goals than revenge against the Aggies. "We've been winning all season," said Odyssey Sims, who led Baylor with twenty-six points in the Big 12 Tournament championship game. "We've been successful. This is great, but now we're focused on six games. That's what we're striving for."

Baylor kept rolling and notched those six wins, finishing with a 40–0 record and a national championship. The Lady Bears defeated Notre Dame 80–61 in the NCAA Tournament final for the title.

MARCH 11, 1989

MARCH 12, 2009

San Antonio Cole seven-foot center Shaquille O'Neal led the Cougars to a 66–60 victory over Clarksville for the Class 3A state championship at the Frank Erwin Center in Austin. O'Neal scored nineteen points, grabbed twenty-six rebounds, blocked three shots, and handed out six assists in the championship game victory.

In what would become his signature smirking-bravado style, O'Neal described Cole's formula for success to a television reporter: "Well, the secret is me blocking shots and getting rebounds and making my shots well. That's the secret."

The future LSU All-American and number 1 overall NBA draft pick by the Orlando Magic averaged twenty-two rebounds a game and set a state record with 791 boards during his senior season at Cole.

Baylor guard LaceDarius Dunn went six for eleven from behind the three-point arc, scoring twenty-four points and leading the ninth-seeded Bears to a 71–64 upset of top-seeded Kansas at the Big 12 Tournament in Oklahoma City.

Baylor surged to a seventeen-point lead in the first half, reaching its largest margin when guard Curtis Jerrells hit a three-pointer with 7:08 left before halftime. But Kansas came all the way back to tie the game at 37 early in the second half. "We kept telling ourselves we can't get down and just can't give up," Dunn said in a postgame press conference. "We just kept fighting, and it turned out great for us."

Kansas took the lead midway through the second half, but Dunn scored eight points in a crucial four-minute span near the end. He made a jumper that gave Baylor a 60–58 edge, and this time the Bears held onto the lead.

Baylor lost to Missouri in the Big 12 Tournament championship game, keeping the Bears out of the NCAA Tournament. But Baylor went into the National Invitational Tournament riding a wave of confidence. The team made the finals before falling to Penn State 69–63 at Madison Square Garden in New York.

MARCH 13, 2007

Dallas Star center Mike Modano controlled a ricocheting puck and stuffed it into the net past Philadelphia Flyer goaltender Antero Niittymäki, lighting the lamp and sending the Stars' fans into an uproar. The Dallas crowd cheered Modano's 500th career goal, and the Stars went on to a 3–2 win over the Flyers on the historic night.

"I wanted to get it over with," Modano said. "I wanted to do it here and celebrate in front of our fans."

Modano, who played sixteen of his twenty-one NHL seasons in Dallas, finished his career with 557 goals and 802 assists. With him in the lineup, the Stars enjoyed twelve playoff seasons and Stanley Cup Finals appearances in 1999 and 2000.

MARCH 14, 1992

The Texas Tech women's basketball team broke new ground by defeating Texas 76–74 in the Southwest Conference Tournament championship game. Texas had controlled the conference from 1983 to 1990 before Arkansas wrested away both the regular season and conference tournament titles in 1991. Texas Tech then seized its turn to sweep both championships in 1992.

Junior forward Sheryl Swoopes led the Lady Raiders with twenty-four points and fourteen rebounds, enough to fend off a valiant challenge from the Lady Longhorns.

"This is a great day for women's basketball at Texas Tech," Lady Raiders coach Marsha Sharp said. "It's a great feeling to beat Texas in a game both teams can be proud of."

MARCH 15, 2003

Texas forward Stacy Stephens led a second-half rally as the fifth-ranked Longhorns defeated eighth-ranked Texas Tech 67–57 for the Longhorns' first Big 12 Conference Women's Basketball Tournament championship. Texas claimed the title in front of a tournament-record crowd of 10,717 at Reunion Arena in Dallas.

Stephens finished with sixteen points, and frontcourt teammate Heather Schreiber scored thirteen points and grabbed eleven rebounds. The duo made most of the key shots during a 16–3 run midway through the second half. The Longhorns' surge erased Texas Tech's nine-point lead and gave Texas the lead for good.

"I had my doubts to as if we could stay on the floor with them," Texas coach Jody Conradt said in a postgame press conference. "We struggled to stay close. I think Stacy's baskets gave us the momentum for us to believe we could win."

The Longhorns and Red Raiders both entered the NCAA Tournament as number 2 seeds. Texas Tech reached the Elite Eight before falling to Duke, while Texas earned a Final Four berth and then lost in the semifinals against the eventual national champion, Connecticut.

MARCH 16, 2006

Texas A&M guard Acie Law scored twelve of his game-high twenty-three points in the final 2:25 of the second half as he led the twelfth-seeded Aggies to a 66–58 upset of fifth-seeded Syracuse in the first round of the NCAA Tournament in Jacksonville, Florida.

Texas A&M, making its first NCAA Tournament appearance in nineteen years, notched its first win in the Big Dance since 1980. The Aggies' victory marked a high point in Billy Gillispie's three-year stint as Texas A&M's head coach. The Aggies lost to fourth-seeded LSU in the next round.

Texas A&M returned to the NCAA Tournament in 2007 with a number 3 seed and advanced to the Sweet Sixteen before being ousted by second-seeded Memphis. Gillispie departed soon after for Kentucky.

MARCH 17, 1996

Texas Tech forward Jason Sasser missed a hook shot in the lane, setting the stage for teammate Darvin Ham's career-defining play.

When Sasser's shot bounced high off the back iron, Ham sprung into action, sprinting in from the free-throw line and vaulting to grab the rebound and slam home a thundering dunk in one motion. Ham's slam tied the Red Raiders with North Carolina at 16 with 12:06 remaining in the first half of an NCAA Tournament second-round tilt. It also shattered the backboard and supplied Texas Tech with a phenomenal momentum boost.

"My teammates were already hyped up, and that play really just set the whole thing off," Ham said after the game. "I was just feeling so good and ready to play that I wanted to run around the court and jump up and down and do some flips. Sasser was giving me chest bumps, and I just wanted to flex."

The Red Raiders ran away with the contest in the aftermath of Ham's dunk. Texas Tech defeated the Tar Heels 92–73 at Richmond Coliseum in Richmond, Virginia.

Sasser scored twenty-seven points, and Ham added fourteen, as Texas Tech improved to 30–1 on the season and advanced to play Georgetown in the Sweet Sixteen. Four days later, Allen Iverson's Hoyas ended the Red Raiders' season with a 98–90 win, but Ham had given the Red Raiders a shining moment for the ages.

MARCH 18, 1967

MARCH 19, 1966

The Houston Cougars fended off a furious second-half rally by SMU and held onto an 83–75 victory in the Midwest Regional final of the NCAA Tournament, played in Lawrence, Kansas. In doing so, Houston earned its first Final Four berth.

Cougars center Elvin Hayes dominated the contest, scoring thirty-one points and pulling down eleven rebounds. But that almost wasn't enough. The Cougars led by twelve points with seven minutes left in the contest before SMU rallied to tie the game at 73. When Hayes hit a jumper from near the free-throw line with 1:57 left, it gave Houston a three-point edge that allowed the Cougars to escape the Mustang surge.

Houston, which did not have a conference affiliation at the time, entered the NCAA Tournament ranked seventh in the nation. The Cougars didn't join the Southwest Conference until the 1975–1976 season, but outdueled SWC champion SMU for the Final Four berth. Coach John Wooden's UCLA Bruins defeated Houston in the national semifinal.

Texas Western coach Don Haskins deployed an all-black starting lineup—guards Bobby Joe Hill, Willie Worsley, and Orsten Artis, forward Harry Flournoy, and center David Lattin—against the all-white Kentucky Wildcats in the NCAA Tournament championship game.

The Miners were the first basketball program to start five African American players in an NCAA Tournament title game, and the team defeated top-ranked and heavily favored Kentucky 72–65 in front of 14,253 at Cole Field House in College Park, Maryland.

Hill scored twenty points and Lattin dominated the boards as they led Texas Western to the historic victory, which inspired the 2006 film *Glory Road*.

The significance of the cultural statement didn't occur to Haskins until the aftermath of the win. "I guess I really didn't give much thought to it, and I didn't give a lot of thought to it before we played Kentucky for the national championship," said Haskins in a famous comment from an interview years after winning the title. "I just thought about beating them. I really didn't know until after the game, and I got bushelsful of hate mail, how important that game was. All I did was play my best people. It was that simple."

The Texas Western Miners are the only men's basketball team from the state of Texas to claim the Division I title as of this writing. Photo courtesy of UTEP Athletics.

MARCH 20, 2016

Northern Iowa's Jeremy Morgan made a pair of free throws to give the Panthers a twelve-point lead over Texas A&M with forty-four seconds left in the second half of a second-round NCAA Tournament game in Oklahoma City. Some Aggies fans who filed out of the arena glanced at their smartphones in the parking lot, turned on their heels, and headed back for one of the craziest comebacks in the history of March Madness.

Aggie guard Admon Gilder got an offensive rebound and made a layup and then stole the ball from UNI. After Texas A&M's Danuel House added another layup, Aggie forward Jalen Jones came up with a steal and threw down a dunk. Then another Panther turnover led to a House three-pointer that cut UNI's lead to three points.

For a moment it appeared as if sanity would prevail when Panther forward Klint Carlson broke away for a dunk with seventeen seconds left. But the Aggies weren't finished. Texas A&M guard Alex Caruso quickly went to the basket and completed a three-point play. Gilder swiped one more steal, off an errant Panther pass, and made a layup to tie the game at 71 with three seconds left. From there, a Texas A&M win seemed inevitable. The Aggies finally grasped a 92–88 victory in double overtime.

UNI guard Paul Jesperson had banked in a half-court buzzer beater to defeat Texas two days earlier in the first round. But it was the Aggies who were in gleeful amazement after the second-round thriller.

"The game, man, I'm still at a loss for words," Jones said in the postgame press conference. "I'm still just shocked. I just know that my teammates and I just continued to fight throughout the game and we kept fighting and the coaching staff just kept telling us to fight. Our bench kept backing us up, the crowd kept backing us up. Man, it was just probably one of the best victories of my life."

MARCH 21, 2014

Stephen F. Austin added to March Madness lore as the twelfth-seeded Lumberjacks upset fifth-seeded Virginia Commonwealth 77–75 in overtime in the round of sixty-four in San Diego.

VCU held a ten-point lead with 3:38 left in the second half, but then the Lumberjacks made their charge. SFA guard Thomas Walkup went to the basket for a layup, and forward Jacob Parker hit a three-pointer to quickly slice VCU's lead to five. But the Rams continued to fend off SFA, and VCU appeared to seal the game when guard Brianté Weber made a layup for a four-point lead with twenty-one seconds left.

That was when magic happened. Walkup drove into the lane in the closing seconds and found Lumberjack teammate Desmond Haymon open on the right wing. Haymon hit a three-pointer and got fouled by VCU guard JeQuan Lewis with three seconds left. Haymon stepped to the free-throw line and sank a shot to tie the game at 67, sending it to overtime.

Haymon hit another key three-pointer in overtime, one that put SFA in the lead for good. "I was struggling shooting the ball, and I knew to get it going I was going to have to continue to try to find it," Haymon said. "I guess I found that groove with the last shot."

Fourth-seeded UCLA ended SFA's run two days later, but it didn't smudge the Lumberjacks' shining moment.

MARCH 22, 2004

The Baylor women's basketball team earned its first trip to the NCAA Tournament's Sweet Sixteen when the fourth-seeded Lady Bears defeated fifth-seeded Florida 91–76 in a Midwest Regional second-round game in Albuquerque, New Mexico.

The win marked a significant leap forward for Coach Kim Mulkey's Baylor squad. Although top-seeded Tennessee defeated the Lady Bears by two points in the next round, Mulkey had built a future powerhouse. After breaking through to the Sweet Sixteen in 2004, Mulkey and the Lady Bears ascended to the national championship at the end of the next season.

MARCH 23, 2001

Texas Tech introduced Bob Knight as its new men's basketball coach at a combination press conference–pep rally held at the United Spirit Arena in Lubbock. The Red Raiders loudly welcomed Knight, despite his controversial dismissal as Indiana's head coach just six months earlier because of incidents of physical abuse of players at IU.

Knight had led the Hoosiers to three national championships and eleven Big Ten regular-season titles in his twenty-nine years at the school. But the red-sweater-clad coach known as the "General" hadn't won a conference title since 1993 and hadn't made it to the Sweet Sixteen since 1994.

Still, Texas Tech hired him to breathe life back into the Red Raiders, and he was up for the challenge. "Without a doubt this is the most comfortable red sweater I've had on in six years," Knight told reporters and the Red Raider crowd at his introductory press conference.

MARCH 24, 1990

MARCH 25, 1993

Southwest Conference rivals Arkansas and Texas met in the Midwest Regional final at Reunion Arena in Dallas. Tenth-seeded Texas had made an improbable run to the Elite Eight of the NCAA Tournament by defeating seventh-seeded Georgia, second-seeded Purdue, and sixth-seeded Xavier to face the fourth-seeded Razorbacks, with a berth in the Final Four at stake. Arkansas had defeated Texas twice during the regular season and won the SWC tournament with a victory over Houston at Reunion Arena just two weeks earlier.

Arkansas kept its good vibe in Dallas going by dismissing Texas from the Big Dance 88–85. Texas guards Travis Mays and Joey Wright scored twenty points apiece, but it wasn't enough to offset the talented Razorbacks. Forward Lenzie Howell led Arkansas with twenty-one points, and guard Lee Mayberry added eighteen points and seven assists.

After the game, Arkansas coach Nolan Richardson lamented that the two teams had been placed in the same regional bracket. "There's no question in my mind that if Texas had gone the other direction (in a different region), we'd probably be meeting (at the Final Four) in Denver," Richardson said.

Duke ousted the Razorbacks from the tournament in the national semifinal.

Sheryl Swoopes bested another future women's basketball superstar when she lifted the Texas Tech Lady Raiders past Lisa Leslie–led Southern California 87–67 in the Sweet Sixteen round of the NCAA Tournament in Missoula, Montana. Swoopes scored thirty-three points and grabbed eleven rebounds in an outstanding performance that spurred Texas Tech's successful run to the 1993 national title. Leslie scored fifteen and added eleven rebounds in the Trojans' losing effort.

Lady Raiders guard Krista Kirkland complemented Swoopes's performance by scoring twenty-six points and handing out eight assists. Texas Tech took control of the game early, holding USC to two points through the first five minutes. The Lady Raiders led 40–22 at halftime.

MARCH 26, 2010

Baylor basketball fans took over the South Regional site and roared their approval as the Bears dismantled Saint Mary's 72–49 in a Sweet Sixteen game at Houston's Reliant Stadium.

While the Baylor women's team found phenomenal success in the 2000s, the Baylor men saw their drought without an NCAA Tournament victory linger on through the decade. But Coach Scott Drew's Bears made history in the first round of March Madness in 2010 by defeating Sam Houston State for Baylor's first NCAA Tournament win in sixty years. Riding that wave of momentum, Bears fans showed up en masse in Houston.

"It's like a home game," Baylor forward Ekpe Udoh said in a postgame press conference. "I mean the whole lower bowl seemed like it was all Baylor fans."

The Bears clearly fed off their fans' intensity as they raced past Saint Mary's in the first half. Baylor hit a barrage of three-pointers, and guard Tweety Carter lobbed a fast-break pass to fellow guard LaceDarius Dunn for a highlight-reel alley-oop as the Bears streaked to a 46–17 halftime lead. Baylor never looked back. Dunn scored twenty-three points, Carter added fourteen, and Udoh contributed eight points and eleven rebounds.

The Bears advanced to the regional final to face Duke two days later. The Blue Devils prevailed 78–71, eliminating Baylor from the tournament.

MARCH 27, 1971

MARCH 28, 2003

UCLA coach John Wooden led the Bruins to their fifth consecutive NCAA Tournament championship, and their seventh title in eight years, as UCLA defeated Villanova 68–62 in the only Final Four held at the Astrodome in Houston. Steve Patterson led the Bruins, scoring twenty-nine points, grabbing eight rebounds, and dishing out four assists.

Villanova returned to the national championship game on the same city block forty-five years and a few days later. The Wildcats defeated North Carolina 77–74 in the 2016 NCAA Tournament championship game at NRG Stadium.

Old Houston-area high school rivals clashed again, and once again T. J. Ford got the better of Emeka Okafor, this time in the NCAA Tournament's Sweet Sixteen round in San Antonio.

Fort Bend Willowridge alum Ford led Texas to an 82–78 victory over Houston Bellaire alum Okafor and Connecticut. Ford, who finished with thirteen points and nine assists, hit a pair of free throws with 11.8 seconds remaining to help the Longhorns seal the win. Okafor scored twenty-one points and grabbed seventeen rebounds for the Huskies, but the sophomore center and the Huskies would have to wait another year before reaching the Final Four.

Instead, Ford led Texas to its first Final Four appearance in sixty years. Two days after the top-seeded Longhorns defeated fifth-seeded Connecticut, Texas ousted seventh-seeded Michigan State in the South Regional final. Syracuse, the eventual national champion, ended Texas's run in the national semifinal, 95–84.

MARCH 29, 1994

The Dallas Cowboys owner, Jerry Jones, and Jimmy Johnson held a joint press conference to announce that Johnson, who had led the team to two consecutive Super Bowl victories, would no longer be the Cowboys' head coach. The next afternoon, Jones held another press conference, announcing the hiring of Barry Switzer as the Cowboys' new head coach.

MARCH 30, 1986

Texas forward Clarissa Davis came off the bench to score twenty-four points and lead the Lady Longhorns past Southern California 97–81 for Texas's first national championship in women's basketball.

The Lady Longhorns (as they were then known) subdued USC superstar Cheryl Miller, who made just two of eleven from the field and finished with sixteen points. Miller, a four-time All-American, fouled out with seven minutes left in the second half.

By defeating USC at Rupp Arena in Lexington, Kentucky, Texas completed a 34–0 season. "I told them in the locker room that I thought this was the best team ever in women's basketball," Lady Longhorn coach Jody Conradt said in a postgame interview.

The Texas team set the tone for women's basketball in the Lone Star State: the Lady Longhorns, Texas Tech, Baylor, and Texas A&M would combine to win five national championships between 1986 and 2012.

(PHOTO, OPPOSITE PAGE)
Texas coach Jody Conradt and forward Clarissa Davis led the Longhorns to the 1986 NCAA National Championship. Photo courtesy of University of Texas Athletics.

MARCH 31, 1984

Michael Young scored seventeen points and Hakeem Olajuwon added twelve points and eleven rebounds as Houston outlasted Virginia 49–47 in the Final Four at Seattle's Kingdome.

The Cougars' national semifinal victory over the Cavaliers would be their last of the Phi Slama Jama era. Two days later, Georgetown defeated Houston in the national championship game, handing the Cougars their second straight loss in the final.

Houston won eighty-eight games in the three seasons leading up to its second consecutive Final Four appearance. Most memorably, the Cougars came heartbreakingly close to grasping the national championship in 1983 before North Carolina State forward Lorenzo Charles caught an errant shot and sent through a buzzer-beating dunk to lift the Wolfpack to the title.

April

APRIL 1, 2003

Texas women's basketball coach Jody Conradt notched her 700th victory at the school as she guided the Longhorns to an Elite Eight, 78–60 victory over LSU at Maples Pavilion in Stanford, California. With the win, Conradt and Texas punched their ticket to the NCAA Tournament Final Four for the third time in program history.

"I've gone into a lot of seasons thinking 'This team is talented enough to get to the Final Four,'" Conradt said in a postgame press conference. "I can't say I ever thought that far ahead with this team. Sometimes the surprises are the best ones."

Texas forward Heather Schreiber scored thirty-two points and grabbed eight rebounds, and fellow forward Stacy Stephens had fourteen points and twelve boards as the second-seeded Lady Longhorns rolled past top-seeded LSU and cut down the nets at the West Regional final.

Texas's men's and women's basketball teams both made the Final Four in 2003. Connecticut defeated the Texas women in the national semifinal, and Syracuse eliminated the Texas men in the same round.

APRIL 2, 1939

Dallas Wilson High School graduate Ralph Guldahl bested Sam Snead by one stroke to win the 1939 Masters green jacket.

Guldahl, who finished as the Masters runner-up in 1937 and 1938, shot a nine-under-par 279 over seventy-two holes at Augusta National Golf Club. He closed the championship with a back nine of three-under on Sunday to edge Snead.

It was Guldahl's third and final major championship, following US Open titles in 1937 and 1938.

Guldahl won sixteen tournaments before the age of thirty, but then his top-notch game deserted him. He never won another professional tournament after the 1940 season.

APRIL 3, 2011

Texas A&M guard Sydney Colson drove into the lane and found guard Tyra White open for a layup with 3.3 seconds remaining to topple number 1 seed Stanford 63–62 in a Final Four semifinal at Bankers Life Fieldhouse in Indianapolis.

It was the second straight game in which the Texas A&M women had dismissed a top seed from the NCAA Tournament: the Aggies ousted Big 12 rival Baylor 58–46 in the Dallas Regional final.

With that momentum, the Aggies charged into the national championship game to meet Notre Dame. "It's time to make history," Colson said. Two days later, Texas A&M defeated Notre Dame 76–70 to claim the national title.

APRIL 4, 1993

Texas Tech star Sheryl Swoopes once again proved unstoppable, leading the Lady Raiders to a national championship victory over Ohio State.

Swoopes scored from inside and out, but her signature move to the basket consistently befuddled and ultimately felled the Buckeyes. Swoopes drove for a layup, drew a foul, and completed a three-point play with fifty-eight seconds left to boost Texas Tech's lead to 80–73. The Lady Raiders hung on for an 84–82 victory.

Texas Tech guard Krista Kirkland pitched in fourteen points to balance Swoopes's offensive show. "Krista and I felt it was time for the two of us to take control," Swoopes said in a postgame interview. "I felt like I would be able to score any time I had the ball."

By pouring in forty-seven points, Swoopes broke Bill Walton's NCAA Tournament championship-game scoring record of forty-four. That performance was the continuation of a trend: three weeks earlier, she had scored fifty-three to lead Texas Tech past Texas in the SWC Tournament final, breaking Larry Bird's Reunion Arena single-game record of fifty points.

Texas Tech women's basketball legend Sheryl Swoopes (22) leaps in celebration of the Lady Raiders' 1993 NCAA National Championship, April 4, 1993. Photo courtesy of Texas Tech University Athletics.

APRIL 5, 2005

Baylor forward Sophia Young scored twenty-six points to lead the Lady Bears basketball team to an 84–62 throttling of Michigan State in the NCAA Tournament championship game. The Lady Bears grasped their first national championship with the victory, and Coach Kim Mulkey became the first woman to win an NCAA title as a player and a coach.

But she deflected the glory onto her players. "What a team I get to coach!" Mulkey exclaimed after the game. "It wasn't the coaching, it's these guys taking me for a tremendous ride."

Baylor forward Sophia Young led the Lady Bears to their first NCAA National Championship in 2005. Photo courtesy of Baylor University Photography.

APRIL 6, 1992

Dallas native Grant Hill (son of Dallas Cowboy standout Calvin Hill) and Lancaster High School alum Thomas Hill bested their Texas counterparts Jimmy King and Ray Jackson of Michigan's Fab Five as the Duke Blue Devils defeated the Wolverines 71–51 in the NCAA Tournament championship game at the Metrodome in Minneapolis, Minnesota. Grant Hill scored eighteen points with ten rebounds and five assists, while Thomas Hill added sixteen points and seven rebounds.

As freshmen, King, from Plano, and Jackson, from Austin, joined Chris Webber, Jalen Rose, and Juwan Howard in a phenomenal recruiting class that lifted the Wolverines to the championship game in their first collegiate season. But Duke held Jackson scoreless and limited King to seven points in the final.

APRIL 7, 1940

Houston native Jimmy Demaret won the first of his three Masters green jackets as he posted a seventy-two-hole eight-under-par 280 at Augusta National Golf Club.

Demaret won again in 1947 and 1950, becoming the first three-time Masters champion. As of this writing, only Jack Nicklaus, Arnold Palmer, and Tiger Woods have surpassed Demaret.

Demaret's win came amid Texas's domination of the Masters. Texans Byron Nelson, Ralph Guldahl, Demaret, Ben Hogan, and Jack Burke Jr. combined to win nine Masters green jackets between 1937 and 1956. They might have added to that total, but the Masters was not played from 1943 to 1945 because of World War II.

APRIL 8, 2014

Connecticut senior guard Shabazz Napier led the Huskies to a 60–54 victory over freshmen-laden Kentucky in the national championship game in front of 79,238 fans at AT&T Stadium in Arlington.

Napier scored twenty-two points and grabbed six rebounds in the final as Connecticut claimed the national title for the third time in eleven years, all in Final Fours played in Texas. The Huskies won the 2011 tournament, played at Reliant Stadium in Houston, and the 2004 championship, contested at the Alamodome in San Antonio.

APRIL 9, 1965

The Houston Astros and New York Yankees played the inaugural game in the Astrodome. President Lyndon B. Johnson and First Lady Lady Bird Johnson were in attendance. Mickey Mantle recorded the first hit and the first home run in the new stadium, though the Astros won the exhibition game 2–1.

APRIL 10, 1993

Richardson native Del Ballard Jr. rolled his way to the Bowling Proprietors' Association of America US Open title, defeating Walter Ray Williams Jr. 237–193 in the title match in Canandaigua, New York. In doing so, Ballard claimed his fourth career bowling major and twelfth tournament championship.

Ballard and his wife, Carolyn-Dorin Ballard, a West Texas State alum who won twenty-one professional titles and was named the Professional Women's Bowling Association Bowler of the Year in 2001 and 2003, are both members of the United States Bowling Congress Hall of Fame.

APRIL 11, 1994

The Texas Rangers officially opened their new home, originally christened The Ballpark in Arlington. The Milwaukee Brewers defeated the Rangers 4–3 in the inaugural game.

APRIL 12, 2015

Dallas native Jordan Spieth finished off four days of domination with a steady final round to win his first Masters green jacket and his first professional golf major at Augusta National Golf Club in Augusta, Georgia. Spieth shot a final-round two-under-par 70 to finish the tournament at eighteen under, four strokes in front of Phil Mickelson and Justin Rose, who tied for second place.

Spieth led the tournament the entire way after an eight-under opening round. He set scoring records through the second round (fourteen-under) and third round (sixteen-under). In the end, he tied Tiger Woods's record for the lowest tournament total, and at twenty-one years and eight months of age, Spieth became the second-youngest winner behind Woods, who won when he was twenty-one and three months.

"It's the most incredible week of my life," Spieth said immediately following his victory. "This is as great as it gets in our sport. It's a dream for me. . . . I'm excited already about coming back. And being the Masters champion. That carries a heavy weight. I hope I'll be ready for it, and what it means."

APRIL 13, 1942

Byron Nelson shot three under par and defeated fellow Fort Worth native Ben Hogan by one stroke in an eighteen-hole playoff for the Masters at Augusta National Golf Club.

Nelson and Hogan, who were caddies at Fort Worth's Glen Garden Country Club in their youth, both finished seventy-two holes of regulation at eight-under-par 280, three strokes in front of the rest of the field. Hogan then grabbed the early advantage in the Monday playoff, going ahead by three shots through the first four holes and taking advantage of Nelson's double bogey on the opening hole. But Nelson began to turn things around with a birdie on the par-three sixth hole and then took the lead with an eagle on the par-five eighth. Nelson stayed hot on the back nine, birdieing the eleventh through thirteenth holes. His birdie on thirteen gave him a three-stroke lead over Hogan with five holes left. Hogan closed to within one stroke but couldn't catch his longtime rival.

By winning the playoff, Nelson claimed his second Masters green jacket, adding to his 1937 championship. Hogan had to wait four years before winning his first major, at the 1946 PGA Championship. Hogan added the Masters to his career grand slam in 1951.

Waxahachie native Byron Nelson, who grew up caddying at Glen Garden Country Club in Fort Worth, went on a historic eleven-tournament winning streak in 1945. The streak included Nelson's fifth and final career major victory, which came at the PGA Championship at Moraine Country Club in Dayton, Ohio. Photo courtesy of the Texas Sports Hall of Fame.

Texas State (then Southwest Texas State) freshman pitcher Nicole Neuerburg enjoyed a perfect day in the circle as she sat down twenty-one straight Texas–San Antonio batters at Bobcat Stadium in San Marcos. Neuerburg struck out eleven, including UTSA's Serena Ormsby for the final out of the perfect game, which was the first Texas State softball no-hitter in more than a decade.

Bobcat catcher Jennie Tomme and shortstop Liz Wissel supplied the offense as Texas State claimed a 6–0 victory over the Roadrunners. Tomme homered to left field, and Wissel hit a two-run double down the left-field line, giving Neuerburg more than enough run support. A day earlier, Neuerburg had a no-hitter going until the final out, when Ormsby broke it up with a single in the seventh.

"I don't know if there's enough you can say about Nicole Neuerburg and the way she threw the ball this weekend," Texas State coach Ricci Woodard told *San Marcos Record* sportswriter Jason Gordon after the game. "She's been capable of this all year and she was really able to put it together."

The twentieth-ranked Bobcats swept UTSA in three straight games, winning by a combined total of 21–0, during a phenomenal stretch of softball. Texas State won eighteen straight games, including thirteen shutouts, between April 4 and May 10. Neuerburg's no-hitter came in the middle of a stretch of eight straight shutouts. The Bobcats finished the 2001 season with a 54–12 record and won the Southland Conference championship. Eventual national champion Arizona ended Texas State's season in the NCAA Tournament regional final with a 6–2 win in Tucson, Arizona.

APRIL 15, 1984

APRIL 16, 1972

Austin High and University of Texas alum Ben Crenshaw shot a final-round four-under-par 68 to hold off Tom Watson for the Masters green jacket. Crenshaw, who edged Watson by two shots, won his tenth PGA Tour tournament and his first major title, posting eleven under for seventy-two holes at Augusta National Golf Club.

In his post-tournament comments, Crenshaw considered his near misses at majors up to that point. "I never thought this moment would come," Crenshaw said. "When you hit in the water on the seventy-first hole to miss a playoff in the US Open ... When you make double bogey on the seventy-first hole to lose the British Open ... When you lose a playoff for the PGA ... When you miss by one shot you start to wonder if you can hold yourself together, if you can ever win it. This is a sweet, sweet win. I don't think there'll ever be a sweeter moment."

Crenshaw went on to win nineteen times in his PGA Tour career. His only other major came at the Masters in 1995, when he once again shot four under in the final round, this time for a tournament total of fourteen under, a stroke better than Davis Love III. Crenshaw's second Masters victory came one week after his longtime coach, Harvey Penick, died at age ninety.

Corpus Christi King and University of Texas alum Burt Hooton threw a no-hitter in his fourth Major League start, pitching the Chicago Cubs to a 4–0 victory over the Philadelphia Phillies at Wrigley Field. Hooton struck out seven and walked seven as his go-to pitch, the knuckle-curve, baffled the Philadelphia lineup.

"I went to (the knuckle-curve) exclusively in the eighth and ninth innings when I pitched my best," Hooton said in a postgame interview. "That's when I felt the adrenaline flowing."

Hooton went on to win 151 games in 377 Major League starts before retiring after the 1985 season. His gem against the Phillies in the second game of the 1972 season remained his only career no-hitter.

APRIL 17, 1994

APRIL 18, 1998

Left wing Brent Gilchrist scored two goals, and goaltender Darcy Wakaluk made thirty-three saves, to lift the Dallas Stars to their first playoff victory, a 5–3 win over the St. Louis Blues at Reunion Arena in Dallas.

The franchise had reached the Stanley Cup Finals three seasons earlier as the Minnesota North Stars and then moved to Dallas in 1993. The Stars went on to sweep the Blues 4–0 in the NHL Western Conference first-round series. The Vancouver Canucks defeated Dallas 4–1 in the conference semifinal series.

Dallas Star center Joe Nieuwendyk and wingers Jere Lehtinen and Jamie Langenbrunner scored a goal apiece to lift the Stars to a 3–1 victory over the Chicago Blackhawks at Reunion Arena in Dallas. With the win, the Stars clinched the Presidents' Trophy, awarded to the NHL team with the best regular-season record, for the first time in franchise history.

Dallas finished the 1997–1998 season 49–22–11, for 109 standings points, two better than the second-place New Jersey Devils. The Stars reached the Western Conference Finals before losing to the eventual Stanley Cup champions, the Detroit Red Wings, four games to two, in their best-of-seven series.

APRIL 19, 1991

Native Texan and forty-two-year-old former heavyweight champion George Foreman went toe-to-toe with current heavyweight champ Evander Holyfield for twelve rounds at the Atlantic City Convention Center. Foreman, who had retired in 1977 and then made a comeback in 1987, after ten years away from boxing, showed he belonged in the ring in the seventh round when he traded punches for a thrilling three minutes of heavyweight action.

Although Holyfield won the fight by unanimous decision and remained the undisputed heavyweight champion, it was Foreman who held up his head and crowed following the bout. "Senior citizens everywhere can be proud of themselves," he said in a postfight interview.

Foreman viewed going the distance against Holyfield as an achievement, and the sports world concurred. Boxing writers speculated that it would be Foreman's last fight, and the man himself predicted it would be a singular event. "We proved that the age forty, fifty, or sixty is not a death sentence," Foreman said. "It will be fifty years until the world sees something like this again."

As it turned out, everyone was wrong. Foreman entered the ring nine more times and regained the heavyweight championship at age forty-five when he knocked out Michael Moorer in the tenth round of a match on November 5, 1994, at the MGM Grand in Las Vegas.

APRIL 20, 2007

Baylor took over hosting the Varsity Equestrian National Championships, but Texas A&M grabbed the spotlight at the Heart O' Texas Fair Complex. The Aggies defeated South Carolina 6–2 in the final match to win the western riding national championship.

Texas A&M rider Caroline Green posted a match-high score of 149.5 in horsemanship, and the Aggies swept all four points in the discipline. Maggie Gratny scored 147 in reining to win a crucial point in that event, which the Aggies and Gamecocks split 2–2. Texas A&M riders Maddi Williams, Tonna Brooks, and Amanda Ryan also won points to help the Aggies win their fourth national title in western riding in the program's eighth year of existence.

"You have to go mistake free," Texas A&M coach Tana Rawson said. "We had a couple of little bobbles in the beginning, but overall they were very, very smart. That's the name of the game."

APRIL 21, 1972

The Texas Rangers played their first home game at Arlington Stadium, defeating the California Angels 7–6.

Ranger second baseman Len Randle brought home four runs with a pair of singles, and Frank Howard and Dave Nelson each homered in the Texas win.

The Rangers, in their inaugural season after the franchise moved from Washington, DC, to the Dallas–Fort Worth Metroplex, were managed by Hall of Famer Ted Williams, but finished last in the American League West with a 54–100 record.

APRIL 22, 1979

SMU senior Payne Stewart shot a final-round two-under-par 70 to tie Houston sophomore Fred Couples at five-under, 211, for the Southwest Conference men's golf individual championships at Briarwood Country Club in Tyler. The two players were officially cochampions. Stewart, however, won a sudden-death playoff on the first hole to earn the berth at the Colonial Invitational, in Fort Worth, that came with the conference medalist title.

Stewart went on to win eleven PGA tournaments, including three major championships, between 1982 and 1999. Couples surpassed Stewart in PGA wins, with fifteen, but won just one major title, the 1992 Masters.

APRIL 23, 1989

With the first pick of the NFL draft, the Dallas Cowboys selected Troy Aikman, quarterback from UCLA.

Dallas's pick of Aikman came a year after it chose wide receiver Michael Irvin with the eleventh selection, and a year before the Cowboys grabbed Emmitt Smith with the seventeenth pick.

Aikman, who went on to lead Dallas to three Super Bowl victories, was the only quarterback selected in the first round in 1989.

APRIL 24, 2012

The Texas Rangers' first-year pitcher Yu Darvish served notice that he was a genuine ace when he struck out ten New York Yankees in the Rangers' 2–0 victory at Globe Life Park in Arlington. Darvish, making his fourth Major League start, boosted his record to 3–0 by scattering seven hits and two walks. He worked out of a bases-loaded, no-outs jam in the top of the third inning by striking out Yankee center fielder Curtis Granderson and then getting designated hitter Alex Rodriguez to ground into a double play.

Darvish knew, though it was early in his first MLB season, that he was starting to find his rhythm. "After my last start, I mentioned my command is starting to come together," Darvish said through an interpreter following his win over the Yankees. "Stuff-wise, there wasn't much difference. I still like to think that there's still more in me."

Texas acquired Darvish before the 2012 season by placing the winning bid of $51.7 million to buy his rights from the Japanese team Hokkaido Nippon-Ham Fighters. In his first year with the team, Darvish began rewarding the Rangers for their investment, posting a 16–9 record with 221 strikeouts in 191⅓ innings pitched.

APRIL 25, 1993

The New York Giants selected Texas Southern defensive end Michael Strahan with the fortieth pick of the NFL draft. Strahan, who played one year of high school football at Houston Westbury, recorded 141.5 sacks in fifteen NFL seasons, all with the Giants. He was inducted into the Pro Football Hall of Fame in 2014.

APRIL 26, 1984

The Dallas Mavericks extended their first foray into the postseason by defeating the Seattle SuperSonics 105–104 in overtime at Moody Coliseum in the deciding game of the best-of-five Western Conference opening-round playoff series. Guard Rolando Blackman, who scored a game-high twenty-nine points, had a steal and two vital baskets in the final minute to send the game to overtime.

Seattle was leading by six points in the final minute of regulation before Mavs center Pat Cummings hit a pair of free throws and Blackman swiped a pass and converted it into a breakaway dunk with twenty-one seconds left. Blackman's jumper with twelve seconds remaining rattled off the rim and kissed the backboard before falling in to tie the game at 95 on its way to overtime.

Dallas forward Mark Aguirre hit a pair of jumpers early in overtime as the Mavs surged ahead 101–95. The Mavericks never trailed again, though they were forced to endure a clock mishap that allowed Seattle two last-second chances to win the game. But Dallas reserve center Kurt Nimphius deflected a long pass on the official final play to end the game and send the Mavericks on to face the Los Angeles Lakers in the Western Conference semifinals.

The Mavericks and SuperSonics played their deciding game in Moody Coliseum because Dallas's usual home court at Reunion Arena had been booked for World Championship Tennis. The Mavs returned to Reunion Arena to defeat the Lakers in game three of the semifinals, but Los Angeles went on to win the best-of-seven series 4–1.

APRIL 27, 2003

University of Houston alum Fred Couples birdied four of the last five holes at the Redstone Golf Club to win the Houston Open, his first PGA Tour victory in almost five years. Forty-three-year-old Couples finished the tournament with a twenty-one-under-par 267, four strokes ahead of three golfers, including Dallas native and SMU alum Hank Kuehne, in a tie for second place.

It was Couples's fifteenth and last (at the time of this writing) PGA Tour victory. Following his birdie on the final hole, Couples became too emotional to conduct a postround television interview. After he composed himself for the trophy presentation, he explained the tears. "I am always emotional when nice things happen to nice people," Couples said. "I haven't played really well in five years, and I worked hard on my game, and it meshed. That's kind of what was going through my mind (in the television interview). Didn't get it out very well."

APRIL 28, 2002

Austinite Andy Roddick won his second consecutive US Men's Clay Court Championship with a 7–6 (11–9), 6–3 victory over Pete Sampras at the Westside Tennis Club in Houston.

APRIL 29, 1984

Tennis superstar John McEnroe held back his infamous temper and instead unleashed one of the finest performances of his career, defeating archrival Jimmy Connors 6–1, 6–2, 6–3 in the World Championship Tennis final on the carpet court inside Reunion Arena in Dallas.

"This is probably one of the greatest matches I have ever played," McEnroe told the crowd of 13,236 in a postmatch speech.

McEnroe used thirteen aces to even his career record against Connors at twelve wins apiece. Connors knew he was seeing his counterpart at his best. "When he's serving as well as he did today, he's dangerous on anything," Connors said afterward. "He's able to hit the ground strokes when he has to, and I thought he played well all-around today."

APRIL 30, 1932

The inaugural Houston Fat Stock Show opened at Sam Houston Hall in downtown Houston. As the event evolved, it migrated from its original location, to the Astrodome and eventually to NRG Stadium.

Now known as the Houston Livestock Show and Rodeo, it is one of the world's largest and most prestigious rodeos. In 2013, the twenty-one-day event had attendance of more than 2.5 million.

May

MAY 1, 1991

Forty-four-year-old Nolan Ryan felt his age as he prepared to face the Toronto Blue Jays, but it didn't stop the Texas legend from making history. After a day of popping Advil to quiet a stiff back and ankle, the Ryan Express tossed the seventh no-hitter of his career as the Rangers notched a 3–0 victory over the Blue Jays. Ryan struck out Toronto second baseman Roberto Alomar swinging to end the game, and the Texas players carried Ryan on their shoulders off the field at Arlington Stadium.

Ryan struck out sixteen and walked two while shutting down Toronto. Right fielder Ruben Sierra hit a two-run home run into the stands in left, scoring first baseman Rafael Palmeiro and capping a three-run Rangers rally in the bottom of the third inning.

After the game, Texas manager Bobby Valentine broke open a bottle of champagne that he had been saving for a World Series celebration. Ryan becoming the oldest pitcher to toss a no-hitter qualified as an accomplishment deserving of a toast.

Despite a miserable lead-up to the game, including a poor warm-up, Ryan came alive early, and the Blue Jays were in trouble. "The key tonight was I had good command of all three of my pitches," Ryan said in a postgame interview. "I had a good fastball, and I was able to establish my changeup and curveball early, which is what we intended to do."

At the time of his seventh no-hitter, and still at the time of this writing in 2016, Ryan was the only pitcher in MLB history to record more than four no-hitters.

MAY 2, 1979

MAY 3, 2001

San Antonio Spur guard George "the Iceman" Gervin hit a pair of free throws with eleven seconds left in the fourth quarter to ice the Spurs' 111–108 victory over the Philadelphia 76ers. By edging Philadelphia in the decisive seventh game, San Antonio won its first seven-game series in franchise history and advanced to the conference finals of the NBA playoffs for the first time.

Julius "Dr. J" Erving scored a game-high thirty-four points, one more than Gervin, who led the NBA in scoring that season. The Spurs advanced on the strength of Gervin's usual output plus Larry Kenon's twenty-seven points and Mike Green's twenty.

The Spurs forced the Washington Bullets to a deciding seventh game in the Eastern Conference finals, in which the Bullets prevailed. Although San Antonio made the playoffs in nine of its first ten NBA seasons, the Spurs didn't break through to the finals until 1999, when they won their first NBA championship.

The Dallas Mavericks, making their first playoff appearance in eleven years, edged the Utah Jazz 84–83 to finish off a 3–2 first-round series victory at the Delta Center in Salt Lake City, Utah.

The Jazz led by fourteen points as the fourth quarter began, but Mavs stars Steve Nash, Michael Finley, and Dirk Nowitzki each contributed points to Dallas's 18–4 run to tie the game. Nash hit a three-pointer with 4:02 remaining to even the score at 79. Dallas reserve guard Calvin Booth made a layup with 9.6 seconds left to give the Mavericks their first lead since early in the fourth quarter, and the Jazz couldn't answer.

The San Antonio Spurs ended Dallas's season in the next round with a 4–1 series victory.

(PHOTO, OPPOSITE PAGE)
Distance runner Sally Kipyego won a combined nine national titles in cross country, indoor track, and outdoor track during her Texas Tech career. Photo courtesy of Texas Tech University Athletics.

MAY 4, 2008

Texas Tech distance runner Sally Kipyego posted an NCAA-record time of 31:25.45 in the 10,000-meter run at the Payton Jordan Cardinal Invitational in Palo Alto, California. Kipyego's scorching pace bested her own personal record in the event by more than thirty seconds and was the fastest time run by a collegian up to that point in the 2008 season by more than forty-five seconds.

Kipyego's victory was a prelude to her national championship in the event later that season. The Kenyan-born distance runner finished her Texas Tech career with a combined nine national titles in cross-country and indoor and outdoor track. She went on to win the silver medal in the 10,000 at the London Olympics in 2012.

MAY 5, 1995

Hakeem Olajuwon and Clyde Drexler stamped Phi Slama Jama's seal on NBA history as the University of Houston alumni became the third set of teammates to each score more than forty points in a playoff game. Drexler poured in forty-one points with nine rebounds and six assists, and Olajuwon added forty and eight rebounds to lift the Houston Rockets to a 123–106 victory over the Utah Jazz in a Western Conference first-round best-of-five series.

The Jazz led the series 2–1 before the Rockets duo lit up the scoreboard. "We couldn't deal with Olajuwon or Drexler at all," Jazz coach Jerry Sloan said in a postgame interview.

Two nights later, the Rockets won the series' deciding game on their way to their second consecutive NBA championship. Houston swept the Orlando Magic in the NBA Finals for the title.

MAY 6, 1998

Grand Prairie High School alum Kerry Wood set a National League record by striking out twenty Houston Astros batters as he led the Chicago Cubs to a 2–0 victory at Wrigley Field. Wood, who was a little more than a month shy of his twenty-first birthday, pumped his fastball, consistently clocked at 95–100 miles an hour, past one Astro hitter after another. He tied fellow Texan Roger Clemens for the Major League record for strikeouts in a game.

Astros manager Larry Dierker compared Wood to yet another flame-throwing Texan. "It reminded me of the first time we ever saw Nolan Ryan," Dierker told reporters after the game. "It seemed like the ball was getting to the catcher's mitt at about the same time he was letting it go."

Astro shortstop Ricky Gutierrez kept Wood from pitching a no-hitter, legging out a grounder to third base for a single in the third inning, the Astros' only hit of the afternoon contest. Wood shut down the heart of Houston's batting order—Jeff Bagwell, Jack Howell, and Moises Alou—as they went zero for nine with nine strikeouts.

MAY 7, 1955

Fabens native Willie Shoemaker won the first of his eleven Triple Crown races as he rode Swaps to victory at the Kentucky Derby.

Shoemaker pushed Swaps into the lead early in the race, and the horse-and-rider team held off Nashua on the home stretch to win by a length and a half at the famed Churchill Downs in Louisville, Kentucky.

Willie Shoemaker won the Kentucky Derby four times—including the 1965 Derby, which he won on this horse, Lucky Debonair—among his eleven Triple Crown titles. Photo courtesy of Texas Sports Hall of Fame.

MAY 8, 1965

Texas A&M multisport athlete Randy Matson threw the sixteen-pound shot put 70 feet, 7 inches on his second throw at the Southwest Conference championships, held in College Station, to win the event. In doing so, he became the first person to break the seventy-foot barrier, setting a world record.

Matson, who had already ascended to world-class status by winning the silver medal in the shot put at the 1964 Tokyo Olympics, won the SWC title by almost fifteen feet. Baylor's Jim Lancaster finished second at 55 feet, 10 inches.

"I really didn't feel I'd do better than sixty-seven feet today," Matson said in an interview held in the Kyle Field press box. "But my first throw went past sixty-eight and kind of rolled off the side of my hand, so I felt like I could do better."

Matson, also a member of the Aggies basketball team, went on to win the gold medal in the shot put at the 1968 Mexico City Olympics with a throw of 67 feet, 5 inches.

(PHOTO, OPPOSITE PAGE)
Texas A&M track and field star Randy Matson won four NCAA national championships (two in shot put and two in discus), six US track and field national titles, and an Olympic gold medal in the shot put at the 1968 Mexico City Games. Photo courtesy of Texas A&M Athletics.

MAY 9, 1997

The fourth-ranked Texas Tech baseball team claimed a 12–9 victory against Texas A&M at Dan Law Field in Lubbock, and in doing so the Red Raiders locked up the first Big 12 baseball regular-season championship.

Texas A&M led for most of the game before Texas Tech put together a rally for the ages, scoring twelve runs in the bottom of the seventh inning. Texas Tech first baseman Joe Dillon, who led off the seventh by walking, later singled and scored twice in the frame. Red Raider catcher and cleanup hitter Josh Bard singled twice and scored twice, but it was six-hole hitter Jason Landreth who did the most damage in the inning. Landreth doubled to bring home two runs, shifting the rally into high gear. He scored after his first at-bat and then walked in his second one of the inning, after which pinch runner Duane Price scored in his place. In all, Texas Tech plated the twelve runs on nine hits, three walks, and an Aggie error.

Texas Tech third baseman Keith Ginter singled in the seventh to extend his school-record hitting streak to twenty-nine games. But he went hitless the next day, and Texas A&M won the final two games of the series.

MAY 10, 2016

San Antonio Spurs center Tim Duncan played in his 250th playoff game. He logged twenty-eight minutes, scoring five points, grabbing three rebounds, and blocking two shots in the Spurs' 95–91 loss to the Oklahoma City Thunder in game five of the Western Conference semifinals. Duncan, who had not scored in game four, ended the drought by going down the lane for a dunk with 2:58 left in the second quarter.

Duncan's 250th playoff game, the equivalent of more than three full NBA regular seasons, put him nine games behind Derek Fisher for the most career playoff games in NBA history. Fisher reached the playoffs with the Los Angeles Lakers, the Utah Jazz, and the Thunder, while Duncan wore a Spurs jersey for all of his playoff appearances.

MAY 11, 2007

Copperas Cove junior Robert Griffin III flew past the competition, setting state records in the 110-meter and 300-meter hurdles at the UIL Class 4A Track & Field Championships at Mike A. Myers Stadium in Austin. Griffin raced to a time of 35.33 seconds in the 300 hurdles, setting a new state record for all classes and finishing just 0.01 of a second slower than the national record. He earlier won the 110 hurdles in a 4A-record time of 13.55 seconds.

With Griffin's performances, a victory in the 4 × 200-meter relay, and a second-place finish in the 4 × 400-meter relay, Copperas Cove claimed the 4A team championship.

It was Griffin's final state meet. After graduating in December, he joined the Baylor football team for spring practice and the Bears track squad for the outdoor season. Griffin won the Big 12 championship in the 400-meter hurdles as a freshman in May 2008.

MAY 12, 1985

Monahans native and Texas women's golf legend Kathy Whitworth posted a fifty-four-hole total of 207, nine under par, to win the United Virginia Bank Classic by one stroke over runner-up Amy Alcott. At the age of forty-five, it was Whitworth's eighty-eighth and final career victory on the LPGA Tour.

MAY 13, 1999

The San Antonio Spurs defeated the Minnesota Timberwolves 85–71 at the Target Center in Minneapolis, Minnesota, to take a 2–1 lead in their Western Conference first-round playoff series. Guard Avery Johnson led the Spurs with twenty-four points, and center David Robinson had a double-double with seventeen points and eighteen rebounds.

The win ignited San Antonio, which went undefeated in its next eleven games. The Spurs tore through the Western Conference, sweeping their second-round series against the Los Angeles Lakers and the Western Conference finals against the Portland Trail Blazers. The New York Knicks ended San Antonio's NBA-record twelve-game playoff winning streak by taking game three of the finals. But San Antonio went on to claim its first NBA championship when it finished off New York two games later, winning the series 4–1.

MAY 14, 1994

Fairfield junior Nanceen Perry added three gold medals to her amazing UIL Track & Field State Meet collection as she won the Class 3A 100-meter and 200-meter dashes and the long jump. Perry clocked a state-record time of 11.3 seconds in the 100 (breaking her own mark of 11.4, set a year earlier) and won the 200 with a time of 23.5. She leapt 19 feet, 5.5 inches to win the long jump, missing the state record by 1.5 inches.

Perry returned to the state meet in 1995 to set the state record in the 200 at 23.49 and went home with a gold medal also in the 100, along with silver medals in the long jump and 4 × 100-meter relay. She finished her high school career with sixteen medals, ten of them gold, at the state track meet.

After a stellar track career at the University of Texas, Perry went on to claim Olympic bronze as a member of the United States 4 × 100-meter relay team at the Sydney Games in 2000.

MAY 15, 1998

The Texas softball team, making its NCAA Tournament debut, blanked Arizona State 6–0 in the regional opener at Bomber Stadium in Clearwater, Florida. That set the tone for the Longhorns' three-game sweep of the regional.

On the second day of competition, Texas went to extra innings versus South Florida before notching a 1–0 victory. In the bottom of the eighth, Nikki Cockrell raced home from third on a grounder by pitcher Christa Williams. South Florida third baseman Ginny Georgantas made a one-hop throw to first base, but first baseman Amanda Whitesell couldn't pick it off the bounce, allowing Williams to reach base and the Longhorns to walk off with the victory.

Texas stayed undefeated in the regional on the final day as it grasped a 4–2 victory over South Florida. With that, the Longhorns earned their first trip to the Women's College World Series in only their second season as a varsity squad. Two seasons earlier, the softball team had played a full season as a non-athletic-department-funded club sport, finishing with a 1–25 record.

"When we won that first game against (University of the Incarnate Word in 1996), it was like we won the World Series," Cockrell told *Austin American-Statesman* reporter Mark Wangrin. "Now we have a chance to really win the World Series."

Texas's phenomenal second season relied on the strength of Williams's arm. The sophomore pitcher won twenty-eight games, including all three at the regional tournament. Williams, who pitched the final five innings of the regional final, finished the three-game sweep in Florida with twenty-six strikeouts and gave up no runs and just six hits in twenty innings of work.

Second-seeded Michigan and fifth-seeded Nebraska ousted Texas from the WCWS after two games, but the Longhorns still finished seventh in the final national rankings.

MAY 16, 1998

The Fort Worth O.D. Wyatt 4 × 100-meter relay team combined speed and precision to shatter the national high school record at the UIL State Track & Field Meet at Darrell K Royal–Texas Memorial Stadium. The Chaparrals' relay team members—Milton Wesley, Montie Clopton, Michael Franklin, and De-Mario Wesley—brought around the baton in 39.76 seconds for a new national-best time, winning the Class 5A race in the process.

Anchor leg DeMario Wesley sensed a special race in the making before he took the baton. But as is often the case with sprinters, he felt the need for still more speed. "When I saw (third leg Franklin), I knew it was a national record," Wesley told reporters after the race. "This makes us feel proud. It felt like a record, but we think we could go a little faster."

MAY 17, 2011

Dallas Mavericks forward Dirk Nowitzki gave an impressive opening salvo, scoring forty-eight points as Dallas defeated the Oklahoma City Thunder 121–112 in game one of the Western Conference finals in Dallas. Nowitzki made twelve of fifteen shots from the field and knocked down all twenty-four free throws he took.

"I thought Dirk was pretty good tonight," Thunder coach Scott Brooks joked in the postgame press conference. "I thought we defended him as close as we can—obviously, too close."

Nowitzki's effort outshined that of University of Texas alum Kevin Durant, who led the Thunder with forty points. The Mavs' forward had scored forty by the end of the third quarter, when Dallas led 90–79. Nowitzki made his fourth-quarter points count, contributing all eight in the final 2:31 after Oklahoma City had sliced the Mavs' lead to six.

Dallas went on to a 4–1 series win over the Thunder to advance to the NBA Finals for the second time in six seasons.

MAY 18, 1997

Tiger Woods fired a final round of 68, two under par, to win the GTE Byron Nelson Classic with a seventy-two-hole total of 263, seventeen under. It was Woods's first and only career victory in Texas through the 2016 golf season.

Woods formed a friendship with Nelson before the Texas golf legend's death in 2006. But Woods didn't develop the same type of relationship with Nelson's home state. Woods eventually removed the Byron Nelson tournament from his annual schedule, along with the other PGA Tour stops in Texas. Because the US Open and the PGA Championship have been absent from Texas since 1969, Woods has seldom played in the Lone Star State.

MAY 19, 1990

Houston sprinter Leroy Burrell clocked blazing fast times on his way to victories in the 100-meter and 200-meter dashes at the Southwest Conference Track and Field Championship at Frank G. Anderson Track and Field Complex in College Station. Burrell's time of 19.61 seconds in the 200 was the fastest time run under any conditions, but the wind at the SWC meet measured 4.0 meters per second, well over the 2.0 that would disqualify a time from world-record certification. The Houston sprinter's time of 9.94 in the 100 was just off the world record.

Still, Burrell was satisfied with his pair of SWC gold medals, especially since he outran Baylor's Michael Johnson to win the 200. "I just had something to prove," Burrell told reporters after the race. "All I've heard is Michael Johnson this. Michael Johnson that. Michael Johnson is the best 200-meter sprinter in the world. I didn't believe it. I'm better."

Johnson, running in his final SWC meet, never won a conference outdoor individual championship. But Johnson went on to win the NCAA national title in the 200 that spring, and he would later eclipse Burrell's wind-aided time on a much grander world stage.

Baylor pitcher Cristin Vitek struck out twenty-eight University of North Carolina batters as she led the Lady Bears to a victory over the Tar Heels in the 2004 NCAA Tournament. Photo courtesy of Baylor University Photography.

MAY 20, 2004

Pitcher Cristin Vitek kept batters guessing, and mostly guessing wrong, as she struck out twenty-eight North Carolina Tar Heels to help Baylor grasp a 1–0 victory in the bottom of the sixteenth inning in an NCAA Tournament game at Getterman Stadium in Waco. Vitek held North Carolina hitless for 10⅓ innings, more than three innings longer than a regulation game, to give the Lady Bears a fighting chance in a scoreless game. She allowed three hits and had just two intentional walks while throwing 185 pitches in a game lasting three hours and fifty-four minutes.

"I've been coaching ten years and that's the most incredible performance I've ever seen," Baylor softball coach Glenn Moore said after the game. "She continued to go out there and do her job despite not getting much production behind her or even many threats."

Baylor broke through in the bottom of the sixteenth when Kim Wilmoth doubled, then scored on a double by Melissa Maler, giving the Lady Bears their first NCAA Tournament win. Baylor defeated Illinois in the next game before losing to LSU and Illinois and exiting the tournament.

MAY 21, 1986

Ralph Sampson caught the in-bounds pass and in the same motion floated the basketball toward the hoop. The Houston Rockets led the Los Angeles Lakers three games to one in the Western Conference finals. The Rockets had the defending world champions on the verge of elimination, and the incomparable Ralph Sampson was on the verge of reaching the pinnacle of his basketball career.

With four seconds remaining, the Lakers' Byron Scott shot and missed off the back iron. The Rockets' Allen Leavell rebounded with one second left and called time-out. By rule, the ball was moved to midcourt, where Rodney McCray threw the in-bounds pass. McCray tossed a high line drive to the seven-foot, four-inch Sampson, who jumped and tipped the ball toward the basket. The shot bounced high off the front of the rim and then through the hoop, stunning the Lakers and sending the Rockets to the NBA Finals to face the Boston Celtics.

MAY 22, 2003

Sweden's Annika Sörenstam became the first woman in fifty-eight years to compete in a PGA Tour event when she teed it up at the Bank of America Colonial in Fort Worth. Sörenstam played in the event on a sponsor's exemption entry, which drew the eyes of the sports world to the famed Texas country club.

The LPGA's biggest star at the time, Sörenstam represented her tour well by opening with a one-over-par 71 on the Colonial course. After winning a battle with nerves, she stood in seventy-third place after eighteen holes.

"Everything is so much bigger and so many more people and the course is so much longer," Sörenstam said in a press conference after her first round. "And I feel like it's almost over my head a little bit. I've been nervous that I wasn't going to perform. In the back of my mind, though, I know I can play. The question is can I play when everybody is looking, when everybody is analyzing every little thing. And that's what made me nervous."

Sörenstam posted another decent score of four-over 74 in the second round. But at five over for the tournament, she was four strokes off the cut line and didn't make it to the weekend.

MAY 23, 2010

Twenty-two-year-old Jason Day won the HP Byron Nelson Championship, but he shared the spotlight with a younger competitor from Texas, who won the hearts of golf fans. Sixteen-year-old Jordan Spieth birdied the par-three tenth hole at TPC (Tournament Players Course) Las Colinas to move three strokes from the lead in the final round. Although Spieth ultimately shot two-over on the back nine on Sunday and finished six strokes behind Day's tournament-winning ten-under, the Texas teenager was good enough for a tie for sixteenth.

"It was awesome . . . the entire round, the entire week," Spieth said in a post-tournament interview. "Starting the week, I definitely would've taken a top-twenty, in a heartbeat. Obviously now, looking back, being a competitor, I look back at the mistakes I made that didn't give me an opportunity to win."

Spieth played as an amateur and was therefore ineligible to claim prize money. The intangible benefits, however, were undoubtedly larger than his sixteenth-place money would have been, since Spieth officially put himself on the golf map.

MAY 24, 1987

Pitcher Shawn Andaya baffled UCLA hitters in two straight games to lead the Aggies to the Women's College World Series championship.

Facing the Bruins in an elimination game, Andaya threw a perfect game, keeping Texas A&M alive with a 1–0 victory. In the championship final, Andaya stepped into the circle again and held UCLA to one run on two hits. At the plate, Andaya drove in two runs to put Texas A&M over the top for a 4–1 victory and the national title.

Andaya's victory in the Women's College World Series final gave her thirty-six victories for her senior season and 114 for her Texas A&M career.

MAY 25, 2003

Kenny Perry shattered the seventy-two-hole tournament scoring record by shooting a nineteen-under 261 to win the Bank of America Colonial in Fort Worth. The final round became a mere formality after Perry blitzed the third round, shooting a course-record nine-under 61 to take an eight-stroke lead over second-place Rory Sabbatini into Sunday. Perry then turned in a smooth two-under 68 on the final round to claim the champion's plaid jacket and another tournament record.

Though Perry won by six strokes, the final round still provided some drama. Dallas native Justin Leonard ascended from a tie for eighteenth place to runner-up with a final round of 61. Leonard took aim at a birdie on the eighteenth hole that would have given him a phenomenal fifty-nine. But his nine-iron shot onto the green came up twenty yards short of the cup, and he eventually took a bogey to tie Perry's course record.

(PHOTO, LEFT)
Texas A&M pitcher Shawn Andaya struck out 1,234 batters in her college career, an NCAA record, and led the Aggies to the 1987 Women's College World Series championship. Photo courtesy of Texas A&M Athletics.

MAY 26, 2007

Baylor first baseman Ashley Monceaux squeezed an infield pop fly in her glove, recording the final out in the Lady Bears' 4–0 victory over Michigan and sending Baylor to its first Women's College World Series.

A day earlier, Monceaux had hit two home runs, including a three-run walk-off shot in the bottom of the fifth inning that secured Baylor's 9–0 run-rule victory over Michigan in the opening game of a best-of-three NCAA Super Regional series in Waco.

After Michigan won the second game of the series, Lady Bear pitcher Lisa Ferguson bore down and shut out the Wolverines in the series final. Baylor batters Kirsten Shortridge and Alex Colyer each hit home runs to drive the offense. Monceaux's final catch sparked a joyous celebration.

"This is the best feeling you can ever have," Ferguson told the *Waco Tribune-Herald* following the game. "After Ashley caught that last popup it took a moment to realize that it actually happened."

MAY 27, 2003

Dallas Maverick forward Michael Finley led a phenomenal comeback as the Mavs overwhelmed in-state rival San Antonio in the second half to claim a 103–91 victory in game five of the Western Conference finals in San Antonio. The Spurs led 44–25 in the second quarter, but Dallas owned the second half. The Mavericks shot 56 percent from the field and made all twenty-three free-throw attempts in the third and fourth quarters. Dallas outscored San Antonio in the final period 29–10.

Finley finished with thirty-one points, guard Nick Van Exel added twenty-one, and guard Steve Nash had fourteen points and six assists as the Mavs staved off elimination. Mavs star forward Dirk Nowitzki was sidelined with an injury. Dallas's come-from-way-behind win cut the Spurs series lead to 3–2. But San Antonio clinched the series two nights later and went on to defeat the New Jersey Nets in the NBA Finals.

MAY 28, 2005

Baylor freshman Zuzana Zemenova became the first unseeded player to win the NCAA women's singles national title when she defeated Northwestern freshman Audra Cohen 4–6, 6–2, 7–5 in the championship match at Henry Feild Stadium in Athens, Georgia.

Zemenova, who came to Baylor from Kosice, Slovakia, went on to win four consecutive Big 12 Player of the Year awards and garnered four straight All-America honors. She posted a 17–3 career record in NCAA Tournament matches, but claimed the singles championship only once.

"I feel great right now," Zemenova told *Waco Tribune-Herald* sports editor Kim Gorum following her championship victory. "I was very tired out there, but I felt like I played my best tennis of the tournament today."

MAY 29, 1977

Houston native A. J. Foyt became the first driver to win the Indy 500 four times as he claimed his fourth and final checkered flag at the Brickyard. "We had our good breaks, we had our bad breaks and still I'm just, oh I can't believe it," Foyt said in a television interview immediately following the race.

Foyt piloted the red no. 14 Gilmore racing car and waved to the crowd during his victory lap after finishing almost thirty seconds in front of second-place Tom Sneva.

After Foyt won sixty-seven Indy car races, seven in the NASCAR series, and more than 155 titles in vehicles of all types, he and Mario Andretti were named codrivers of the century by the Associated Press in December 1999.

MAY 30, 2003

Six Texas schools began the NCAA Division I Baseball Tournament, and one of them would be the last team standing. Rice edged McNeese State 3–2 in ten innings at its home field, Reckling Park in Houston, in the tournament opener. In doing so, the Owls took their first step on a twelve-game twenty-five-day journey to the College World Series championship.

Rice defeated Houston two games to one in a best-of-three Super Regional series to reach the College World Series in Omaha, Nebraska. The Owls then defeated Texas twice in their three-win surge to the CWS championship versus Stanford. In the third and deciding game of the series, Rice pitcher Philip Humber pitched a complete game to hold the Stanford Cardinal to two runs on five hits as the Owls claimed a 14–2 national championship victory. Second baseman Enrique Cruz, the son of former Astro star Jose Cruz, sparked the Rice offense by going two for three and driving in four runs in the championship game.

The 2–1 series win over Stanford gave Rice its first national championship in a team sport. "It means something to Houston," Rice coach Wayne Graham said in a postgame press conference. "They're proud of the academic tradition of Rice. This was merely a quest to maintain honor and to do things the right way, which has always been so important at Rice. Giving them an athletic championship means a lot."

MAY 31, 2014

The Baylor softball team won a pair of elimination games, including coming from a 7–0 deficit against Kentucky, to stay alive in the Women's College World Series at the ASA Hall of Fame Stadium in Oklahoma City.

The Lady Bears defeated Florida State 7–2 in the first game of the day, advancing to play Kentucky. The Wildcats surged ahead by seven runs in the middle of the sixth inning. But Baylor began to chip away at the lead, scoring three runs in the bottom of the sixth. In the seventh, second baseman Ari Hawkins led off with a home run over the left-field fence, third baseman Sarah Smith doubled to drive in a run, and designated player Robin Landrith came up with the most important hit, a two-run double to left, to tie the game at 7 and force extra innings.

After Baylor pitcher Heather Stearns retired Kentucky in order in the top of the eighth, Lady Bear right fielder Kaitlyn Thumann doubled to start the bottom of the eighth. Thumann darted to third on a sacrifice bunt by Hawkins, and Kentucky committed a costly error by trying to throw out Hawkins at first. The miscue allowed Thumann to score the walk-off run.

Baylor lost to Florida 6–3 in the semifinals the next day, but the thrill of the journey stayed with Baylor coach Glenn Moore. "Wow, I won't forget that until I forget who I am," Moore said in a postgame press conference following the win over Kentucky. "These girls are incredible. They just didn't quit believing. Just unbelievable fight and execution from these girls."

June

JUNE 1, 2008

Texas A&M left fielder Kelsey Spittler, batting in the ninth slot, sent a ninth-inning triple down the right-field line to drive in shortstop Macie Morrow for the only run the Aggies would need to advance to the Women's College World Series championship. Texas A&M pitcher Megan Gibson finished off top-seeded Florida in the bottom of the inning, and the Aggies grasped a 1–0 victory over the Gators.

Gibson, who gave up five hits and struck out six in the complete-game shutout, earned her forty-first win of the season. This one put Texas A&M in college softball's ultimate series for the first time since the Aggies won the national title in 1987. Arizona State, however, won the next two games to claim the WCWS championship.

JUNE 2, 1997

The Houston Astros selected Rice junior Lance Berkman with the sixteenth pick in the first round of the Major League Baseball draft.

The Astros grabbed Berkman one day after his junior season at Rice ended at the College World Series. Berkman and pitcher Matt Anderson, the first overall pick of the draft by the Detroit Tigers, had led Rice to a 47–16 record and its first CWS appearance.

Berkman's first-round selection in the draft was the culmination of his college baseball career, in which he hit .385 with 67 home runs and 272 RBIs.

The Astros' pick of the native Texan and local college star paid huge dividends. Berkman hit 313 home runs and drove in 1,090 runs in an Astros uniform from 1999 to 2010.

JUNE 3, 2012

University of Texas golfers Dylan Frittelli, Cody Gribble, and Jordan Spieth won championship-round matches as the Longhorns defeated Alabama 3–2 and claimed the NCAA Division I national championship at the Riviera Country Club in Pacific Palisades, California. Frittelli rolled in a thirty-foot birdie putt on the eighteenth hole of his match to defeat Alabama's Cory Whitsett and clinch the title.

The Longhorns' national championship was the program's first since Texas golfers Ben Crenshaw and Tom Kite tied for the individual title and led the Longhorns to the team crown in 1972.

JUNE 4, 2011

It was just past eight-thirty in the evening when Baylor pitcher Whitney Canion struck out Missouri's opening batter of the night. More than three hours later, just past midnight, Lady Bear first baseman Holly Holl blasted a two-out, walk-off, solo home run over the wall in left field, giving Baylor a 1–0 victory over the Tigers after thirteen innings at the Women's College World Series in Oklahoma City.

Canion struck out eleven and gave up just two hits and two walks in going the entire thirteen innings for Baylor. That standout performance, combined with Holl's clinching effort at the plate, sent Baylor into the national semifinals to face Arizona State. Though the Sun Devils claimed a 4–0 win the next day, the Lady Bears had reached a significant high point, which wasn't lost on their ace pitcher.

"I heard the fans, but I didn't want to look into the stands because I knew I would get emotional," Canion said in an interview after the Arizona State game. "This is the most fun I've ever had playing in my life. All I want to do is come back here."

JUNE 5, 1999

JUNE 6, 1999

Texas women's 4 × 400-meter relay anchor leg Suziann Reid brought home an NCAA Outdoor Track & Field Championship victory as well as helped the Longhorns set a collegiate record with a time of 3:27.08.

Reid, along with relay teammates Angel Patterson, Aminah Haddad, and Tanya Jarrett, vaulted Texas into first place in the team standings, clinching the Longhorns' second consecutive national championship. It also marked the second straight year that winning the 4 × 400 relay pulled Texas into first place in the team standings.

Texas finished the meet with 62 points, two in front of second-place UCLA. Also contributing valuable points to the Longhorns effort was the 4 × 100 relay team of Kim McGruder, Nanceen Perry, Lakeesha White, and LaKeisha Backus.

Texas A&M pitcher Casey Fossum struck out Clemson center fielder Patrick Boyd with two out and two Tigers on base in the bottom of the ninth inning to preserve a 5–4 victory that sent the Aggies to the College World Series.

In the top half of the ninth, Aggie shortstop Steve Scarborough had led off with a solo home run off Clemson reliever Chris Heck to tie game three of the NCAA Tournament Super Regional best-of-three series at Pat Olsen Field in College Station. "I was just trying to get on base for the other guys to get me in," Scarborough said in a postgame interview. "(Heck) left one kind of up in the zone and I got under it a little bit and it fell over the fence, I guess. I didn't remember even running around the bases. I was floating."

Texas A&M center fielder Steven Truitt followed with another solo homer off of Heck, which boosted the Aggies into the lead. That set the stage for Fossum, who had already won the opening game of the Super Regional. He came on in the seventh inning and finished the job to earn both wins in the series.

Florida State and Cal State Fullerton each defeated Texas A&M in Omaha, Nebraska, ending the Aggies' season at the CWS.

JUNE 7, 1980

UTEP distance runner Suleiman Nyambui won the 5,000-meter run, sprinter Bert Cameron claimed the 400, and Steve Hanna leapt to victory in the triple jump as the Miners surged to their second straight NCAA Men's Outdoor Track & Field National Championship at Memorial Stadium in Austin.

Nyambui, who had won the 10,000 the previous day, led the way for the Miners with twenty points. UTEP tallied 69 team points, finishing twenty-three ahead of second-place UCLA. The Miners, who won their first NCAA outdoor title in 1975 and tied UCLA for the championship in 1978, claimed six altogether between 1975 and 1982.

(PHOTO, OPPOSITE PAGE)
UTEP's Suleiman Nyambui (center) led the way by winning both the 5,000-meter and 10,000-meter races as the Miners claimed the NCAA Men's Outdoor Track & Field national championship in 1980. Photo courtesy of UTEP Athletics.

JUNE 8, 2014

Texas Tech used four pitchers to shut out the College of Charleston and claim a 1–0 victory that sent the Red Raiders to their first College World Series. It was the third straight shutout for the Texas Tech pitching staff, which had blanked Miami six days earlier and then the College of Charleston in the opening game of the best-of-three Super Regional series held in Lubbock. Red Raiders designated hitter Adam Kirsch doubled down the right-field line in the fourth inning to drive in outfielder Tyler Neslony for the only run that Texas Tech needed in the series-clinching win.

Texas Tech's victory came the day after the University of Texas won its Super Regional over Houston, and the day before TCU did the same against Pepperdine. As a result, the state of Texas sent three teams to the College World Series in Omaha, Nebraska.

JUNE 9, 2011

The Dallas Mavericks won pivotal game five of the NBA Finals, thwarting the Miami Heat 112–103 at the American Airlines Center in Dallas. Mavericks power forward Dirk Nowitzki scored twenty-nine points, outdueling LeBron James and Dwyane Wade of the Heat as Dallas took a 3–2 series lead.

Guard Jason Terry pulled Dallas through the game's critical juncture in the fourth quarter. Terry made two three-pointers and dished out assists to Nowitzki and Jason Kidd, driving a Mavericks' 11–1 run that gave them a 108–101 lead with thirty-three seconds left. "I said to myself, I said to my teammates, 'We're not going to continue to miss those open shots that we're getting,'" Terry said after the game.

Nowitzki and the Mavs, realizing how important their final game of the series in Dallas would be, seized the moment. "We didn't want to go to Miami and give them basically two shots to close us out," Nowitzki said. "So we kept plugging there in the fourth. So definitely a big win for us. And now we have to go down there and basically approach Sunday's game as Game Seven."

Three days later, Dallas clinched the series and grasped the Larry O'Brien Trophy with a 105–95 victory in game six in Miami.

JUNE 10, 1990

Texas Ranger pitcher Kevin Brown kept his head in the game despite taking a line drive to the skull in the third inning against the California Angels at Anaheim Stadium. With two out in the bottom of the third inning, Angel left fielder Luis Polonia smacked a pitch right back at Brown. It hit the pitcher and then deflected into right field.

Somehow, Brown was uninjured. He got Angel designated hitter Chili Davis to fly out to end the inning. Brown came back to the mound for the fourth inning and went on to pitch a complete game. Brown jokingly dismissed the line drive off his head when he spoke to reporters after the game. "It probably would have done more damage if it hit me in the arm or foot," he said.

Ranger right fielder Ruben Sierra drove in two runs to give Brown all the run support he needed. Angel right fielder Dave Winfield homered with one out in the bottom of the ninth inning, but Brown recorded the final two outs to finish off a 2–1 victory.

Brown took the mound again five days later, again going the distance. He then did the same in his next start, giving him three straight complete games in ten days, in which he allowed a total of four runs in twenty-seven innings pitched.

JUNE 11, 1950

Ben Hogan defeated Lloyd Mangrum and George Fazio in an eighteen-hole playoff at the Merion Golf Club in Ardmore, Pennsylvania, to win the US Open.

The victory capped Hogan's comeback from a catastrophic car accident just sixteen months earlier that left him nearly crippled (see the entry for February 2). Hogan was not expected to make a full recovery from multiple broken bones, but willed himself back to health and onto the golf course again. He returned to the PGA Tour in January 1950 and lost in a playoff against Sam Snead at the Los Angeles Open before claiming the US Open title, his fourth of nine career major victories. Hogan's triumph in the 1950 US Open soon came to be known as the "Miracle at Merion."

Ben Hogan, who grew up caddying at the Glen Garden Country Club in Fort Worth, won eight career major championships and served as the nonplaying captain of the victorious US team in the 1967 Ryder Cup at the Champions Golf Club in Houston. Photo courtesy of the Texas Sports Hall of Fame.

JUNE 12, 2010

Nacogdoches native Clint Dempsey sent a shot from twenty-five yards out and straight on toward England goalkeeper Robert Green on the second day of play at the 2010 World Cup. Team USA trailed 1–0 when Dempsey took his fateful shot, which Green initially stopped but then fumbled over the goal line. Dempsey tied the match, and the US team went on to earn a 1–1 draw at Royal Bafokeng Stadium in Rustenburg, South Africa.

The goal continued a hot streak in Africa for Dempsey, who had scored in three straight games during the FIFA Confederations Cup in 2009 in Africa. Dempsey appeared to add another goal in group play in the 2010 World Cup when he scored against Algeria, but the goal was disallowed on a controversial offside call.

JUNE 13, 2009

The Texas A&M men's 4 × 400 relay team finished second at the NCAA Outdoor Track & Field Championships, securing the points the Aggies needed to grab the team title.

By clinching the team championship in the final race, the Texas A&M men equaled the achievement of the Aggie women, who had won their national championship by the time the 4 × 400 relay began. The Texas A&M women had made their mark on the previous day when the 4 × 100 relay team of Khrystal Carter, Porscha Lucas, Dominique Duncan, and Gabby Mayo won the national title with a time of 42.36 seconds, 0.03 of a second in front of second-place Florida State. Lucas also scored key points for the Aggies with a victory in the 200-meter dash.

The Aggie men trailed Oregon by six points and Florida by one going into the 4 × 400 relay. But the Ducks didn't have an entry in the event, meaning Texas A&M's squad—Tran Howell, Bryan Miller, Kyle Dykhuizen, and Justin Oliver—needed to stay ahead of Florida to win the team championship. Florida State won with a time of 2:59.99. Texas A&M finished a little less than a second behind the Seminoles, but two places ahead of the Gators.

"When it got to the 300 mark and I saw I was still second place, I see the finish line,

JUNE 14, 1975

I see the trophy at the finish line waiting on me," Oliver said. "We're the national champions. Texas A&M. No one else. That's all I could say. We did it."

Texas A&M's sweep of the men's and women's NCAA outdoor national titles set off a wave of domination as the Aggies swept the team championships again in 2010 and 2011.

Texas first baseman Mickey Reichenbach smacked a two-run homer over the right center-field wall at Rosenblatt Stadium, helping lift the Longhorns to a 5–1 victory over South Carolina and the College World Series championship in Omaha, Nebraska. Longhorn starting pitcher Richard Wortham struck out nine Gamecocks as he threw a complete-game four-hitter.

With the win, Texas claimed its third national championship, and the first since 1950. Coach Bibb Falk had led the Longhorns to back-to-back titles in 1949 and 1950. By guiding the 1975 Horns to the championship, Texas coach Cliff Gustafson claimed the first of his two CWS crowns.

JUNE 15, 2003

San Antonio center Tim Duncan scored twenty-one points, grabbed twenty rebounds, and dished out ten assists for an astounding triple-double that lifted the Spurs to an NBA Finals–clinching 88–77 victory over the New Jersey Nets. Duncan, who was named the Finals MVP, finished just two blocks shy of a quadruple-double.

Duncan played the starring role in helping San Antonio win game six and the series, 4–2. At the same time, his frontcourt teammate David Robinson put the most emphatic of exclamation marks on his career. Robinson scored thirteen points and grabbed seventeen boards in the final game of his fourteen-year NBA career. "To finish my career in the NBA Finals and to win the championship is a play written only by God," Robinson said.

The Spurs' twin towers of Duncan and Robinson, who had helped San Antonio win its first world championship in 1999, claimed their second title with the Finals triumph over the Nets. Despite Robinson's retirement, it was only the beginning for the Spurs, who added NBA championships in 2005, 2007, and 2014.

JUNE 16, 1968

Lee Trevino posted his first PGA Tour win at the age of twenty-eight, finishing four shots ahead of Jack Nicklaus for the 1968 US Open championship at Oak Hill Country Club in Rochester, New York. Trevino shot a five-

Dallas native Lee Trevino won the 1968 US Open at Oak Hill Country Club in Rochester, New York. Photo courtesy of Texas Sports Hall of Fame.

JUNE 17, 2009

under-par 275, tying the tournament scoring record, set a year earlier by Nicklaus.

Bert Yancey began the final round with a one-stroke lead, but Trevino overtook him on the front nine and went on to his fourth straight round in the 60s with a final-round 69.

Afterward, Trevino sensed that his initial victory was a sign of things to come. "I'm going to keep on playing as well as I can and as long as I can," Trevino said. "I'm going to play some bad rounds. I've played bad rounds before. But I'll keep playing. I'll be playing this game when I'm one hundred years old."

Trevino went on to win six major titles among his twenty-nine PGA Tour victories in a career that spanned three decades.

Houston Astro catcher Iván Rodríguez caught his 2,227th game as the Astros faced the Texas Rangers, for whom Rodriguez caught from 1991 to 2002. The Ballpark in Arlington therefore made a fitting setting as Rodriguez passed Carlton Fisk for most games behind the plate.

The Rangers enjoyed the occasion and a win as David Murphy hit a walk-off single to score Ian Kinsler in the bottom of the tenth to give Texas a 5–4 victory.

JUNE 18, 1999

SMU alum Payne Stewart solved a baffling Pinehurst No. 2 golf course and posted one of only three under-par scores in the second round of the US Open in Pinehurst, North Carolina. Stewart's second-round one-under 69 elevated him to a first-place tie with Phil Mickelson and David Duval at three-under through thirty-six holes.

The three leaders were part of an elite group of seven players who shot par or better in the second round. Pinehurst No. 2 brought out the worst in many of the world's greatest golfers. Spain's José María Olazábal, the 1999 Masters champion, was so disgusted with his first-round score, a five-over 75, that he punched a hotel room wall and broke a bone in his right hand.

Stewart kept his composure through the weekend and stayed in front. He sunk a fifteen-foot par putt on the eighteenth hole of the final round to edge Mickelson by one stroke. With that, the former SMU Mustang grasped his second US Open championship. He spread out his arms in victory and then immediately went to console Mickelson, his playing partner.

"When I looked up, it was about two feet away from the hole and breaking right into the center of the cup," Stewart said in a post-round interview. "I couldn't believe my eyes. I couldn't believe I had accomplished my dream."

It was the last shot Stewart ever played in a US Open.

JUNE 19, 1999

JUNE 20, 1992

Dallas Star right wing Brett Hull tucked a rebounded puck into the net, beating Buffalo Sabre goalie Dominik Hašek and giving the Stars a 2–1, triple-overtime victory in game six of the Stanley Cup Finals. Hull's goal ended the longest Cup-clinching game in Finals history. The Stars celebrated their first Stanley Cup title after a 4–2 series win.

A controversy about the ending did little to diminish Dallas's enthusiasm for its hockey team. Hull's game-winning goal was viewed as an illegal play by some, especially Buffalo fans, who rallied with the slogan "No goal!" Hull's left skate was in the crease when he took the shot. But officials deemed it a legit score, and the Stars held a victory parade and rally three days later at Reunion Arena.

With the wind swirling, waves crashing, and golfers' hopes rising and falling like roller coasters, Austin native and University of Texas alum Tom Kite stayed unshaken and posted a two-under-par 70 at Pebble Beach on Saturday at the US Open.

Second-round leader Gil Morgan appeared to be running away with the major championship, shooting nine under through thirty-six holes. Morgan kept it going for a while on Saturday. He became the first man to reach ten under in the US Open and got to twelve under with a seventh-hole birdie. But then Morgan's train derailed: he made three bogeys and three double bogeys in the next seven holes. Although Morgan led at the end of the day at four under, Kite, fellow Texan Mark Brooks, and Welshman Ian Woosnam trailed by only one shot going into the final round.

Kite held steady on Sunday, carding an even-par 72 to edge second-place Jeff Sluman by two strokes. With that, Kite won his first and only major title.

JUNE 21, 2015

Jordan Spieth hugged his mom and dad while a look of utter disbelief still adorned his face.

A few seconds earlier, Dustin Johnson missed a four-foot putt that would have tied Spieth at the end of seventy-two holes at the US Open.

A few minutes earlier, Spieth two-putted the eighteenth green at Chambers Bay near Seattle, Washington, to take a two-stroke lead in the 115th playing of America's national championship.

A half hour earlier, Spieth sank a nineteen-foot downhill right-breaking birdie putt that gave him a three-stroke lead with two holes to play in the final round.

The prevailing feeling at the end of the 2015 US Open, as is often the case with the grueling event, was gut-punched sadness for Johnson as well as South African Branden Grace, who sliced his tee shot on the par-four sixteenth out of bounds, falling out of the hunt.

But once the dust settled, everyone realized the twenty-one-year-old Spieth was halfway to immortality. Spieth began the 2015 golf season by winning the Masters, so when he grabbed the US Open title as well, he became the sixth man to pull off the double. He joined the likes of Jack Nicklaus, Tiger Woods, Ar-nold Palmer, Craig Wood, and fellow Texan Ben Hogan.

Spieth tied for fourth at The Open Championship, in Scotland, and then took second at the PGA Championship at Whistling Straits in Wisconsin. Spieth posted a record-setting fifty-four under par in his sixteen rounds at the majors in 2015.

JUNE 22, 1994

Hakeem Olajuwon scored twenty-five points, grabbed ten rebounds, and dished out seven assists to lead the Houston Rockets to a seventh-game victory over the New York Knicks in the NBA Finals.

Olajuwon, the Finals MVP, scored at least twenty-one points in every game of the series while lifting the Rockets to their first NBA championship and bringing the Larry O'Brien NBA Championship Trophy to Texas for the first time. "If you write a book, you can't write it any better," Olajuwon said in the *Houston Chronicle*'s game story. "It has been a great season for us and I'm so happy to bring a championship to this city, Houston. That means a lot."

JUNE 23, 1926

Winters native and St. Louis Cardinals second baseman–manager Rogers Hornsby hit a seventh-inning grand slam off the Pittsburgh Pirates' Don Songer, lifting the Cardinals to a 6–2 victory. With the home run, Hornsby reached two thousand hits for his career.

Hornsby amassed 2,930 hits and batted .358 over twenty-three seasons of playing for the Cardinals, New York Giants, Boston Braves, Chicago Cubs, and St. Louis Browns.

JUNE 24, 1950

JUNE 25, 1997

Beaumont native Babe Didrikson Zaharias defeated Peggy Kirk in the match-play final at the Cherry Hills Country Club in Denver, Colorado, to become the first four-time winner of the Women's Western Open. Zaharias claimed the title also in 1940, 1944, and 1945 at the Western Open, considered a women's golf major from 1930 until it was discontinued after the 1967 tournament. She and Patty Berg of Minnesota had each won three titles going into the 1950 tournament. Zaharias edged Kirk in the final, taking a five-hole lead with three to play to clinch the match.

Zaharias's victory set off Texas's domination of the event in years to come. Betsy Rawls of Arlington won the Western Open in 1952 and 1959, and Betty Jameson of Dallas, the runner-up in 1952, won it in 1954.

The San Antonio Spurs drafted Wake Forest power forward Tim Duncan with the first overall selection of the NBA draft. The Spurs paired Duncan with center David Robinson in one of the most dominant frontcourts in basketball history. With Duncan and Robinson in the starting lineup, San Antonio claimed its first world championship in 1999.

Duncan played an integral role in the Spurs' five NBA title wins between 1999 and 2014. He was the NBA Finals MVP in 1999, 2003, and 2005.

JUNE 26, 2005

Texas coach Augie Garrido joined Bibb Falk and Cliff Gustafson as the only Longhorn skippers to win a pair of College World Series titles when Texas defeated Florida 6–2 for a two-game sweep in the championship best-of-three series in Omaha, Nebraska.

The Longhorns won the series opener, and in the second game, third baseman David Maroul and first baseman Chance Wheeless each homered to supply all the runs Texas needed for a clinching victory. Longhorns starting pitcher Kyle McCulloch struck out eight while holding the Gators to two runs in 6⅔ innings.

Texas won its sixth national championship in baseball by surviving a roller-coaster NCAA Tournament. Leading up to the CWS, the Longhorns lost to Arkansas and Mississippi, but won five elimination games. Texas then went undefeated in Omaha to secure the CWS championship.

"We got hot at the right time," Horns reliever J. B. Cox said. "It was hard to stop us. It all came together at the right time for us. It definitely wasn't easy."

JUNE 27, 1994

Fellow Houston natives and friends Zina Garrison-Jackson and Lori McNeil each won fourth-round matches to advance to the Wimbledon quarterfinals. The Texans made certain neither of the Grand Slam tournament's top seeds made it to the semifinals: Garrison-Jackson ousted second-seeded Arantxa Sanchez Vicario 7–5, 4–6, 6–3 in their fourth round match, and earlier in the tournament, McNeil took out top-seeded Steffi Graf in the first round with a 7–5, 7–6 (7–5) victory. McNeil won her fourth-round match over Florencia Labat of Argentina 7–6 (7–4), 7–6 (7–4).

The Texans were two wins apiece away from fulfilling the lofty vision of their Houston-based coach John Wilkerson. "John used to talk about it a lot," Garrison-Jackson said in a postmatch interview. "It is really weird. I can remember actually the first time we came over here and John used to say to us his dream was for Lori and me to be in the finals and then for him to just sit back and relax for the first time in his life and not worry about who wins."

The dream derailed in the quarterfinals when Gigi Fernández defeated Garrison-Jackson 6–4, 6–4. McNeil defeated Larisa Neiland of Latvia in the quarterfinals 6–3, 6–4. She lost a grueling match to eventual champion Conchita Martinez of Spain in the semifinals as Martinez prevailed 3–6, 6–2, 10–8.

JUNE 28, 2007

Craig Biggio, who played his entire Major League Baseball career for the Houston Astros, went five for six versus the Colorado Rockies and, in doing so, rolled past the 3,000-hit mark for his career.

Biggio began the game with 2,997 hits and reached 3,000 with a single to right center field in the bottom of the seventh. Biggio's single drove in Brad Ausmus from second base. But Rockies center fielder Willy Taveras threw out Biggio when he tried to stretch his hit into a double.

Biggio's first hit in the majors was recorded on June 29, 1988, and his 3,000th came on nearly the same day of the same month, nineteen years later. When he retired at the end of the 2007 season, Biggio had played in 2,850 games and recorded 3,060 hits.

JUNE 29, 1985

The Birmingham Stallions defeated the Houston Gamblers 22–20 in the first round of the United States Football League playoffs, bringing an end to USFL play in Texas.

The league disbanded before the start of the 1986 season, and its top players were welcomed by the NFL. The Buffalo Bills had retained the rights to Gambler quarterback Jim Kelly after drafting him in 1983. Kelly eventually signed with the Bills and led them to four consecutive Super Bowls.

JUNE 30, 2005

The Texas Rangers rocked the Anaheim Angels' pitching staff for a team-record-tying eight home runs. Ranger left fielder Kevin Mench led the way as he homered in the fifth, sixth, and seventh innings. By the time Mench had belted his third round-tripper, Texas was leading 18–3 on the way to an 18–5 rout of the rival Angels at Ameriquest Field in Arlington.

"It was a combination of things," Mench told reporters after the game. "It was a hot day, there was a breeze, but we also put together some good at-bats."

Texas first baseman Mark Teixeira smashed two home runs, and designated hitter David Dellucci, second baseman Alfonso Soriano, and third baseman Hank Blalock had a homer apiece.

On May 21, the Rangers had gone deep eight times in an 18–3 win over the Astros.

July

JULY 1, 1990

Waco native and Midway High School alum Andy Hawkins threw a no-hitter for the New York Yankees, but lost the game to the Chicago White Sox 4–0 at Comiskey Park in Chicago. Hawkins struck out three and gave up no hits in eight innings of work against Chicago, but he walked five, and the Yankees committed three costly errors.

With two outs in the bottom of the eighth, White Sox right fielder Sammy Sosa reached base on an error by Yankees third baseman Mike Blowers. Hawkins then walked short-stop Ozzie Guillén and center fielder Lance Johnson, loading the bases. That set the table for Chicago third baseman Robin Ventura, who hit a fly ball to left field that Jim Leyritz couldn't handle for New York. Leyritz's error allowed Sosa, Guillén, and Johnson to score. Ventura would later come home on an error by Yankees right fielder Jesse Barfield.

White Sox relief pitcher Scott Radinsky sat down the Yankees in order in the top of the ninth to end the game, preserving Chicago's win and Hawkins's no-hitter in a losing effort, since the White Sox didn't come to bat in the ninth.

Hawkins finished his career with eighty-four Major League wins but, officially, no no-hitters. In 1991, Major League Baseball changed the definition of a no-hitter to exclude Hawkins's gem against the White Sox.

JULY 2, 1976

Houston Astros center fielder César Cedeño recorded his 1,000th hit by smacking a single to right field off Cincinnati Reds pitcher and Waco native Pat Zachry in the top of the third inning in Cincinnati, Ohio. Cedeño went seven for eleven to help the Astros win both games of a doubleheader against the Reds, 3–2 and 10–8.

Cedeño hit a two-run double in the top of the eighth of the first game to put Houston in front. Then in the nightcap, he blasted a game-winning two-run homer in the top of fourteenth inning.

JULY 3, 1961

Trinity University sophomore Chuck McKinley defeated Bobby Wilson of England 6–4, 6–4, 4–6, 6–4 in the quarterfinals at Wimbledon. Two days later, McKinley ousted Mike Sangster, another Englishman, 6–4, 6–4, 8–6 to reach the finals at the All-England Club. Second-seeded Rod Laver, from Australia, overcame the eighth-seeded McKinley in the championship match 6–3, 6–1, 6–4.

McKinley made a victorious return to that stage when he defeated England's Fred Stolle 9–7, 6–1, 6–4 for the 1963 Wimbledon championship.

JULY 4, 1910

Jack "the Galveston Giant" Johnson landed a right to the jaw of Jim Jeffries that sent him through the ropes in the fifteenth round of the "Fight of the Century" in Reno, Nevada. Johnson, who in 1908 had become the first African American world heavyweight champion, finished off the previously retired champion Jeffries later in the round, making the Galveston native the undisputed heavyweight champion of the world.

Prefight prognosticators favored Jeffries, who went undefeated with fourteen knockouts in nineteen career victories before his 1904 retirement, which he returned from in 1910 specifically to take on Johnson. But Johnson had a better feel for how the fight would unfold. "I won from Mr. Jeffries because I outclassed him in every department of the fighting game," Johnson told reporters after the fight. "Before I entered the ring I was certain I would be the victor. I never changed my mind at any time."

Johnson held his world championship title through four bouts until being defeated by Jess Willard on April 5, 1915, in Havana, Cuba.

JULY 5, 1990

Houston native Zina Garrison defeated Steffi Graf 6–3, 3–6, 6–4 in a Wimbledon semifinal. "It feels really good, like the last point, I mean, I couldn't have won it better, hitting an ace on match point to get into my first Grand Slam final," Garrison said in a post-match interview.

Garrison had ousted Monica Seles a round earlier, 3–6, 6–3, 9–7, snapping Seles's thirty-six-match unbeaten streak. But Martina Navratilova defeated Garrison in the final 6–4, 6–1, ending the Texan's best chance at a Grand Slam singles title. It was Garrison's only career appearance in a singles final at a Grand Slam event, although in doubles play she claimed two Grand Slams and an Olympic gold medal.

Zina Garrison won fourteen singles and twenty doubles titles in her pro tennis career. Photo courtesy of Texas Sports Hall of Fame.

JULY 6, 2003

Saginaw native and TCU alum Angela Stanford sunk a curling twenty-foot birdie putt on the final green to get into an eighteen-hole playoff at the US Women's Open at Pumpkin Ridge Golf Club in North Plains, Oregon. Stanford's birdie on the par-five eighteenth put her at 283, one under par for the seventy-two-hole tournament, tied with Kelly Robbins and Hilary Lunke.

The world's top-ranked player, Annika Sörenstam, had a chance to either win the tournament or make it a four-player playoff, but she sliced her second shot on the eighteenth hole into trees on the right and then struggled to a bogey finish that left her one shot behind the leaders.

Lunke edged Stanford by one stroke in the playoff to keep the Texan from claiming her first major championship.

JULY 7, 1971

Lee Trevino grabbed a share of the lead by shooting a four-under-par 69 in the opening round of The Open Championship, known to most Americans as the British Open, at the Royal Birkdale Golf Club in Southport, England. Trevino finished the first eighteen holes in a tie with three others at 69, but the Texan would prove to be the most consistent player in the tournament over the next fifty-four holes of links golf.

Trevino led the tournament from start to finish, posting a seventy-two-hole score of fourteen under, a stroke in front of Taiwan's Lu Liang-Huan in second place. With that, Trevino claimed his first Open title and his second major of the 1971 season, having won the US Open championship less than three weeks earlier.

Trevino joined Ben Hogan as the only Open champions from Texas at the time.

JULY 8, 1965

Houston Astro second baseman and Bonham native Joe Morgan tied the modern-era National League record for hits in a game by going six for six against the Braves at Milwaukee County Stadium. Morgan smashed two home runs and a double, drove in three runs, scored four times, and made a diving catch of a line drive to put out Brave first baseman Joe Torre.

Morgan's heroics were not enough to lift Houston to the win. Brave outfielders Hank Aaron and Felipe Alou each homered, helping Milwaukee keep pace with Morgan. Then Brave second baseman Frank Bolling singled in the bottom of the twelfth to score Mike de la Hoz for a 9–8 victory. "I thought we had it won," Morgan told reporters after the game. "I'm glad I got six hits, but losing takes a lot out of it."

JULY 9, 1994

Brazil defender Branco sent a left-footed free kick into the right corner of the goal to lift the Brazilians to a 3–2 victory over the Netherlands in a World Cup quarterfinal match at the Cotton Bowl in Dallas. Branco's goal came in the eighty-first minute—Brazil had squandered a 2–0 lead in the second half. "I looked at the scoreboard and I saw there were ten minutes left," Branco said in a postmatch interview. "I had to try something and I figured now was the time. It was predestined."

Eight days later, Brazil claimed the World Cup championship with a 3–2 penalty-kicks victory over Italy at the Rose Bowl in Pasadena, California.

JULY 10, 1953

Ben Hogan shot a course-record four-under-par 68 at Carnoustie to win The Open Championship in his only career appearance at the event.

Hogan, who traveled to Scotland two weeks before the Open in order to practice links golf, opened the tournament with a one-over 73 in the first round, then fired descending rounds of 71, 70, and 68 for a seventy-two-hole total of 282. He finished four shots ahead of four golfers tied for second.

The win gave Hogan a unique Triple Crown, since he already had won the 1953 Masters and US Open. He could not have claimed the Grand Slam in a calendar year because the Open Championship overlapped with the PGA Championship. Hogan joined Bobby Jones and Gene Sarazen as the only golfers to win the US Open and The Open Championship in the same year.

Masters founder Jones, who in 1930 won the tournaments that made up the Grand Slam at that time—the US Open, the US Amateur Championship, The Amateur Championship (in Britain), and The Open Championship—was reached in New York and reacted to Hogan's Triple Crown. "If they are calling Hogan the greatest golfer of all time, it is not for me to say otherwise," Jones said.

JULY 11, 1940

North manager Rogers Hornsby sent Dizzy Dean to the mound to start the Texas League All-Star Game in Fort Worth. Dean, who played in four straight MLB All-Star Games from 1934 to 1937, gave up a leadoff double, but then sat down three South batters. He left after one inning of work.

But it was North left fielder Hank Oana of the Fort Worth Cats who proved to be the hero. Oana hit a sacrifice fly to tie the game at 6 in the bottom of the ninth inning. The Hawaii-born Oana then hit a walk-off double in the eleventh to give the North a 7–6 victory.

JULY 12, 1972

Defending champion Lee Trevino began The Open Championship by shooting an even-par 71 at Muirfield Golf Links in Gullane, Scotland. Trevino moved into a tie for first place with Tony Jacklin in the second round with a one-under 70 and then grabbed the lead by shooting 66 in the third round.

With Jack Nicklaus charging in the final round, Trevino made the key shot of the championship when he chipped in for par from thirty yards out on the par-five seventeenth hole. Trevino carded a final-round 71 to hold off Nicklaus by one stroke.

The Texan's victory kept the Golden Bear from placing the Claret Jug alongside the Masters and US Open trophies he had already won in 1972. "Well, that's life," Nicklaus told reporters after the round. "If I had to get beaten by somebody, I'm glad it was Lee. He's some player."

By successfully defending his 1971 title, Trevino became the first Texan to win The Open Championship twice.

JULY 13, 1995

Texas Ranger catcher Iván "Pudge" Rodríguez hit a pair of home runs over Fenway Park's "Green Monster" off Boston ace Roger Clemens as the Rangers edged the Red Sox 9–8 in Boston. Rodríguez, batting seventh, went three for five with the two homers, three runs scored, and four RBI.

In his fifth Major League season, Rodríguez was just finding his swing as a power hitter. His two blasts off Clemens brought him to 45 career home runs. He finished his twenty-one years in the majors with 311 homers.

But Pudge wasn't the only player to leave the yard that day at Fenway. Rangers Juan Gonzalez and Mike Pagliarulo, as well as Boston's Jose Canseco, hit home runs. The Rangers deployed seven pitchers to limit Boston to eight runs. Texas relief pitcher Ed Vosberg retired the only batter he faced in the eighth, grabbing the win, and closer Jeff Russell sat down the Red Sox in order in the ninth inning to earn a save.

JULY 14, 2008

Texas Ranger outfielder Josh Hamilton blasted an amazing twenty-eight home runs in the first round of the Major League Baseball Home Run Derby, breaking the single-round record of twenty-four set by Philadelphia Phillie Bobby Abreu in 2005.

Hamilton had fifteen homers before recording his eighth of ten outs (any swing that doesn't result in a homer is an out in Home Run Derby rules). Then he went on a tear, smashing thirteen home runs without an out, to the delight of a crowd of 53,716 at Yankee Stadium. Television announcers Chris Berman and Joe Morgan marveled not only at Hamilton's consistency, but also at the length of the blasts. Hamilton hit most of his homers well beyond the right center-field wall, which was 385 feet from home plate, and launched three shots more than five hundred feet.

After his first-round exertion, Hamilton hit just four homers in the second round, but easily made it into the finals to duel with Minnesota Twin Justin Morneau. Although Hamilton finished the contest with thirty-five home runs, Morneau won the final round 5–3. Hamilton hit thirteen more homers than anyone else in the contest, but finished second.

Morneau, recognizing the glitch in the scoring system, saluted Hamilton after the competition. "This was his show," Morneau said. "He deserved to win it. That was one of the best performances I've ever seen."

JULY 15, 1945

Fort Worth native Byron Nelson won his fifth and final major tournament by claiming the PGA Championship in a four-and-three match-play final-round victory over Sam Byrd at the Moraine Country Club in Dayton, Ohio. Nelson trailed Byrd in the thirty-six-hole final match until the Texan won the twenty-ninth through thirty-second holes to clinch the win.

By winning the only golf major held in 1945—the US Open, The Open Championship, and the Masters were not played in deference to World War II—Nelson extended his tournament-winning streak to eight. By the time he was finished, Nelson won eleven straight tournaments in his historic 1945 run.

JULY 16, 1971

The Houston Astros recorded the first triple play in team history on their way to a 9–4 victory over the New York Mets. With runners on first and second and no outs in the top of the third, Mets left fielder Cleon Jones hit a sharp ground ball to shortstop, which Astro Roger Metzger handled and then stepped on second for the first out. Metzger fired a bullet to first baseman Denis Menke for the second out. Menke in turn threw a laser to third baseman Doug Rader, who tagged out sliding Met Ken Boswell to end the half inning.

Nolan Ryan played a bit part in the Astros' historic game. Houston scored four runs on three hits and an error off Ryan in the first 1⅓ innings, chasing the Met starter and future Astro from the game in the second inning.

JULY 17, 1997

Dallas native and Texas alum Justin Leonard posted a first-round two-under-par 69 in The Open Championship at Royal Troon Golf Club in Troon, Scotland. Leonard's tidy first eighteen holes put him in a tie for third place with Fred Couples and Greg Norman, two shots behind coleaders Jim Furyk and Darren Clarke. But Leonard was only getting started.

The Longhorn fired a second-round 66 to get to seven under through thirty-six holes and keep close to Clarke, who was the leader at nine under through two rounds. After a slight bobble in the third round, in which Leonard went one-over par, he roared to the finish on Sunday.

Leonard started the final round five strokes out of the lead, but scorched the Troon course with a six-under 65. The Texan sunk a thirty-five-foot birdie putt on the par-three seventeenth hole to wrest the lead from Sweden's Jesper Parnevik while Parnevik watched from the tee.

"Just to be able to come through with the tournament on the line, that's the kind of confidence I'll be able to take away from here," Leonard said in a post-tournament interview.

Leonard cruised through the final hole and wound up three strokes ahead of second-place finishers Clarke and Parnevik, who bogeyed the seventeenth after witnessing Leonard's birdie.

JULY 18, 1963

Jack Nicklaus began the PGA Championship by firing a two-under-par 69 at the Dallas Athletic Club's Blue Course. Nicklaus had already won the Masters that year, and he was within striking distance after eighteen holes in Dallas as he stood tied for second, three strokes behind first-round leader Dick Hart.

Three days later, Nicklaus shot a three-under 68 in the final round to claim the championship by two strokes. It was the Golden Bear's first PGA Championship title and the third of his eighteen career majors.

JULY 19, 1984

Houston Astro left fielder Jose Cruz went three for three with a pair of doubles to lead the Astros to a 3–2 victory over the Montreal Expos at the Astrodome. Cruz was in the middle of the best statistical month of his outstanding career. During July 1984, Cruz drove in fifteen runs and batted an eye-popping .443, with eleven doubles and three home runs among his forty-seven hits that month.

Cruz, whose number 25 was retired by the Astros in 1992, played nineteen MLB seasons and collected 2,251 hits. He wore an Astros jersey for thirteen seasons and had more hits, 1,937, than any Houston player before him.

Cruz made the All-Star Game in 1980 and 1985. In July 1984, he was snubbed in All-Star voting in favor of outfield starters Tony Gwynn of the San Diego Padres, Dale Murphy of the Atlanta Braves, and Darryl Strawberry of the New York Mets. Perhaps responding to the snub, Cruz won the National League Player of the Month award.

JULY 20, 2003

Houston Astro first baseman Jeff Bagwell hit home runs in the fourth and sixth innings to reach 400 career homers. Bagwell tagged fastballs by Cincinnati Red starting pitcher Danny Graves for both shots, which led the Astros to a 6–3 victory in Cincinnati.

Bagwell played all fifteen of his Major League seasons in an Astros uniform and finished with 449 career home runs.

JULY 21, 1968

Julius Boros shot a one-over-par 281 to win the PGA Championship at Pecan Valley Golf Club in San Antonio. Boros narrowly escaped the late heroics of Arnold Palmer.

After hitting his ball into the left rough on the par-four eighteenth hole in the final round, Palmer nailed a dramatic three-wood shot from the high grass. His approach stopped twelve feet from the hole. But Palmer's birdie try missed by inches, and Boros survived. Palmer and Bob Charles tied for second at two-over.

It was Boros's third major victory. Palmer never won the PGA Championship, the only trophy not included among his seven career major titles.

JULY 22, 1984

Kathy Whitworth claimed the Rochester International in Pittsford, New York, for her eighty-fifth career professional golf victory, surpassing Sam Snead as the career leader in pro titles. Whitworth shot a three-under-par 69 in the final round and then made par on the first hole of a sudden-death playoff to beat Rosie Jones for the tournament championship. Whitworth and Jones each shot seven under through seventy-two holes of regulation.

Whitworth won three more times in her career, retiring with eighty-eight titles, including six majors.

JULY 23, 1985

Texas center fielder Oddibe McDowell became the first Ranger to hit for the cycle as he helped Texas roll past the Cleveland Indians 8–4 at Arlington Stadium. McDowell led off the game for the Rangers with a double in the first inning. He then reached base on a bunt single in the bottom of the third to get halfway to the cycle. McDowell tripled in the fourth, driving in the fourth run of the Rangers' five-run rally to take control of the contest.

Needing a home run to complete the cycle, McDowell went deep off Indian relief pitcher Tom Waddell with two outs in the eighth inning. McDowell finished the game five for five with three RBIs.

JULY 24, 1999

Plano native Lance Armstrong won the penultimate stage of the Tour de France with a time of one hour, eight minutes, and seventeen seconds in the Futuroscope time trial in the Tour de France. It was Armstrong's fourth stage win and virtually ensured his first Tour de France title.

Less than three years earlier, Armstrong had been diagnosed with testicular cancer. He not only survived the disease, but also ascended to the top of his sport.

"I don't even have the words to describe this," Linda Armstrong, Lance's mother, told Suzanne Halliburton of the *Austin American-Statesman*. "We were facing death in the eye and to come back at this level . . . This proves that there is hope."

The next day, Armstrong completed the first of his seven consecutive Tour de France victories. He won his first title by a margin of 7:37. At the time, Armstrong's story of surviving cancer to win cycling's premiere event was considered an inspiring answer to a recent drug scandal within the sport.

JULY 25, 1972

Bonham native and Cincinnati Red second baseman Joe Morgan hit a walk-off single in the bottom of the tenth inning to score San Diego Padre Nate Colbert from second and lift the National League to a 4–3 victory over the American League in the All-Star Game.

Morgan led off a National League lineup that included Willie Mays, Hank Aaron, Willie Stargell, and Johnny Bench. Although Morgan went zero for three before his tenth-inning single, the hit elevated him to the game's MVP honor. That made Morgan the second straight native Texan to be named All-Star Game MVP after Beaumont's Frank Robinson earned the honor in 1971.

JULY 26, 1976

Conroe High School and Rice alum Dave Roberts passed on an attempt at 18 feet, 2½ inches in the pole vault at the Montreal Olympics. Roberts, who had cleared the Olympic-record height of 18-0½, along with Poland's Tadeusz Slusarski and Finland's Antti Kalliomäki, aimed instead at the 18-4½ mark. It proved to be a tactical error: none of the competitors cleared 18-2½, and Roberts missed his three attempts at the higher mark.

Earlier that summer, Roberts had set the pole vault world record by clearing 18-8¼ at a meet in Eugene, Oregon. But he took bronze in the 1976 Summer Olympics because Slusarski (gold) and Kalliomäki (silver) had fewer misses at 18-0½.

Roberts, who won three NCAA national titles while at Rice, saw his next chance at Olympic gold wiped out when the United States boycotted the 1980 Moscow Olympics. Though he retired without winning an Olympic gold medal, he was inducted into the Pole Vault Hall of Fame in 2006.

JULY 27, 1969

Betsy Rawls won her eighth and final major title as she shot a one-over-par 293 to claim the LPGA Championship at the Concord Golf Club in Kiamesha Lake, New York. Rawls finished four strokes in front of Carol Mann and Susie Maxwell Berning, who tied for second place. Kathy Whitworth, from Monahans, tied for sixth at eight over.

Rawls won three more LPGA Tour events before retiring in 1975 with fifty-five career victories.

JULY 28, 1994

Texas Ranger pitcher Kenny Rogers threw a perfect game and the Rangers defeated the California Angels 4–0.

While Rogers earned a place in baseball lore by tossing the fourteenth perfect game in MLB history, rookie outfielder Rusty Greer won over Ranger fans in the top of the ninth inning. Greer sprinted in from his center-field spot, stretched out, and made a diving catch of Rex Hudler's slicing line drive to right center field, recording the first out of the ninth.

"I never thought he was going to get it," Rogers said in a postgame interview. "I thought that ball was going to drop, no matter what. Then, I thought the ball was going to pop out."

Two batters later, Greer made a much easier catch of a Gary Disarcina pop fly to center, and the Rangers celebrated Rogers's gem, the first perfect game in team history, in the inaugural season played at The Ballpark in Arlington.

Rogers, who won 219 career games, including seventy as a Ranger, struck out eight batters in the process of sitting down twenty-seven straight Angels.

JULY 29, 2012

Granbury native Dana Vollmer swam to a world-record time of 55.98 seconds in the 100-meter butterfly to win an Olympic gold medal at the London Games. Vollmer reached the turn along with a pack of swimmers, but she dominated the final fifty meters.

After pulling off her goggles and looking at the clock, Vollmer tilted her head back with a wide smile of amazement. The release of excitement followed an intense focus on keeping cool in the battle. "I kept telling myself that my strength is my second fifty," Vollmer said in a postrace interview. "I kept really calm."

Vollmer, who first won Olympic gold in 2004, as a member of the 4 × 200-meter freestyle relay team in Athens, added gold medals in the 4 × 100-meter medley relay and the 4 × 200-meter freestyle relay in London to bring her career collection of Olympic gold medals (up to that point) to four.

JULY 30, 1996

Texas Ranger right fielder Juan Gonzalez went five for five with a pair of home runs to lead the Rangers' 15–2 drubbing of the New York Yankees at The Ballpark in Arlington. Gonzalez's second home run of the contest gave him fourteen for the month of July. "The way he's swinging the bat, I expect Juan Gonzalez to drive a run in every at-bat, even when there's nobody on base," Rangers manager Johnny Oates told reporters after the game.

The next night, Gonzalez homered again, boosting his team record for home runs in a month to fifteen. He tied Joe DiMaggio, Hank Greenberg, and Joe Adcock for the most July home runs in Major League Baseball history. Gonzalez finished the 1996 season with a career-best forty-seven homers.

JULY 31, 1932

Port Arthur native Babe Didrikson launched the javelin 143 feet, 4 inches, to claim the gold medal in her debut event at the Los Angeles Olympics. Germany's Ellen Braumüller took the silver medal after her best throw came up nine inches short of Didrikson's mark.

Didrikson went on to set a world record while winning the 80-meter hurdles with a time of 11.7 seconds. She also claimed the silver medal in the high jump.

Going into her second day of competition, an International News Service report quoted Didrikson explaining, as only the brassy Texan could, how she started her athletic career. "It was the result of a cat-fight: you know, a row between two girls," Didrikson said. "I was one of the girls.

"The other was a girl down in Texas who thought she was pretty good; she had run a few good races. So I made up my mind to go out and beat her. And when we met, Babe Didrikson won. That was good enough for me!"

Babe Didrikson, a star in basketball, track and field, and golf, set a world record in the 80-meter hurdles to win one of three medals at the 1932 Los Angeles Olympics. Photo courtesy of the Texas Sports Hall of Fame.

August

AUGUST 1, 1996

Michael Johnson flew out of the blocks, running the first half of the 200-meter dash in 10.12 seconds and gaining speed through the end of the race.

When Johnson crossed the finish line, he wowed the Atlanta Olympics crowd of 82,884 by posting a new world record of 19.32 seconds. Johnson broke his own world record in the event, 19.66 seconds, set less than six weeks earlier on the same track during the US Olympic Trials. "I can't describe what it feels like to break the world record by that much," Johnson said in a postrace interview. "I thought 19.5 was possible, but 19.3 is unbelievable."

Johnson had set the Olympic record in the 400 meters three days earlier with a time of 43.49 seconds. His effort in the 200 so awed his competitors that the *New York Times* reported that bronze medalist Ato Boldon of Trinidad bowed to Johnson rather than shake his hand after the race.

Dallas native and Baylor alum Michael Johnson won two gold medals at the Atlanta Olympics in 1996. Photo courtesy of Baylor University Photography.

AUGUST 2, 1980

Bob "Mr. Cowboy" Lilly was enshrined in the Pro Football Hall of Fame in Canton, Ohio. Lilly, the Cowboys' first-ever draft pick, in 1961, played his entire fourteen-year career in Dallas, helping the Cowboys win their first Super Bowl in 1972.

Though Lilly played in an era before sacks were a recorded statistic, the Cowboys defensive tackle still posted one of the most memorable sacks of all time. During the Cowboys' victory over the Miami Dolphins in Super Bowl VI, Lilly dropped Dolphins quarterback Bob Griese for a twenty-nine-yard loss.

Lilly served as the heart of the Cowboys' famed Doomsday Defense, earning seven All-Pro and eleven Pro Bowl selections. He was the first player to see his name go up in the Cowboys' Ring of Honor and the first player who played his entire career with the Cowboys to be inducted in the Pro Football Hall of Fame.

AUGUST 3, 1984

Mary Lou Retton flung her arms into the air, in an instant defining the moment and becoming the icon of American gymnastics.

Retton took on a Tsukahara—a back flip with a 360-degree twist—the vault she needed for a perfect ten that would pass Ecaterina Szabo of Romania for the Olympic women's gymnastics all-around gold. When she stuck it, Retton knew the gold medal was hers. "I work better under pressure," Retton said following her gold-medal performance. "I knew I had to stick it and I did."

Bela Karolyi cheered and squealed from the sideline. Bela and Marta Karolyi had defected from Romania in 1981 and soon after established a gym in Houston. Retton, a native of Fairmont, West Virginia, moved to Houston to train at the Karolyis' camp. Together, the adopted Texans put American gymnastics on the map. In the following decades, the Karolyis trained Olympians Kim Zmeskal, Dominique Moceanu, and Kerri Strug, among others.

Retton was inducted into the Texas Sports Hall of Fame in 2004, and Bela and Martha Karolyi followed in 2005.

AUGUST 4, 1993

Texas troubadour Terry Allen penned the lines "I don't wear no Stetson, / But I'm willing to bet, son, / That I'm as big a Texan as you are." Nolan Ryan embodied those words more than any athlete in Texas sports history.

Though Ryan recorded 5,714 strikeouts, 324 wins, and 7 no-hitters, his defining moment in the hearts and minds of Texas sports fans came in the third inning of an early-August game versus the Chicago White Sox.

On August 4, 1993, Nolan Ryan dealt with a mound-charging Robin Ventura as only Ryan could. Photo courtesy of AP Photo/Linda Kaye.

Chicago third baseman Robin Ventura stepped to the plate for his second at-bat of the game, having singled and driven in a run in the first inning. According to Rob Goldman's book *Nolan Ryan: The Making of a Pitcher*, a feud had been brewing between Ryan's Rangers and the White Sox for years. It reached a fever pitch when Ryan's first offering to Ventura plunked him just below his right shoulder blade.

In the next few seconds, Ventura's heat-of-the-moment decision led to one of the most glorious highlights in the Rangers' history. Ventura stopped three steps into his trip to first base, discarded his bat and helmet, turned, and began running toward Ryan. But the White Sox batter's charge of the mound was as poorly executed as it was ill conceived.

When Ryan saw Ventura heading to the mound, the forty-six-year-old, already-legendary pitcher calmly tossed aside his glove and met Ventura head on. Ryan quickly wrapped him in a headlock and delivered a series of punches to the top of the White Sox player's head.

A sprawling brawl on the Arlington Stadium field resulted as both benches cleared. It took more than three minutes to restore order.

Ventura was ejected. Ryan stayed in the game.

The National Basketball Association officially merged with the American Basketball Association, ushering the San Antonio Spurs, Denver Nuggets, New York Nets, and Indiana Pacers into the NBA. Texas's stock of NBA teams doubled from one to two, since the Spurs joined the Houston Rockets, which had moved from San Diego to Houston in 1971.

The Spurs enjoyed success from the start in the NBA, making the playoffs in their first seven seasons and reaching the conference finals three times in that span.

AUGUST 6, 1984

University of Houston alum Carl Lewis soared 28 feet, 0.25 inches on his first attempt in the long jump finals at the Los Angeles Olympics. That leap proved enough to win Lewis his second gold medal of the games, and, assured of that, he moved on to loftier goals.

Lewis faulted on his second jump and then passed on his four remaining attempts and the possibility of a world record. The decision didn't sit well with the crowd at the Los Angeles Coliseum, which booed when Lewis left the competition area.

Lewis was focused on his quest to match Jesse Owens and win four gold medals. He had already won the 100-meter dash. He won the long jump by almost a foot (Gary Honey of Australia claimed the silver medal at 27 feet, 0.5 inches), and went on to add the 200 title. Lewis finished with an appropriate exclamation point as he anchored the US 4 × 100-meter relay team to a world-record time of 37.83 seconds. "To end the meet with a world record makes it real special," Lewis said in a television interview. "This has been the time of my life."

Lewis went on to win nine Olympic gold medals in his career, including the long jump at the next three Summer Olympics.

Carl Lewis soars through the air as a Houston Cougar. Lewis was a member of the Houston track and field team from 1979 to 1981. Photo courtesy of University of Houston Athletics.

AUGUST 7, 2004

AUGUST 8, 1992

San Angelo native Greg Maddux notched his 300th Major League victory as the Chicago Cubs defeated the San Francisco Giants 8–4.

Maddux, known for his unparalleled ability to win the chess match between pitcher and batter, finished his career with 355 wins, 3,371 strikeouts, and a 3.16 ERA.

In reaching 300, Maddux leaned heavily on a good offensive day for the Cubs. He gave up four runs in five innings of work, with three strikeouts and three walks. Maddux exited the game with a 6–3 lead, and Chicago held on for an 8–4 victory.

Houston alumni Leroy Burrell and Carl Lewis formed half of the 4 × 100-meter relay team that sprinted to a world record at the Barcelona Olympics. Leadoff leg Michael Marsh handed the baton to Burrell, who gave it to third leg Dennis Mitchell. When Mitchell handed off to Lewis as the anchor, momentum and history took over.

The Associated Press account of the race stated that Lewis had about a one-step lead on the Nigerian team at the last exchange. Lewis had stretched that margin to six meters by the finish line. Lewis ran the final hundred meters in less than nine seconds, helping the US team set a world record at 37.40 seconds.

Lewis credited his teammates with getting him the baton in excellent position. "I've never experienced three legs of a relay like that," he said. "I almost wanted to go up to the stands to watch that anchor."

The race marked Lewis's final Olympic victory on the track, though he added a gold medal in the long jump at the Atlanta Games in 1996.

AUGUST 9, 1995

AUGUST 10, 1976

Michael Johnson won his second consecutive world championship in the 400-meter dash by clocking his eighth career time under forty-four seconds, 43.39, in Gothenburg, Sweden. Johnson, who finished 0.83 seconds in front of world-record holder Butch Reynolds, was just off Reynolds's world-record time of 43.29. "I have to admit that I wanted to break the world record," Johnson said following the race. "But I'm very pleased with my time. I think I'll eventually break it."

Two days later, Johnson claimed the title in the 200 meters with a time of 19.79, becoming the first man to sweep the 200 and the 400 at the IAAF World Championships.

Johnson eclipsed Reynolds's world record in 1999 by clocking 43.18 at the World Championships in Seville, Spain. That time stood for more than sixteen years, until Wayde van Niekerk of South Africa ran 43.03 to win the Olympic gold medal in Rio in 2016. Fellow Baylor alum Jeremy Wariner, from Arlington, came close to Johnson's mark by posting a time of 43.45 in 2007 at the World Championships in Osaka, Japan.

Emotions erupted into fisticuffs between the Dallas Cowboys' starting quarterback, Roger Staubach, and backup Clint Longley after a training camp practice in Thousand Oaks, California. Staubach and Longley began jawing at each other during a drill after Longley criticized wide receiver Drew Pearson. Multiple accounts of the incident reported that the two quarterbacks then moved behind a baseball dugout, where Longley landed a glancing punch to Staubach's head.

Dallas assistant coach Dan Reeves said Staubach was on top of the scuffle when he separated the two players. The next day, both players downplayed the significance of the scrape. "It's a new form of conditioning," Longley jokingly told reporters. "We do it after running sprints and before lifting weights. We get so little contact, we decided to roll over and push each other. We probably could fight for hours and not hurt each other."

Staubach dismissed the incident as well. "No big deal," he said. "It was just the frustration of five weeks of training camp."

Longley was entering his third NFL season. As a rookie in 1974, he had led Dallas to a second-half comeback victory over the Washington Redskins on Thanksgiving Day at Texas Stadium. With less than a minute left in the fourth quarter, Longley hit Pearson for a fifty-yard game-winning touchdown in the 24–23 triumph.

But a few weeks after the training camp brawl, Dallas traded Longley to the San Diego Chargers.

Texas track and field alum Sanya Richards-Ross claimed four Olympic gold medals, including two at the 2012 London Games. Photo courtesy of University of Texas Athletics.

AUGUST 11, 2012

Sanya Richards-Ross anchored the gold-medal-winning Team USA 4 × 400-meter relay as it posted a time of 3:16.87 at the London Olympics. In doing so, Richards-Ross claimed her second gold medal of the Games and the fourth Olympic gold of her career.

She was quick to credit her relay teammates, DeeDee Trotter, Allyson Felix, and Francena McCorory, for putting her in position. "By the time I got the stick, it was basically a victory lap," Richards-Ross said.

Six days earlier, Richards-Ross claimed her first Olympic individual gold in the 400 meters with a time of 49.55. The result eclipsed her disappointing bronze-medal finish four years earlier in the Beijing Olympics, when she entered the race as the favorite.

"It's a huge weight off my shoulders," Richards-Ross said of the individual title. "I kept telling myself, 'You are the champ. You are the champ.' To go out there and actually accomplish it is really fantastic."

Upon winning the race in London, Richards-Ross was embraced by her husband, fellow Texas alum and NFL defensive back Aaron Ross.

AUGUST 12, 2016

Red Oak High School and Texas graduate Michelle Carter threw the shot 20.63 meters (67 feet, 8¼ inches) in her dramatic final toss to claim the gold medal at the Rio Olympics.

Valerie Adams of New Zealand held the lead with a best mark of 20.42 through the first five throws of the competition. Carter's best throw before the final round was 19.87. But she put together a winning spin and released the shot that flew high and far enough to claim the first US Olympic gold medal in women's shot put. Not coincidentally, Carter's final throw set a new American record.

"Everybody wants to come out and win the gold. Sometimes it takes a personal best, sometimes it doesn't," Carter told the media after the event. "To be able to have all those pieces finally come together that you've been working on, it's a great feeling."

Carter's father and coach, Michael Carter, a Dallas native, won the silver medal in the shot put at the 1984 Los Angeles Olympics. He was also a standout defensive lineman at Dallas Jefferson High School and SMU before going on to a nine-year NFL career with the San Francisco 49ers.

AUGUST 13, 1931

The Houston Buffaloes wrapped up the Texas League championship with a 5–2 victory over the Beaumont Exporters. Houston and Beaumont tied for the first-half championship, necessitating a best-of-five in-season playoff series, which the Buffaloes won 3–1. By then, the Buffaloes were on a tear of twenty-one wins in twenty-three games in the second half of the season, which locked up the second-half title as well.

Houston pitcher Tex Carleton won the clinching game against the Exporters, improving his season record to 20–7. Teammate and fellow right-handed pitcher Dizzy Dean compiled a 26–10 record for the Buffaloes that season. Both Dean and Carleton, along with outfielder Joe "Ducky" Medwick, were members of the St. Louis Cardinals the following season.

AUGUST 14, 2004

The US Olympic women's basketball team, including Texans Sheryl Swoopes and Tamika Catchings, opened the Athens Games with a 99–47 victory over New Zealand.

Swoopes, a Brownfield native and Texas Tech alum, was playing in her third and final Olympics. She scored fourteen points in the opener. Duncanville native Catchings was playing in her first Olympics. She pitched in six points and eight rebounds in the victory over New Zealand.

The two Texans contributed as role players, but still earned gold medals as Team USA went 8–0 in the tournament and defeated Australia 74–63 in the gold-medal game.

AUGUST 15, 2008

Nastia Liukin of Parker edged US teammate Shawn Johnson for the gymnastics all-around gold medal at the Beijing Olympics.

Liukin's astounding uneven bars routine was crafted with the help of her father, Soviet Union Olympic gold medalist Valeri Liukin. The rotation, which earned her a 16.650, was her key move in the competition. When all four rotations were complete, Liukin posted an all-around score of 63.325, 0.6 of a point better than Johnson.

Both Liukin and Johnson scored 15.525 in the floor exercise routine, demonstrating just how close the two Americans had become during training. "We have both wanted it so bad that we've pushed each other so much and I think that we became a better and a stronger gymnast because of each other," Liukin said after her victory.

Two days before the two Americans finished first and second in the individual all-around, Liukin and Johnson helped the US team earn the silver medal in the team competition.

AUGUST 16, 1990

Rumblings that the Southwest Conference's days were numbered began to surface as the annual football media tour convened in College Station. *Waco Tribune-Herald* sports editor and *Texas Football* magazine creator Dave Campbell reported that an unnamed master of ceremonies opened the media tour with the salutation "Welcome to the last football press tour the Southwest Conference will ever have." The cryptic welcome was a response to a meeting between Texas A&M athletic director John David Crow, Texas AD DeLoss Dodds, and Pac-10 officials a day earlier. While meeting with media at the press tour, Crow confirmed the Pac-10 confab, but gave no specific details. Campbell also reported on rumors that Texas A&M would rather go to the Southeastern Conference, while Texas was still interested in the Pac-10.

The MC presumed too much. Although Arkansas had escaped to the Southeastern Conference in 1992, there were five more SWC media tours before the conference finally disbanded, following the 1995–1996 academic year. The Big Eight brought in Texas, Texas A&M, Texas Tech, and Baylor to form the Big 12. SMU, TCU, and Rice joined the Western Athletic Conference. Houston became a member of the new Conference USA. It would be another sixteen years before Texas A&M followed its heart to the SEC.

AUGUST 17, 1977

Texas Ranger catcher Jim Sundberg singled to left field to drive in third baseman Toby Harrah in the bottom of the tenth inning, and the Rangers walked off with a 6–5 victory over the Toronto Blue Jays at Arlington Stadium. With the win, the Rangers moved into first place in the American League West, holding a half-game lead over the Chicago White Sox and the Minnesota Twins.

Texas finished the 1977 season with a 94–68 record, but couldn't hold off a charge from the Kansas City Royals. Kansas City was a game behind the White Sox and Twins when the Rangers moved into first on August 17. Then the Royals caught fire, going 37–9 for the rest of the season (the Rangers went 27–18 in the same span) to finish eight games in front of Texas for the AL West title.

AUGUST 18, 1935

The nine Deike brothers from the Hill Country town of Hye faced the Stanczak brothers of Waukegan, Illinois, in the All-Brothers Championship at the National Baseball Congress World Series in Wichita, Kansas. According to Carlton Stowers's documentary book *Oh Brother, How They Played the Game*, the Deike brothers, who composed the entire team from Hye, were playing in their first night game and their first game on a manicured grass field. Nonetheless, the Deikes took an early 3–0 lead on the more seasoned Stanczaks.

But the Stanczaks bounced back by scoring seven runs in the second inning, and claimed an 11–5 victory. "We were beaten fair and square," center fielder Ernest Deike said. "They had a couple of big ol' boys who were just better ballplayers than we were."

Stowers noted that shortstop Levi Deike framed the loss in the context of the all-brother team's legacy. "I don't remember anybody getting too down in the dumps over the fact we lost," Levi Deike said. "It wasn't the first time we'd been beaten, you know. Back in those days we had our hands full just trying to whip town teams like Dripping Springs, Blanco, and Johnson City."

AUGUST 19, 1960

Baltimore Colt quarterback Johnny Unitas welcomed the expansion Dallas Cowboys to the NFL by throwing a last-minute, sixty-two-yard touchdown pass to Lenny Moore, giving the Colts a 14–10 preseason victory over the Cowboys. Although it was the third pre-season game for Dallas, it drew an exceptionally large audience: 40,000 spectators showed up to see the 1959 NFL champion Colts face the Cowboys at the Cotton Bowl.

(PHOTO, RIGHT)
Monahans native Kathy Whitworth compiled a record eighty-eight victories on the LPGA Tour. Her collection of trophies included six major championships. Photo courtesy of the Texas Sports Hall of Fame.

AUGUST 20, 1967

Kathy Whitworth fired a final-round four-under-par 71 to win her first LPGA Western Open at Pekin Country Club in Pekin, Illinois. Whitworth's seventy-two-hole total of 289 (eleven under) was an LPGA record and gave her a three-stroke victory over Sandra Haynie of Fort Worth.

Whitworth's Western title, her sixth win of the season, gave her three major victories through the first seven years of her pro career, and she won the Western Open just in time, since it disappeared from the LPGA schedule in 1968.

AUGUST 21, 1926

Former Baylor basketball and baseball standout Ted Lyons threw the only Major League no-hitter of the 1926 season as he led the Chicago White Sox to a 6–0 victory over the Red Sox at Fenway Park in Boston. Lyons struck out two and walked one in an impressively efficient performance on the mound. The game lasted just one hour and forty-five minutes.

Lyons, who was elected to the Baseball Hall of Fame in 1955, added to the stellar day by going one for four at the plate, with an RBI.

AUGUST 22, 1989

Rickey Henderson of the Oakland Athletics stepped to the plate with his customary bravado, never mind—or maybe more accurately, because of—the fact that he was facing Nolan Ryan, pitching for the Texas Rangers, in a historic moment.

Henderson led off the fifth inning, having struck out in the third to become Ryan strikeout victim 4,998. (Ryan caught Ron Hassey looking in the same inning, and he became number 4,999.) Henderson worked the count full, but couldn't avoid history. Ryan threw a fastball low and away. Henderson swung and missed.

"If somebody had asked me how I'd have liked to get it (his 5,000th strikeout), I would have said with a fastball swinging," Ryan said in a postgame interview. "That's my bread-and-butter pitch."

According to the *Dallas Morning News*, Ryan's pitch that struck out Henderson matched his highest velocity of the game, 96 mph.

Ryan entered the game with 4,994 career strikeouts. He struck out thirteen in a 2–0 Ranger loss. Though Texas lost the game, a sellout crowd of 42,869 got what they came for as the Strikeout King passed a momentous milestone. Ryan finished his career with 5,714 Ks, 839 in front of second-place Randy Johnson.

AUGUST 23, 1992

Family, friends, and fans from the towns of Hewitt and Woodway welcomed home their conquerors as the Little League Softball World Series champion Midway All-Stars returned to Broughton Field in Woodway.

A day earlier, Midway defeated Gresham, Oregon, 4–1 in Kalamazoo, Michigan, to clinch its first World Series title, becoming the first softball team from Texas ever to win the crown. By breaking through, the Midway girls set off more than a decade of domination: the Little Leaguers from the Waco area claimed the championship ten more times in the next twelve years.

Although the team of eleven- and twelve-year-olds flew home as a squad, many of the girls' families drove through the night from Michigan in order to make it to the homecoming celebration.

The Midway Little League Softball All-Stars won the 1992 Little League World Series, launching a streak of eleven World Series titles in the next twelve years. Photo courtesy of Conine family.

AUGUST 24, 2002

The NFL returned to Houston when the Texans played their first game at Reliant Stadium. A crowd of 69,432 saw the team lose to the Miami Dolphins 24–3 in a preseason game. The Texans were playing their inaugural season after the NFL awarded the city an expansion team in 1999. The Houston Oilers had played in the Astrodome from 1968 to 1996 before owner Bud Adams took the franchise to Tennessee.

Two weeks later, the Texans won their first regular-season game at Reliant by defeating the Dallas Cowboys 19–10. The magnificent start turned out to be a rare bright spot for the Texans, who went 4–12 in their first campaign.

AUGUST 25, 1946

Ben Hogan claimed his first major by defeating Ed Oliver 6-and-4 in the match-play final of the PGA Championship at the Portland (Oregon) Golf Club.

Hogan went on to win nine major championships, including another PGA title in 1948, four US Opens, two Masters green jackets, and an Open Championship.

AUGUST 26, 1992

AUGUST 27, 2004

Seventh-ranked Texas A&M opened the college football season with a 10–7 victory over seventeenth-ranked Stanford in a rare Wednesday night game in the Disneyland Pigskin Classic at Anaheim Stadium.

Stanford began the fourth quarter with a 7–0 lead, but Texas A&M quarterback Jeff Granger threw a twenty-one-yard touchdown pass to Greg Schorp early in the period. Aggie kicker Terry Venetoulias booted a thirty-nine-yard field goal with 4:27 left to put Texas A&M in front for good.

The Aggies spoiled Bill Walsh's return to college football. The former 49ers coach had taken over as the Cardinal head coach before the 1992 campaign.

Houston native Nia Abdallah became the first US woman to medal at the Olympics in taekwondo when she won the silver at the Athens Games.

Abdallah began her groundbreaking performance in the 57-kilogram division by defeating Russia's Margarita Mkrtchyan in the first round, becoming the first American woman to win an Olympic taekwondo match. She followed that with wins over Cristiana Corsi of Italy and Thailand's Nootcharin Sukkhongdumnoen. "Just me winning my first fight was putting myself in the record books," Abdallah said. "I'm happy for what I got."

Jang Ji-won of South Korea defeated Abdallah in the final 2–1.

AUGUST 28, 2006

AUGUST 29, 1981

Richardson High School alum Carla Overbeck was inducted into the National Soccer Hall of Fame.

Overbeck played an integral role in Team USA's defense as a member of the 1991 and 1999 Women's World Cup championships. She played every minute of the national team's matches in the 1995 World Cup, the 1996 Olympics, and the 1999 World Cup, and posted a streak of sixty-three consecutive starts in international play.

"Thank you to my teammates, my coaches, my parents, and my family, all of whom supported me as I strived to achieve my goals," Overbeck said upon induction into the Hall of Fame. "Goals for myself and goals for the teams on which I played—there is no way I would be here without your support."

The Houston Astros swept the Philadelphia Phillies in a doubleheader at the Astrodome, 6–1, 2–1.

Houston hitters Denny Walling, Jose Cruz, and César Cedeño sparked the Astros in the second game with back-to-back-to-back hits in the bottom of the first inning. Cedeño's single to left scored Walling, giving Astro starting pitcher Billy Smith a 1–0 lead. Smith took off from there, shutting out the Phillies for seven innings and allowing just five hits. Astro catcher Alan Ashby homered in the bottom of the seventh for a crucial insurance run.

The Astros' twin killing of Philadelphia helped propel their surge during the second half of the season. Houston won nine straight from August 28 to September 4 on its way to the National League West second-half championship.

A player strike cut two months out of the 1981 schedule from mid-June until mid-August. The Astros were 28–29 before the strike, but finished the season 61–49.

The strike caused the first MLB postseason division series, which pitted the Astros against the NL West first-half champion, the Los Angeles Dodgers, in a best-of-five set. Although the Astros won the first two games of the series, the Dodgers responded with three straight victories to advance on their way to the 1981 World Series title.

AUGUST 30, 1997

The Houston Comets defeated the New York Liberty 65–51 to win the inaugural WNBA Championship.

Regular-season and playoff MVP Cynthia Cooper scored twenty-five points, grabbed four rebounds, dished out four assists, and swiped three steals to propel Houston to the title.

The Comets went on to claim the first four WNBA titles, defeating the Liberty three times and the Phoenix Mercury once.

AUGUST 31, 1996

Eighth-ranked Texas defeated Missouri 40–10, and twenty-first-ranked Kansas State edged Texas Tech 21–7, as the Big 12 officially began on the football field.

The formation of the Big 12 was announced on February 25, 1994, as the Big Eight merged with four members of the Southwest Conference: Baylor, Texas, Texas A&M, and Texas Tech.

September

SEPTEMBER 1, 2012

Texas State Bobcat running back Marcus Curry rushed for 131 yards and two touchdowns and caught a twenty-one-yard touchdown pass to propel the Bobcats to a 30–13 season-opening victory over the University of Houston at Robertson Stadium in Houston. Texas State notched a win in its first official game as a Football Bowl Subdivision member program and avenged a forty-point loss to the Cougars from two years earlier on the same field.

The Bobcats moved from the Southland Conference to an independent program in 2011, and then to the Western Athletic Conference in 2012. The Bobcats' victory served as a promising FBS debut. But Texas Tech stomped Texas State the next week 58–10, and the Bobcats failed to reestablish the momentum from the Houston win during a 4–8 season.

SEPTEMBER 2, 1989

SMU played its first football game in more than thirty-three months, beginning a long road back after being assessed the death penalty. The NCAA imposed the harsh sanctions on SMU's football program in February 1987, banning the Mustangs from competing that year and stripping them of their 1988 home games.

The NCAA Committee on Infractions determined that SMU football players received a total of $61,000 in monthly payments from boosters in 1985 and 1986. Those violations came immediately after SMU had been put on probation in August 1985 for similar infractions, offenses that led the NCAA to reduce the number of scholarships the Mustangs could offer and to ban them from bowl games in 1985 and 1986.

SMU eventually canceled the entirety of its 1988 campaign, meaning the Mustangs would go without a football team for two seasons as a result of the NCAA ruling. SMU's football players were allowed to transfer to other schools without losing any eligibility.

The long-term effects of SMU's two-year ban were severe. The Mustangs did not enjoy another winning season until 1997 and didn't earn a bowl-game appearance until 2009.

SEPTEMBER 3, 1978

In SMU's return to action, Rice dismantled the Mustangs 35–6 at Ownby Stadium in Dallas.

By defeating the reborn Mustangs, Rice snapped an 18-game losing streak that dated to September 26, 1987.

"We just wanted one thing out of this game: to stop the losing streak," Rice defensive end Tim Fitzpatrick said in a postgame interview. "It's hard to know what to expect from a team that hasn't played in two years. It's like the Trojan horse. We didn't know what they were bringing in."

Rice won just one more game the rest of the season. The Owls, who finished with a 2-8-1 record in 1989, tied Wake Forest, 17–17, on September 30, and defeated Baylor, 6–3, on November 18.

SMU notched its first post-death-penalty win two weeks later with a 31–30 victory over Connecticut. The Mustangs also defeated North Texas, 35–9, on October 28, and finished the season with a 2–9 mark.

Earl Campbell made his Houston Oilers debut, running seventy-three yards for a touchdown in the first quarter and giving Houston a 7–0 lead over the Atlanta Falcons. The Falcons ultimately won the game 20–14, but Campbell posted 137 rushing yards on fifteen carries.

Campbell finished his rookie season with 1,450 rushing yards and thirteen touchdowns, earning Offensive Rookie of the Year and Offensive Player of the Year honors. The Oilers finished the season 12-7, falling to the Pittsburgh Steelers in the AFC Championship game.

SEPTEMBER 4, 2010

TCU quarterback Andy Dalton ran four yards for a touchdown late in the third quarter, putting the sixth-ranked Horned Frogs ahead for good on their way to a 30–21 season-opening victory over Oregon State at Cowboys Stadium in Arlington. Dalton passed for 175 yards with one touchdown and two interceptions, and ran for 64 yards and two scores. Those were pedestrian statistics, but TCU coach Gary Patterson said that wasn't the point of his quarterback's performance.

"We just beat the twenty-fourth-ranked team that I think should be ranked higher," Patterson said in a postgame press conference. "I think it was a pretty good game. That's how I judge quarterbacks. A game like this, it didn't have to be style points."

The Horned Frogs earned plenty of style points during the rest of the 2010 season, going 13–0. TCU finished the season with a 21–19 victory over Wisconsin in the Rose Bowl and earned the number 2 ranking in the final Associated Press poll.

SEPTEMBER 5, 1996

Waco University High School senior running back LaDainian Tomlinson made the most of his first game as the Trojans' featured ball carrier. Tomlinson, who had served primarily as a blocker as a junior, rushed for 181 yards and five touchdowns to help University defeat Austin LBJ 48–0 in a Thursday night season-opener at Nelson Field in Austin.

"This was a dream come true," Tomlinson told *Austin American-Statesman* sportswriter Olin Buchanan. "My linemen did a good job. All I had to do was run through big holes."

Tomlinson started fast, running for 128 yards in the first quarter and scoring touchdowns of thirty-seven, two, twenty-five, and thirty-one yards. The icing on the cake came when Tomlinson, playing defense in the second quarter, intercepted a pass and returned it sixty yards for a touchdown.

With the phenomenal season-opening game as a catalyst, Tomlinson went on to rush for 2,554 yards and thirty-nine touchdowns in leading the Trojans to a 12–2 season in 1996.

SEPTEMBER 6, 2008

Twelfth-ranked Texas Tech sidestepped a challenge from Colin Kaepernick–led University of Nevada as the Red Raiders defeated the Wolf Pack 35–19 in Reno, Nevada. Red Raider quarterback Graham Harrell passed for a relatively paltry 297 yards, but he hooked up with wide receiver Michael Crabtree for an eighty-two-yard touchdown early in the fourth quarter that helped Texas Tech pull away from upset-minded Nevada.

Kaepernick passed for 264 yards and a touchdown, and rushed for 92, but he fumbled on a would-be go-ahead touchdown run in the third quarter, which allowed the Red Raiders to retain the lead and momentum.

Texas Tech wide receiver Eric Morris caught only two passes for 8 yards, but he played a huge role by returning a punt eighty-six yards for a touchdown and running thirteen yards for another score. Crabtree finished the game with seven catches for 158 receiving yards and the long touchdown.

SEPTEMBER 7, 1992

SEPTEMBER 8, 1990

The Dallas Cowboys' triplets were out in full force to begin the 1992 season. Emmitt Smith rushed for 140 yards and a touchdown, Troy Aikman passed for 216 yards and a touchdown, and Michael Irvin caught five passes for 89 yards as the Cowboys defeated reigning Super Bowl champion Washington 23–10 on *Monday Night Football* at Texas Stadium.

Aikman hit Alvin Harper for a twenty-six-yard score in the second quarter, and Kelvin Martin returned a punt seventy-nine yards for a touchdown in the third to put the Cowboys comfortably in control. Defensive end Charles Haley, in his Dallas debut, posted a sack.

San Antonio Southwest High School product Ty Detmer passed for 406 yards and three touchdowns in leading the BYU Cougars to a 28–21 upset of top-ranked Miami at Cougar Stadium in Provo, Utah. Detmer tossed a seven-yard touchdown pass to Mike Salido in the third quarter and then hit Andy Boyce for the two-point conversion, giving BYU a lead it didn't relinquish.

Chicago Tribune reporter Ed Sherman inquired in the lead paragraph of his game story, "Is it possible to win the Heisman Trophy in September?" Sherman reckoned it was, and he was correct.

Detmer passed for 5,188 yards and forty-one touchdowns during his junior season in leading the Cougars to a 10–3 record. For that he won the Heisman Trophy and the Davey O'Brien Award.

(PHOTO, OPPOSITE PAGE)
Texas Tech wide receiver Michael Crabtree (5) holds the ball aloft after scoring a touchdown in the Red Raiders' 2008 season opener versus Eastern Washington. Crabtree, from Dallas Carter High School, caught ninety-seven passes for 1,165 yards and nineteen touchdowns as he helped the Red Raiders ascend to the number 2 national ranking in the 2008 season. Photo courtesy of Texas Tech University Athletics.

SEPTEMBER 9, 2006

SEPTEMBER 10, 2005

The UTEP Miners pushed twenty-fourth-ranked Texas Tech to the brink of an early-season upset at the Sun Bowl in El Paso. Miner quarterback Jordan Palmer hit wide receiver Johnnie Lee Higgins for a thirty-nine-yard touchdown to tie the game at 35 with 1:04 remaining in the fourth quarter.

But Texas Tech kicker Alex Trlica, who missed field goal attempts of thirty-four and fifty-one yards in the fourth quarter, kicked a forty-nine-yarder in overtime that bounced off the left upright and through to lift the Red Raiders to a 38–35 victory. "When it came off my foot, I thought it was going down the middle," Trlica said in a postgame interview. "Then I saw it tail off and it hit the upright. Everybody was in my way and I couldn't see. I bent over and saw the ref give the signal."

UTEP QB Palmer finished the game with 334 passing yards, three touchdowns, and a pair of interceptions, including a costly one that ended UTEP's overtime possession. His counterpart, Texas Tech QB Graham Harrell, passed for 376 yards, two TDs, and one pick. The Red Raiders' and Miners' offenses combined for 964 yards of total offense.

Texas quarterback Vince Young lofted a twenty-four-yard touchdown pass to Limas Sweed, lifting the Longhorns to a 25–22 victory over Ohio State in Columbus, Ohio. The second-ranked Longhorns claimed bragging rights in the teams' first meeting. By defeating the fourth-ranked Buckeyes, the Horns launched themselves on a campaign for the national championship.

Young passed for 270 yards and rushed for another 76 in the win at Ohio State. In one of the most memorable quarterbacking performances in Longhorn history, Young completed the 2005 season with 3,036 passing yards, 1,050 rushing yards, and thirty-eight total touchdowns. He finished second in Heisman voting to USC's Reggie Bush.

Young had the last laugh in the win column. After the Longhorns defeated Ohio State by three points, none of Texas's next ten opponents came within double digits of the Horns. Texas finished the season by winning the BCS National Championship Game 41–38 over Bush and USC.

SEPTEMBER 11, 1976

SEPTEMBER 12, 2009

The Houston Cougars won their Southwest Conference football debut by rallying in the second half for a 23–5 victory over Baylor in Waco. The Bears led 5–0 as the bands marched at halftime, but the Cougars owned the third and fourth quarters.

Houston quarterback Danny Davis ran four yards for a touchdown that boosted the Cougars to a 6–5 lead with 6:07 left in the third quarter. Houston shut out Baylor for the entire second half, bottling up the Bears in their own end of the field. Cougar running back Dyral Thomas scored on runs of one and five yards as Houston pulled away for the win.

"This is history, pure history," Houston senior defensive tackle Wilson Whitley told *Waco Tribune-Herald* sportswriter John McClain after the game. "I've played in two bowl games, and when you finish (11–1 in the 1973 season) you've really done something. But this win tops everything I've experienced here. This is history being made."

Houston went on to tie for the SWC championship in its first season as a member. The Cougars topped it off by defeating Maryland 30–21 in the Cotton Bowl.

Houston quarterback and Abilene Wylie alum Case Keenum passed for 366 yards and three touchdowns as the Cougars upset fifth-ranked Oklahoma State 45–35 in Stillwater, Oklahoma. Keenum hit Bryce Beall for a six-yard touchdown that gave Houston a 38–35 lead with 6:42 left in the fourth quarter. Then Cougar defensive back and Schertz Clemens alum Jamal Robinson locked up the win by intercepting a pass from Cowboy QB Zac Robinson and returning it twenty-six yards for a touchdown with 3:14 remaining.

"There's no doubt that one win does not make a season," Houston coach Kevin Sumlin said in a postgame interview. "We've got a whole bunch of football to go. But I think any time that you can go on the road and win and beat a Top Ten team, it really helps your confidence as a program and it helps your pride as a university."

Houston kept up the momentum by defeating Texas Tech two weeks later in Houston. The Cougars went on to a 10–4 season after falling in the Conference USA championship game against East Carolina and the Armed Forces Bowl versus Air Force.

SEPTEMBER 13, 1975

Emory Bellard's Texas A&M football team cranked up its season opener by driving fifty-four yards for a touchdown on its first possession against the Ole Miss Rebels at Kyle Field in College Station. Aggie quarterback David Shipman ran four yards for the apparent tone-setting first-quarter score and a 7–0 lead.

But underdog Mississippi fought bravely the rest of the way, and Texas A&M had to hold on to a 7–0 victory. The Rebels had one last chance to tie the game in the final minute of the fourth quarter on a fourth-and-ten from the Texas A&M eleven-yard line. But Aggie defender Pat Thomas knocked a pass away from Mississippi running back Rick Kimbrough, allowing Texas A&M to regain possession and run out the final thirty-nine seconds of action.

Texas A&M took off from there, winning its first ten games before falling in the regular-season finale against Arkansas. Still, the Aggies claimed a share of the Southwest Conference tri-championship with Arkansas and Texas. Southern California handed Texas A&M its second loss of the season 20–0 in the Liberty Bowl.

SEPTEMBER 14, 1991

Baylor kicker Jeff Ireland booted a thirty-five-yard field goal to lift the Bears to a 16–14 victory over defending national champion and twelfth-ranked Colorado in Boulder, Colorado. Baylor's monumental road victory ended the Buffaloes' eleven-game winning streak.

Ireland's game-winning kick was made possible when Bear defensive tackle Santana Dotson dashed through the middle of the Colorado line and blocked Buffalo kicker Jim Harper's twenty-four-yard field goal attempt, which, if successful, would have given Colorado a four-point lead with a little more than three minutes to play. As the Baylor offense moved in position for the win, Ireland's gut began to rumble.

"To be quite honest, I was scared to death," Ireland told *Waco Tribune-Herald* sportswriter Jerry Hill. "I just tried to stay focused. Coach (Grant) Teaff came up and told me, 'Just put it through the uprights and let's win this game.'"

Ireland's kick gave the Bears the lead with fifty-one seconds left, and Baylor held on. Legendary *Tribune-Herald* sports editor Dave Campbell correctly predicted the 16–14 final score, but he had the winning team wrong—he picked Colorado to edge Baylor.

SEPTEMBER 15, 1984

Texas quarterback Todd Dodge passed for 215 yards, ran ten yards for a score, and threw a thirty-two-yard touchdown pass to Brent Duhon to lead the fourth-ranked Longhorns past eleventh-ranked Auburn 35–27 at Memorial Stadium in Austin. Texas escaped with a win despite its inability to slow down Auburn running back Bo Jackson, who rushed for 103 yards and a touchdown on fourteen carries.

Jackson was on his way to leading the Tigers to a huge come-from-behind road win in the third quarter. But after he broke loose for a fifty-three-yard run to the Texas twenty-three, Longhorn defensive back Jerry Gray made a touchdown-saving tackle that caused Jackson to separate his shoulder and brought an end to his promising season. Jackson left the field under his own strength and attempted to return to the game, but was ineffective because of the injury.

The win helped the Longhorns climb to the number 1 national ranking by early October. Jackson's injury sidelined him for most of his junior season. He returned to health for his senior campaign and won the Heisman Trophy in 1985.

SEPTEMBER 16, 1993

Emmitt Smith ended his holdout by signing a four-year, $13.6 million contract with the Dallas Cowboys in time to join the team for the third game of the season.

Smith had rushed for 1,713 yards in the previous season and played a leading role in Dallas's Super Bowl victory. With Smith out of the lineup because of the contract dispute, the defending-champion Cowboys lost their first two games of the 1993 campaign.

"I got what I wanted," Smith said. "I wanted to be the highest-paid running back in the NFL. But it was the hardest thing for me to do to sit in the living room and watch my teammates play on television."

Smith immediately proved his value. Dallas won seven straight after his return. The Cowboys' star running back rushed for 1,486 yards in the first year of his new contract, winning the rushing title and earning NFL MVP honors as Dallas marched to another championship.

SEPTEMBER 17, 1953

Dallas native Ernie Banks made his debut as the first African American to play for the Chicago Cubs. Playing shortstop and batting seventh, Banks had an unproductive first game, going zero for three and committing an error in a 16–4 loss to the Philadelphia Phillies.

But Banks, whose unbridled enthusiasm for the game led to his catchphrase "Let's play two!" was undeterred. He went on to bat .274 for his career and hit 512 home runs in nineteen seasons, all for the Cubs. Banks was inducted into the National Baseball Hall of Fame in 1977.

SEPTEMBER 18, 1966

Dallas Cowboy quarterback Dandy Don Meredith threw two long touchdown passes to "Bullet Bob" Hayes and three short ones to Dan Reeves as Dallas crushed the New York Giants 52–7 in the season opener at the Cotton Bowl.

With the score tied at 7 early in the second quarter, Meredith sensed a blitz coming from the Giants' defense and took advantage of it. He threw over the top to Hayes, who caught the pass and raced the rest of the way for a seventy-four-yard touchdown. Hayes finished the game with six catches for 195 yards, and Reeves caught another six for 120 as Meredith completed fourteen of nineteen for 358 yards.

The hot start launched Dallas on a 10–3-1 season and its first playoff appearance in the NFL Championship game.

(PHOTO, OPPOSITE PAGE)
Legendary Dallas Cowboys coach Tom Landry gives instructions to quarterback Don Meredith (17). Landry was the Cowboys' head coach for the team's first twenty-nine seasons. He led them to five Super Bowl appearances, including victories in Super Bowls VI and XXII. Photo courtesy of the Texas Sports Hall of Fame.

SEPTEMBER 19, 1970

University of Texas quarterback Eddie Phillips showed the Memorial Stadium crowd that he was capable of following the act of James Street and continuing the Longhorns' long winning streak. Phillips spearheaded the wishbone offense by rushing for 129 yards and scoring two touchdowns as second-ranked Texas, the defending national champion, hammered California 56–15 in the season opener.

The Longhorns' gouging of the Bears extended their winning streak to twenty-one games as they charged into the 1970 campaign. Texas won nine more in succession, including victories over thirteenth-ranked UCLA and fourth-ranked Arkansas, on the way to an undefeated regular season. Sixth-ranked Notre Dame halted the Longhorns' winning streak at thirty when the Fighting Irish won the 1971 Cotton Bowl 24–11.

SEPTEMBER 20, 2009

The Dallas Cowboys played their first regular-season game in their new stadium in Arlington. Originally called Cowboys Stadium and often referred to colloquially as "Jerry World," after Cowboy owner Jerry Jones, the stadium featured a massive seating capacity and a gargantuan 160-feet-high-by-72-feet-tall video board. The inaugural regular-season game set an NFL attendance record of 105,121 for the Sunday-night game.

Cowboy coach Wade Phillips had a unique perspective on the opening of the massive new stadium. Phillips played linebacker for the University of Houston when the Cougars played the first football game in the Astrodome in 1965. He compared that event to the debut of the new Cowboys Stadium in an article posted on the Cowboys' official website. "This is similar (to the Astrodome), but probably tenfold," Phillips said. "This stadium is like the (Egyptian) pyramids or something. It's unbelievable. The Astrodome was different because it was a baseball stadium and they'd already opened it for baseball. It wasn't like it was football only. So yeah, this is bigger than something like that."

Unfortunately for the Cowboys, the New York Giants tarnished the debut by defeating Dallas 33–31. Giant kicker Lawrence Tynes nailed a thirty-seven-yard field goal with no time remaining to keep the Cowboys from celebrating a win in their new digs.

SEPTEMBER 21, 1957

First-year Texas coach Darrell Royal guided his team to a 26–7 victory over Georgia in the season opener in Atlanta. Fullback Mike Dowdle led the way for the Texas offense as he ran for four- and three-yard touchdowns in the first half to give the Longhorns a commanding 13–0 lead at the break.

Texas held on for a win that impressed pollsters, and the Longhorns jumped to number 13 in the national rankings the next week. At the end of the roller-coaster first season for Royal, the 6–4–1 Longhorns earned a trip to the Sugar Bowl, but lost to Mississippi 39–7 in New Orleans.

SEPTEMBER 22, 2015

Plano East Senior High and TCU alum Jake Arrieta threw a complete-game three-hitter and led the Chicago Cubs to a 4–0 victory over the Milwaukee Brewers. It was Arrieta's twentieth win of the season and one of many gems in the second half of the season for the Cubs' Cy Young winner. Arrieta finished the season with a 1.77 ERA, 236 strikeouts, and a 22–6 record. He won fourteen games after the All-Star break, including a no-hitter against the Los Angeles Dodgers on August 30 and a complete-game shutout of the Pittsburgh Pirates in the National League wild-card game. The Cubs' manager, Joe Maddon, compared Arrieta's 0.75 ERA in the second half of the season with the 1968 performance of St. Louis Cardinal Hall of Famer Bob Gibson, who posted a 1.12 ERA on his way to the National League Cy Young.

SEPTEMBER 23, 1989

Martina Navratilova defeated Manuela Maleeva in straight sets, and Monica Seles did the same versus Anne Smith, in the semifinals of the Virginia Slims of Dallas at Moody Coliseum. The semifinals results set up the first meeting between thirty-two-year-old tennis legend Navratilova and fifteen-year-old rising star Seles.

The next day, Navratilova edged Seles 7–6, 6–3 to win the tournament for the second consecutive year and the ninth time overall. But Seles's prowess impressed Navratilova. "If she keeps improving we'll all be in trouble," Navratilova said in a postmatch interview.

The two tennis stars' first meeting brought a dramatic end to the Dallas tournament, which relocated the following year.

SEPTEMBER 24, 2000

Houston native Laura Wilkinson put together a miraculous day of diving as she went from the middle of the pack to the gold medal in the ten-meter platform at the 2000 Olympic Games in Sydney, Australia.

Despite breaking three bones in her right foot just six months before the games and competing in her first Olympics, Wilkinson came from eighth place to finish 1.74 points ahead of China's Li Na for gold.

"We had a lot of trials and tribulations to get here," Wilkinson said in her postevent interview. "The day I broke my foot, I thought my dreams were over. But God works in mysterious ways."

Wilkinson nailed a reverse two-and-a-half somersault on her third dive of the final round, propelling her to a final-round five-dive total of 370.71 points. After the final dive of the competition, Wilkinson realized she had won the gold medal and, with tears of joy in her eyes, waved to her parents in the grandstands. Wilkinson had become the first American woman in thirty-six years to win the event at the Olympics.

SEPTEMBER 25, 1986

SEPTEMBER 26, 1965

Houston Astro right-hander Mike Scott pitched a no-hitter versus the San Francisco Giants for a 2–0 victory in which the Astros clinched the National League West division title. Scott dominated the Giants by using his signature pitch, the split-fingered fastball, to strike out thirteen with two walks.

The Giants' manager, Roger Craig, could see midway through the contest what was about to happen. "I've never seen a no-hitter pitched under these circumstances," Craig said to reporters in the clubhouse after the game. "I told one of my coaches in the fourth or fifth inning, 'We're not going to get a hit off of him.'"

Scott's gem capped three straight brilliant pitching performances by the Astros. Jim Deshaies had shut out the Giants two nights earlier, and on the night before Scott's no-hitter, Nolan Ryan gave up one hit in eight innings to lead the Astros to another shutout victory.

Scott led Major League Baseball in 1986 with 306 strikeouts. He combined with Ryan to strike out 500 batters that season. Scott continued his stellar 1986 season into the playoffs by winning two games in the National League Championship Series versus the New York Mets. The Mets, however, won the best-of-seven series 4–2.

Fort Worth native Sandra Haynie nabbed her first major victory by posting a five-under-par 279 through seventy-two holes at the LPGA Championship. Haynie edged Clifford Ann Creed by one stroke at the Stardust Country Club in Las Vegas, Nevada, for the title.

At twenty-two, Haynie had already won six LPGA tournaments before notching her first major. She went on to claim forty-two tournament titles and four majors, including the US Women's Open and the LPGA Championship in 1974.

SEPTEMBER 27, 2003

Texas Tech quarterback B. J. Symons out-dueled his Mississippi counterpart, Eli Manning, as the Red Raider passed for 661 yards and six touchdowns to lead Texas Tech to a 49–45 victory in Oxford, Mississippi. Symons hit wide receiver Carlos Francis for a nine-yard game-winning touchdown with 1:04 left in the fourth quarter.

The Rebels' bid to answer was stopped when Texas Tech defensive back Ryan Aycock intercepted a Manning pass to seal the win.

SEPTEMBER 28, 1968

Texas Tech held off a third-quarter come-back attempt by sixth-ranked Texas as the Red Raiders posted a 31–22 victory. Texas Tech running back Roger Freeman caught a touchdown pass from quarterback Joe Matulich and ran for two more scores, including a two-yard run in the third quarter that offset the Longhorns' twenty-two-point onslaught in that period, which was led by reserve QB James Street.

The next Saturday, Street led Texas to a 31–3 victory over Oklahoma State that began a thirty-game winning streak.

SEPTEMBER 29, 1985

SEPTEMBER 30, 1988

Dallas sacked Houston Oiler quarterback Warren Moon an NFL-record-tying twelve times, and the Cowboys left the Astrodome with a 17–10 victory in Houston. "I lost count after about seven (sacks)," said Moon, who also threw four interceptions.

While the Dallas defense was tormenting the Oilers' quarterback, Cowboy running back Tony Dorsett gave Dallas the burst it needed to overcome an otherwise inefficient contest on offense. Dorsett rushed for 159 yards and set up the go-ahead touchdown in the fourth quarter with a thirty-one-yard run to the Houston one-yard line. From there, Dallas quarterback Danny White threw a one-yard touchdown pass to Fred Cornwell for the score that proved to be the difference.

"Dorsett was just exploding," White said. "He was busting up their 3-4 defense. They've usually held us pretty well in the past, but Tony turned on his jets and moved."

Dorsett's effort proved to be a catalyst for his last great season. He rushed for 1,307 yards, reaching the 1,000-yard mark for the final time in his career.

Red Oak native and Texas Woman's University alum Louise Ritter defeated Bulgaria's Stefka Kostadinova in a jump-off to claim the gold medal in the high jump at the Seoul Olympics. Ritter cleared 6 feet, 8 inches in the jump-off, tying the American record she had set earlier in the year and setting a new Olympic mark.

Ritter and Kostadinova each cleared 6′-7″ on her first attempt. Then both jumpers failed in three attempts at 6′-8″, necessitating the jump-off. Kostadinova went first and again failed to clear 6′-8″. Ritter grazed the bar as she went over, but it stayed on the standard and she was victorious.

With that, Ritter became the first American woman in thirty-two years to win Olympic gold in the event.

October

OCTOBER 1, 1950

OCTOBER 2, 1954

Babe Didrikson Zaharias blistered the Rolling Hills Country Club course in Wichita, Kansas, shooting a seventy-two-hole score of nine-under-par 291 and winning the US Women's Open. Zaharias finished nine strokes in front of fellow Texan Betsy Rawls from Arlington.

Rawls, then playing as an amateur, became a student of Austin legend Harvey Penick during her time at the University of Texas. She turned pro in 1951 and claimed the 1951 US Women's Open title at the Druid Hills Golf Club in Atlanta, Georgia.

Rawls finished her career with four US Women's Open championships. Zaharias won her third and final one in 1954.

Texas A&M's legendary "Junction Boys" won their only game of the 1954 season, claiming a 6–0 triumph over Georgia.

The Aggies earned their nickname and their place in sports history when first-year coach Paul "Bear" Bryant took the squad to the Hill Country town of Junction for a ten-day preseason training camp. Bryant's intent was to build stronger, tougher players. A drought and the heat served as coconspirators. The Texas A&M football program, which at one point had more than a hundred players going into the 1954 season, was whittled down by desertions and injuries. The Aggies had twenty-five healthy players by the end of the camp according to Jim Dent, author of the 2000 book *The Junction Boys: How 10 Days in Hell with Bear Bryant Forged a Championship Team.*

But the brutal training didn't produce an immediate payoff on the field, since Texas A&M opened the season with a 41–9 loss to Texas Tech and went on to lose nine times in the 1954 campaign.

The Aggies' one moment of glory came in Athens, Georgia, when Texas A&M handed the Bulldogs their first loss of the season. Aggie quarterback Elwood Kettler connected on back-to-back passes on the game's only scoring drive. Kettler hit Jack Pardee for a fourteen-yard gain and then threw to Gene Stallings for a sixteen-yard touchdown.

Following the 1954 season, the new attitude ingrained in the Aggies began to make an impact on the scoreboard. Bryant coached three more seasons at Texas A&M, compiling a 24–5–1 record during that time, including a 9–0–1 record and the Southwest Conference championship in 1956.

Texas A&M quarterback Jeff Granger ducked to avoid an almost sure sack by Texas Tech defensive lineman Dusty Beavers near the fifty-yard line at Kyle Field. When Granger remained on his feet, the third-and-eight play was still alive, and he passed to tight end Greg Thorp for a fifteen-yard gain that revived the Aggies' Cotton Bowl hopes.

"On that third-down play, we knew that was it," Texas A&M offensive lineman John Ellisor said in a postgame interview. "That play was for the Cotton Bowl. If we don't make that, we didn't have a chance."

Moments later, Aggie kicker Terry Venetoulias booted a twenty-one-yard field goal on the final play of the game, lifting Texas A&M to a 19–17 victory over the Red Raiders. The win preserved the fifth-ranked Aggies' unblemished season. Texas A&M finished the regular season 12–0, the win over Texas Tech standing as its closest call. But Notre Dame spoiled the Aggies' bid for a perfect campaign when the Fighting Irish defeated Texas A&M 28–3 in the Cotton Bowl.

OCTOBER 4, 2015

OCTOBER 5, 2002

The Texas Rangers hammered the Los Angeles Angels 9–2 on the last day of the regular season to clinch the American League West title and guarantee a wild-card playoff berth for the Houston Astros. Ranger third baseman Adrián Beltré swatted a two-run homer, and designated hitter Prince Fielder, first baseman Mitch Moreland, and outfielder Josh Hamilton also drove in runs. Texas starting pitcher Cole Hamels threw a complete game, giving up two runs on three hits.

The Rangers finished the season with an 88–74 record, two games in front of Houston in the standings. The Astros defeated the New York Yankees in the wild-card play-in game. But the Kansas City Royals ousted Houston, and the Toronto Blue Jays eliminated Texas in the American League Division Series.

Texas Tech rained down a deluge of points in the fourth quarter to erase Texas A&M's eighteen-point lead and tie the game at 41. Even in overtime, the Aggies couldn't muster enough points to stay afloat. Texas A&M quarterback Dustin Long threw his seventh touchdown pass of the game in overtime, but kicker John Pierson missed the extra point wide left, opening the door for the Red Raiders.

Texas Tech quarterback Kliff Kingsbury threw a ten-yard touchdown pass to Nehemiah Glover on the Red Raiders' overtime possession. Then Texas Tech kicker Robert Treece added the extra point to secure the Red Raiders' 48–47 victory at Kyle Field in College Station.

Kingsbury finished the game with 474 passing yards and five touchdown passes to five receivers. "This is the most thrilling victory," Kingsbury said. "It is nice to be on the winning side of an overtime game. I think this is my best game ever."

Texas Tech wide receiver Wes Welker caught ten passes for 120 yards and a score and, most critically, returned a punt eighty-eight yards for a fourth-quarter touchdown to add momentum to the Red Raider rally. Welker finished the game with 166 punt-return yards, a school record. Texas Tech outscored the Aggies 24–6 in the fourth quarter to force overtime.

OCTOBER 6, 2001

Oklahoma safety Roy Williams appeared to be flying as he jumped over Texas running back Brett Robin and soared toward Longhorn quarterback Chris Simms. Williams descended upon Simms and caused the Texas QB to release an errant pass, which Sooner linebacker Teddy Lehman intercepted and returned two yards for a touchdown, delighting half of the crowd at the Cotton Bowl in Dallas.

The score gave the third-ranked Sooners a 14–3 lead over fifth-ranked Texas with 2:01 remaining in the fourth quarter, and Oklahoma went on to win by that score.

The 2001 Red River Showdown was the second game in a streak of five in which both the Sooners and Longhorns came into the contest with a national ranking of eleven or higher. Oklahoma won all five of those games from 2000 to 2004.

OCTOBER 7, 1995

Texas Tech linebacker Zach Thomas stepped in front of a pass from Texas A&M quarterback Corey Pullig and then raced into Red Raider lore. Thomas returned the interception twenty-three yards for a touchdown that lifted Texas Tech to a 14–7 victory over the eighth-ranked Aggies.

"I faked the blitz and read the quarterback's eyes and cut the ball off," Thomas said. "I saw the end zone and just ran for the line."

Thomas's pick-six came with thirty seconds left in the fourth quarter, all but ensuring a Red Raider victory. With that win, Texas Tech defeated Texas A&M for the first time since 1989, setting off a run of eleven Red Raider triumphs over Texas A&M in the next fourteen seasons.

OCTOBER 8, 1977

OCTOBER 9, 2015

Texas running back Earl Campbell raced around the left side of the offensive line, broke through a crease in the Oklahoma defense, hurdled a Sooner defensive back near the twenty-yard line, and flew toward the end zone on a twenty-four-yard touchdown romp that proved pivotal in the fifth-ranked Longhorns' 13–6 victory over second-ranked Oklahoma.

"Campbell is just unbelievable," Oklahoma coach Barry Switzer said in a postgame interview. "I told him I hope he wins the Heisman Trophy. When you get down to Campbell and one defensive guy, it's impossible."

Campbell, well on his way to the 1977 Heisman, rushed for 124 yards in leading Texas to its first win over rival Oklahoma in seven years.

Texas Rangers Hanser Alberto and Delino DeShields each singled in the top of the fourteenth inning, driving home Rougned Odor and Chris Gimenez to boost the Rangers to a 6–4 lead they would hold onto against the Toronto Blue Jays. Texas relief pitcher and Austin native Ross Ohlendorf struck out Toronto batters Troy Tulowitzki, Justin Smoak, and Kevin Pillar in the bottom of the fourteenth for the save and a game-two victory in the American League Division Series.

Texas took the first two games of the series in Toronto, but that was as close as the Rangers came to advancing. The Blue Jays, with no room for error, won the next three games to claim the best-of-five series.

OCTOBER 10, 2015

Fans of the four Texas schools in the Big 12 could all smile at the same time for once as TCU edged Kansas State, Texas Tech demolished Iowa State, Baylor ripped Kansas, and Texas upset archrival Oklahoma.

In particular, Texas quarterbacks took center stage. Texas Tech QB Patrick Mahomes, from Whitehouse, passed for 428 yards and five touchdowns as the Red Raiders won 66–31. TCU's Trevone Boykin, from Mesquite, passed for 301 yards and two TDs and rushed for 124 yards and two scores in the Horned Frogs' 52–45 victory. Baylor QB Seth Russell, from Garland, threw for 246 yards and three touchdowns as the Bears made short work of the Jayhawks, 66–7. Longhorn quarterbacks Jerrod Heard, from Denton, and Tyrone Swoopes, from Whitewright, didn't have statistics as sparkling as the others, but properly managed the biggest win of the day as Texas defeated the tenth-ranked Sooners 24–17.

OCTOBER 11, 1969

Trailing archrival Oklahoma 14–0 in the first quarter, Texas quarterback James Street ignited a comeback with a twenty-four-yard touchdown pass to wide receiver Charles "Cotton" Speyrer, and the Longhorns surged to a 27–17 victory at the Cotton Bowl.

The Sooners stood strong against the Longhorns' rushing attack, so Street beat Oklahoma through the air. He finished with 215 passing yards, including the TD to Speyrer and a key fifty-five-yard completion to halfback Jim Bertelsen that set up Bertelsen's one-yard touchdown run to tie the game early in the second quarter.

The Texas defense clamped down on Oklahoma, holding the Sooners to three points in the final forty-six minutes of action. Texas kicker Happy Feller booted a pair of field goals, and running back Steve Worster added a one-yard touchdown run in the fourth quarter for the Longhorns' final tally.

"It was a gut check, no doubt about that," Texas coach Darrell Royal said after the game. "I'm so pleased that we had the stuff to come back from a 14–0 deficit. It's tough to do against a team like Oklahoma."

OCTOBER 12, 1989

Second-ranked Texas upped its winning streak to thirteen games with the victory over the eighth-ranked Sooners. The Longhorns stayed undefeated throughout the 1969 campaign on their way to the national championship.

The Dallas Cowboys traded Herschel Walker and four draft picks to the Minnesota Vikings for five players and eight draft picks. The Cowboys would parlay the acquired players and draft picks into the building blocks for three Super Bowl champions. Among the players who became Cowboys as a result of the trade were running back Emmitt Smith, wide receiver Alvin Harper, and safety Darren Woodson. Viewed at the time as the Cowboys' dealing away their best player, it would later appear on lists of the most lopsided trades in sports history, aka the "Great Trade Robbery," all of it working in Dallas's favor.

OCTOBER 13, 2005

OCTOBER 14, 1971

The Houston Astros turned the tide in the National League Championship Series by defeating the St. Louis Cardinals 4–1 in game two at Busch Stadium in St. Louis.

Astro ace Roy Oswalt stuck out six and held the Cardinals to one run in seven innings. Houston reliever Brad Lidge held up his end by striking out three during two shutout innings. Craig Biggio, Chris Burke, and Adam Everett each drove in runs to get the job done at the plate for the Astros.

After tying the best-of-seven series at a game apiece, the Astros won the next two games in Houston. The Cardinals won game five, forcing another game to be played in St. Louis, but the Astros prevailed 5–1 in game six to clinch the series. With that, Houston became the first team from Texas to play in a World Series.

But the Astros would not become the first team from Texas to win a World Series game, since they were swept in four games by the Chicago White Sox.

The NBA came to Texas when the Houston Rockets played their first regular-season game versus the Philadelphia 76ers at Hofheinz Pavilion in Houston. But 76ers center Billy Cunningham put a damper on the Rockets' debut by scoring forty-one points in Philadelphia's 105–94 victory. Forward Rudy Tomjanovich scored twenty-eight to lead the Rockets, Stu Lantz pitched in sixteen, and Elvin Hayes added fifteen.

The San Antonio Spurs joined the Rockets as a Texas NBA team when the ABA and NBA merged in 1976. The Dallas Mavericks made it a Texas threesome when the NBA expanded in 1980.

(PHOTO, OPPOSITE PAGE)
Center–power forward Elvin Hayes (44), when he was a member of the Houston Cougars, played in the first college basketball game at the Astrodome. In addition, he played in the first NBA game involving a Texas team, as a member of the Houston Rockets. Photo courtesy of the Texas Sports Hall of Fame.

OCTOBER 15, 1986

New York Met reliever Jesse Orosco struck out Houston Astro right fielder Kevin Bass swinging for the final out in the bottom of the sixteenth inning, stranding Glenn Davis and Denny Walling and giving New York a National League Championship Series–clinching 7–6 victory at the Astrodome.

The Mets won the series 4–2 by claiming back-to-back extra-inning games that totaled twenty-eight frames. New York defeated Houston 2–1 in twelve innings in the fifth game of the series at Shea Stadium the previous day. Darryl Strawberry and Lenny Dykstra produced key hits during a three-run Mets rally in the top of the sixteenth of game six. New York needed all those runs to keep the series from going to a deciding seventh game.

"It was a great game," Astro manager Hal Lanier told reporters after the game. "If we had to lose, I'm glad we went down like we did—battling and swinging."

The Mets went on to defeat the Boston Red Sox in seven games to win the World Series.

OCTOBER 16, 1912

Hubbard native Tris Speaker hit a one-out single off New York Giant pitcher Christy Mathewson in the bottom of the tenth inning of game eight of the World Series. Speaker's hit plated Boston Red Sox teammate Clyde Engle, tying the game at 2.

A few moments earlier, Mathewson and Giant teammates first baseman Fred Merkle and catcher Chief Meyers surrounded but failed to catch a foul pop-up by Speaker, prompting the Texan to taunt, "Well, you just called for the wrong man and it's gonna cost you the ballgame!"

After Speaker singled in the tying run, the Giants intentionally walked Duffy Lewis to load the bases. Larry Gardner then hit a fly ball to right field that allowed Steve Yerkes to tag up and score from third base. With that, the Red Sox claimed the World Series championship, four games to three.

The 1912 World Series was a best-of-seven contest, but went to an eighth game because game two, tied at 6 apiece after eleven innings, was called for darkness.

Tris Speaker became the first Texan elected to the National Baseball Hall of Fame. He was inducted in 1937 as part of the Hall's second class. Photo courtesy of the Texas Sports Hall of Fame.

OCTOBER 17, 2012

Lance Armstrong resigned as chairman of the Livestrong Foundation amid the blood-doping scandal that had swirled around him for more than seven years. Armstrong released a statement announcing his resignation, and Nike, one of his major sponsors, quickly severed ties with the seven-time Tour de France champion. "Due to the seemingly insurmountable evidence that Lance Armstrong participated in doping and misled Nike for more than a decade, it is with great sadness that we have terminated our contract with him," read the Nike statement. "Nike does not condone the use of illegal performance-enhancing drugs in any manner."

Armstrong and Nike had teamed together to create and distribute the yellow Livestrong wristbands that became iconic in the fight against cancer. Armstrong survived testicular cancer before going on his historic cycling winning streak in the sport's biggest event. But accusations that Armstrong was blood doping surfaced in 2005 and followed the Texan cyclist from that point forward.

In June 2012, the US Anti-Doping Agency charged Armstrong with doping and with trafficking performance-enhancing drugs. The International Cycling Union, having reviewed the charges, stripped Armstrong of his seven Tour de France titles and banned him for life.

Armstrong's rise and fall came to an apparent conclusion in January 2013 when he admitted in a televised interview with Oprah Winfrey that he used banned substances to enhance his performance.

OCTOBER 18, 2015

OCTOBER 19, 1929

Mansfield native and New York Met rookie Noah Syndergaard struck out nine and held the Chicago Cubs to one run in 5⅔ innings to help the Mets win 4–1 and take a 2–0 lead in the National League Championship Series at Citi Field in New York. Syndergaard earned the win and added yet another gem to his outstanding Major League debut season.

Syndergaard, a Mansfield Legacy High School alum, made it to the big show before his twenty-third birthday. He went 9–7 in his rookie season, striking out 166 in 150 innings while walking just 31 batters in the regular season.

Syndergaard's first postseason win came in a matchup against Jake Arrieta, a Plano East and TCU alum, of the Cubs. Syndergaard credited the Mets' offense with giving him a huge advantage in the Texan-versus-Texan pitching duel. New York second baseman Daniel Murphy hit a two-run homer to highlight the Mets' three-run first inning.

"It makes pitching a lot more easy when you go out there and the offense puts a three-spot on one of the best pitchers in the game right now," Syndergaard told reporters after the game.

He added another postseason win in game three of the World Series, though the Kansas City Royals claimed the championship, four games to one.

Texas defeated Oklahoma 21–0 as the Red River rivalry resumed in Dallas. The Longhorns and Sooners first faced off in 1900 and played in various locations, including Norman, Austin, Dallas, and Houston, between 1900 and 1923. The two schools put the series on hold from 1924 through 1928 before resuming in 1929 and continuing in perpetuity.

The Red River Showdown, as it came to be called, moved into the Cotton Bowl in 1932.

OCTOBER 20, 1967

The US duo of Arnold Palmer and Gardner Dickinson won their morning and afternoon matches to help the Americans take a lead of 5½–2½ over the British on the opening day of Ryder Cup competition at the Champions Golf Club in Houston. Palmer hit the highlight shot of the opening day when he drilled a six-iron shot lying in the trees and 166 yards from the green to 7 feet from the cup. Palmer's amazing shot set up a relatively easy birdie for Dickinson, helping the US pair claim a 2-and-1 victory over the British team of Peter Alliss and Dave Thomas. Dickinson and Palmer went on to defeat Malcolm Gregson and Hugh Boyle in the afternoon to sweep their opening-day matches.

The US team, led by nonplaying captain Ben Hogan, retained the Ryder Cup with a 23½–8½ victory over the three days of the event. Palmer and Dickinson proved to be the American heroes, each going undefeated in five matches.

OCTOBER 21, 2012

The Circuit of the Americas racetrack, a motorsports course near Austin, officially opened with a first-lap ceremony. Racing icon Mario Andretti took a few laps in a Lotus 79 Cosworth to christen the track. Four weeks later, British driver Lewis Hamilton won the first race at COTA. He qualified in second and then won the Formula One US Grand Prix.

OCTOBER 22, 2010

OCTOBER 23, 1982

Texas Ranger reliever Neftalí Feliz froze Alex Rodriguez with a 1–2 curveball, striking out the Yankee shortstop and sending the Rangers to their first World Series. In striking out Rodriguez, Feliz put the icing on a 6–1 Ranger win in game six of the American League Championship Series at The Ballpark in Arlington.

The Rangers dogpiled in the infield while fireworks shot from the roof of the stadium and the Pat Green song "I Like Texas" blasted from the stadium speakers. Ranger fans roared in celebration.

"The World Series is coming to Texas," Ranger third baseman Michael Young said. "These fans have waited longer than we have. I know how bad we wanted it, and they must have wanted it more."

Although Texas would become the first Major League team in the state to win a World Series game, with a 4–2 victory over San Francisco in game three, the Giants ultimately took the series in five games.

The SMU Mustangs stampeded past Texas, breaking a 10–10 tie with a fortunate bounce for a spectacular touchdown and gliding from there to a 30–17 victory at Memorial Stadium.

On a crucial third-and-eight play, SMU quarterback Lance McIlhenny rolled out and threw for wide receiver Bobby Leach, who was covered by Texas cornerback Jitter Fields. But Fields, in position to intercept the pass, instead saw it bounce off his hands and into Leach's waiting arms. Leach scampered the rest of the way for a seventy-nine-yard touchdown that gave the fourth-ranked Mustangs a 17–10 lead and turned momentum in their favor.

"That freak play was the ballgame," Texas coach Fred Akers said in a postgame interview. "We had an interception and it bounced off for a touchdown. That hurt. That really hurt."

SMU rolled behind star running back Eric Dickerson in 1982. Though Dickerson had a stellar day, rushing for 118 yards and a touchdown against the nineteenth-ranked Horns, it was McIlhenny and the passing game that ultimately lifted SMU. McIlhenny hit Craig James for a forty-six-yard touchdown in the final minute to drive home the point for the Ponies.

SMU improved to 7–0 for the season with the win. The Mustangs went undefeated and tied Arkansas 17–17 in the final game of the regular season. SMU capped the phenomenal season with a 7–3 victory over sixth-ranked and Dan Marino–led Pittsburgh in the Cotton Bowl. The Mustangs were ranked second in the final Associated Press poll despite being the only undefeated team in the nation.

The TCU Horned Frogs made a statement by pounding sixteenth-ranked BYU 38–7 in Provo, Utah. Quarterback Andy Dalton passed for 241 yards and three touchdowns to lead the Frogs as they validated their eighth-place standing in the Bowl Championship Series rankings.

Dalton threw a twelve-yard touchdown pass to Jimmy Young that gave TCU a 21–0 lead midway through the second quarter. Though BYU got on the scoreboard before halftime, the Horned Frog defense shut down the Cougars in the second half to secure a huge road win.

TCU boosted its record to 7–0 and pleased head coach Gary Patterson. "I don't think anyone would have predicted this and that's why I told the players to enjoy the moment," Patterson told reporters after the game.

The Horned Frogs kept up the intensity on the way to a 12–0 season and a berth in the Fiesta Bowl. But Boise State ended TCU's bid for a perfect season by winning 17–10 on January 4, 2010, in Arizona.

OCTOBER 25, 1999

Payne Stewart and five others were killed when the Learjet they were aboard lost cabin pressure somewhere over the southern United States. Stewart and his group left Orlando intending to fly to Dallas. But everyone in the plane apparently lost consciousness, and the aircraft took a long detour before crashing in a field near Mina, South Dakota.

Stewart, the reigning US Open champion, had helped the US team win the Ryder Cup a month earlier in Brookline, Massachusetts. He missed the cut at the Disney / National Car Rental Classic the weekend before his death, but stayed in Orlando through the weekend. News of the tragedy ripped through the golf world.

"There is an enormous void and emptiness I feel right now," Tiger Woods said in an Associated Press story reacting to Stewart's death. Woods had won in Orlando on the previous day.

Stewart, along with being one of the most well-liked players on the PGA Tour, was distinctly recognizable, since he played in knickerbockers, or plus-fours, and an ivy cap.

"That smooth swing, the plus-fours, his tongue-in-cheek wit . . . that's what I'll remember most about Payne," said Jack Nicklaus in the AP reaction article. "He always had a little bit of a needle out. He always had fun with you."

Stewart, who tied Fred Couples for the Southwest Conference title in 1979, won eleven times on the PGA Tour, including the US Open in 1991 and 1999 and the PGA Championship in 1989.

OCTOBER 26, 1985

OCTOBER 27, 1984

Baylor's quarterback duo of Cody Carlson and Tom Muecke combined for 297 passing yards and three total touchdowns to lead the thirteenth-ranked Bears to a 45–0 victory over TCU at Baylor Stadium. Baylor's throttling of the Horned Frogs was its most lopsided win in a Southwest Conference game since the Bears rocked Arkansas 60–13 in 1922.

Baylor led 3–0 after the first quarter, but then enforced its will. Horace Ates ran three yards for a touchdown, Muecke hit Darnell Chase for a forty-five-yard touchdown pass, Charles Perry ran seven yards for a touchdown, and Carlson threw a thirty-seven-yard touchdown pass to Leland Douglas to give the Bears a 31–0 lead by the time they were ready to crown a homecoming queen at halftime.

The Baylor defense took the ball away from TCU five times with three fumble recoveries and two interceptions to pitch a shutout. "The offense owes a great debt to the defense," Baylor coach Grant Teaff said.

The Bears improved to 7–1 and 5–0 in SWC play to sit atop the conference, but they would soar no higher that season. Baylor stayed at number 13 in the national rankings the next week and then lost a pivotal game at Arkansas. The Bears defeated LSU in the Liberty Bowl to finish the season with a 9–3 record and the number 17 spot in the final AP poll.

Hakeem Olajuwon made his debut as a Houston Rocket, and thus the Twin Towers of Olajuwon and Ralph Sampson took the court for the first time, versus the Mavericks in Dallas.

Olajuwon led the Rockets with twenty-four points, and Sampson had a double-double with nineteen points and thirteen rebounds, as Houston defeated the Mavs 121–111.

OCTOBER 28, 2011

OCTOBER 29, 1994

The St. Louis Cardinals finished off the Texas Rangers by winning game seven of the World Series 6–2 at Busch Stadium in St. Louis. Cardinal starting pitcher Chris Carpenter gave up a pair of runs in the first inning but then shut down the Rangers after that. Carpenter, along with Waco native Arthur Rhodes, Octavio Dotel, Lance Lynn, and Nick Punto held Texas scoreless for the final eight innings. New Braunfels Canyon and Rice alum Lance Berkman went one for three at the plate and scored two runs to help propel the Cardinals' offense.

One day earlier, Texas held a 7–5 lead with two out in the bottom of the ninth before St. Louis third baseman David Freese hit a 1–2 pitch from Ranger closer Neftalí Feliz. Freese's fly ball flew just out of the reach of Ranger right fielder Nelson Cruz for a triple, scoring Albert Pujols and Berkman to tie the game and ultimately send it to extra innings. Freese homered in the bottom of the eleventh to give the Cardinals a 10–9 victory and force the deciding seventh game.

SMU quarterback Ramon Flanigan threw a touchdown pass and ran for two more as the Mustangs stunned seventh-ranked Texas A&M by tying the Aggies 21–21 at the Alamodome in San Antonio. The Ponies snapped Texas A&M's twenty-six-game Southwest Conference winning streak, putting the only blemish on the Aggies' 1994 record.

Texas A&M, which had been banned by the NCAA from playing on television or in a bowl game in 1994, finished 10–0–1. Conversely, the Mustangs' only win that season came in non-conference action versus New Mexico. SMU's tie versus the Aggies broke an eight-game losing streak in SWC play.

Both SMU and Texas A&M took a kick at winning the game in the final minute. Mustang kicker Ben Crosland missed a forty-seven-yard field goal wide right with thirty seconds left. The Aggies attempted to respond by moving near midfield, but Texas A&M kicker Kyle Bryant's last-second sixty-seven-yard kick fell short.

OCTOBER 30, 1948

OCTOBER 31, 2009

SMU Mustang running backs Doak Walker and Kyle Rote combined for three touchdowns as the Ponies defeated Texas 21–6 in Austin. Walker broke loose for a sixty-seven-yard touchdown on the third play of the game, setting the tone for an SMU victory that helped it claim the Southwest Conference championship.

Walker added a two-yard touchdown run to cap the Mustangs' second scoring drive. Rote caught a lateral and scampered eighteen yards for the Ponies' final touchdown of the afternoon. Walker, who went on to win the Heisman Trophy for the 1948 season, also kicked the three extra points for the Mustangs.

The Texas defense haunted Oklahoma State quarterback Zac Robinson, intercepting four passes en route to third-ranked Texas's 41–14 thrashing of the thirteenth-ranked Cowboys on Halloween night in Stillwater, Oklahoma. Texas safety Earl Thomas returned a pick thirty-one yards for a touchdown that put the Horns ahead 34–7 midway through the third quarter, effectively icing the game.

Earlier in the night, Texas cornerback Curtis Brown returned an interception seventy-seven yards for a score.

"We just try to put it in the end zone as much as possible and create turnovers," Thomas said in a postgame interview.

While the Texas defense more than did its part, the Horns were efficient on offense as well. Texas quarterback Colt McCoy completed sixteen of twenty-one passes for 171 yards, including an eleven-yard touchdown to Malcolm Williams with nine seconds left in the second quarter to put the Horns ahead 24–7 at halftime.

McCoy, who finished his career with the most wins for a quarterback in NCAA history with 45, led the Longhorns to a win over a ranked opponent for the tenth time in his career.

November

NOVEMBER 1, 2008

Texas Tech quarterback Graham Harrell saw single coverage right where he wanted it.

The seventh-ranked Red Raiders trailed top-ranked Texas by a point in the closing minutes of a clash that drew ESPN's *College GameDay* spotlight. Though Texas Tech led for most of the game, the Longhorns pulled ahead 33–32 when Vondrell McGee scored on a four-yard run with 1:29 left in the fourth quarter.

Was it enough time for the Red Raiders?

Harrell went to work, throwing darts for four straight completions that moved Texas Tech into Texas territory. The drive almost ended in disaster for the Red Raiders when Texas safety Blake Gideon lunged to intercept a tipped ball, but it fell through his hands to the turf. The incomplete pass gave Texas Tech a second-and-ten at the Texas twenty-eight at the left hash mark with eight seconds remaining. That was when Harrell saw the Longhorns manned up against Michael Crabtree on the far sideline.

Harrell threw a strike to Crabtree's back shoulder. The junior Red Raider receiver came back to the ball to catch it, then ducked past Texas defensive back Curtis Brown at the sideline while staying in bounds. Crabtree darted into the end zone and then sprinted across the width of it as the Jones Stadium crowd roared. Fans stormed the field prematurely, befuddling an already rattled group of Longhorns. Penalties on the home crowd forced Texas Tech to kick off from its own five-yard line with one second left, but the Red Raiders managed to snuff out Texas's chance at a return touchdown.

Harrell, Crabtree, and company prevailed 39–33 in one of the most glorious victories in Red Raider history.

NOVEMBER 2, 1985

Just a couple of fourth-quarter minutes after Texas A&M's Eric Franklin missed an extra point versus twentieth-ranked SMU, the Aggies' kicker redeemed himself by nailing a forty-eight-yard field goal that lifted Texas A&M to a 19–17 victory over the Mustangs. Franklin's long kick cleared the crossbar between the uprights with 1:46 remaining in the fourth quarter, but the Aggies didn't wait until the game was over to mob their kicker in celebration.

Despite Franklin's earlier point-after miss and his shaky record on field goals up to that point in the season, Texas A&M coach Jackie Sherrill didn't flinch from sending Franklin on to try the game winner. "Franklin went in with all the marbles on the line and kicked it," Sherrill said. "I didn't put him out there to miss."

Texas A&M's win over the Ponies sparked a surge in the second half of the season. The Aggies won five straight games, including victories over ninth-ranked Arkansas and eighteenth-ranked Texas, to claim their first outright Southwest Conference championship since 1967. But Texas A&M didn't stop there. The eleventh-ranked Aggies defeated sixteenth-ranked Auburn in the Cotton Bowl and stayed on a tear that saw them win three straight SWC crowns.

NOVEMBER 3, 1990

University of Houston quarterback David Klingler lost the passing-yards battle but won the game as the Cougars defeated TCU 56–35 in a Southwest Conference shootout at the Astrodome. TCU backup quarterback Matt Vogler stepped into the spotlight by passing for an NCAA-single-game-record 690 yards. But Klingler tossed seven touchdown passes to go along with his 563 passing yards as he led Houston to the victory.

Both quarterbacks surpassed 1989 Heisman winner Andre Ware's SWC record of 517 passing yards in a game.

"You can take all these numbers and throw them out the window," Vogler said in a postgame interview. "Without a victory, they mean nothing. I'd rather have the game."

After TCU tied the game at 28, Klingler responded by throwing a forty-six-yard touchdown pass to Chuck Weatherspoon and TD passes of fifty-nine yards and two yards to Marcus Grant to help the Cougars pull away.

Houston entered the game ranked sixth in the nation and had the nation's longest winning streak, twelve games, dating back to the 1989 campaign. But fourteenth-ranked Texas handed the Cougars their first loss of the season the following week in Austin.

NOVEMBER 4, 1989

Texas Tech quarterback Jamie Gill threw over the top of the Texas defense to wide receiver Anthony Manyweather for a sixty-five-yard touchdown pass that shocked the Memorial Stadium crowd and lifted the Red Raiders to their first win in Austin in twenty-two years. Gill and Texas Tech were facing third-and-twenty-six at the snap, but they had taken command of the game by play's end as the Red Raiders suddenly led 21–17 with 4:26 left in the fourth quarter.

"It was an out-and-up," Manyweather said in a postgame interview. "I told the coaches that number twenty-two (cornerback Paul Behrman) was covering the out so well, why not try the out-and-up. When I made my cut, he came in for the interception. That's when I knew I had a TD. I looked up and said 'Come on ball. Hurry up and get here.'"

Texas Tech's defense came up with two interceptions in the final four minutes, and Red Raider kicker Lin Elliott added a field goal to wrap up a 24–17 victory.

NOVEMBER 5, 1927

Walter Hagen won his fourth consecutive PGA Championship by defeating Joe Turnesa 1-up in the final thirty-six-hole match at Cedar Crest Country Club in Dallas. Turnesa led the match until the twenty-ninth hole, when Hagen tied it. Hagen then edged into the lead on the thirty-first hole and held off Turnesa down the stretch.

Hagen, who won five PGA Championships between 1921 and 1927, holds the record for most match-play victories in the event (the PGA Championship switched from match-play to stroke-play competition in 1958). In his tournament trophy acceptance speech, Hagen heaped praise on his final opponent. "(Turnesa) showed that he is a player of rare mettle and I hope that if I ever do have to relinquish my title, Turnesa will be the man that receives my congratulations," Hagen said. He did not get his wish, however, as Leo Diegel defeated Hagen on the way to the 1928 title.

NOVEMBER 6, 2005

Belton native Justin McBride stayed on for eight seconds, spending much of that time hanging off the side of a wildly spinning bull named Camo, to claim his first Professional Bull Riders world championship at the Thomas and Mack Center in Las Vegas, Nevada.

McBride's spectacular last ride gave him a PBR-record 13,415 points for the season, a million-dollar bonus for the world title, and season earnings of $1,479,230. He added another PBR world championship in 2007 and retired after the 2008 season with career earnings of more than $5 million. McBride was inducted into the Texas Cowboy Hall of Fame in 2016.

NOVEMBER 7, 1953

The Wayland Baptist University Flying Queens, from Plainview, defeated Dowell's Dolls, an Amateur Athletic Union team from Amarillo, 51–31, thus beginning one of the most amazing streaks in the history of basketball.

The Flying Queens, so named because the team traveled in an airplane supplied by team sponsor Claude Hutcherson and flown by coach Harley Redin, won 131 consecutive games. Wayland Baptist went undefeated until March 20, 1958, when it was beaten by Nashville Business College in the AAU national semifinals. The streak encompassed four of the Flying Queens' ten AAU national titles.

(PHOTO, OPPOSITE PAGE)
Wayland Baptist guard Rita Alexander heads up the floor with a rebound as Flying Queens teammate Kay Garms watches. Photo courtesy of Wayland Baptist University Sports Information Department.

NOVEMBER 8, 2002

NOVEMBER 9, 1974

Pilot Point coach G. A. Moore guided his team to a 27–13 victory over Van Alstyne and in doing so became the winningest coach in Texas high school football history.

Moore, who spent most of his career going back and forth between his alma mater, Pilot Point, and nearby Celina, reached his 397th career win, one ahead of Brownwood legend Gordon Wood, in the final regular-season contest of 2002. "This is not an accomplishment for one person," Moore said in Carlos Mendez's *Fort Worth Star-Telegram* game story. "It's an accomplishment for two towns and a whole lot of people."

Moore finished his career with eight state titles, including two at Pilot Point and six at Celina. He took one more job by coming out of retirement to coach three seasons in Aubrey and then finally hung up his whistle for good with a career record of 423–97–9.

Baylor quarterback Neal Jeffrey led a furious Bear comeback versus twelfth-ranked Texas that came to be known to green-and-gold-clad fans as the "Miracle on the Brazos."

Baylor was trailing the Longhorns 27–7 when the third quarter began, but the Bears quickly turned the momentum when special-teams player Johnny Greene blocked a punt on the fourth play of the second half. Greene's play allowed the Bears to take over at the Texas seventeen-yard line and set up Jeffrey's one-yard touchdown run.

Near the end of the third quarter, Jeffrey tossed a forty-six-yard touchdown pass to Ricky Thompson, cutting the Longhorns' lead to three. The Bears owned the fourth quarter just as they had the third. Baylor wingback Phillip Kent ran six yards for a touchdown to push the Bears into the lead 28–24 with 12:36 left. The Baylor defense shut out the Horns in the second half.

Baylor kicker David Hicks added insurance with field goals of twenty-five and thirty-five yards in the fourth quarter. With that, the Bears grabbed their first victory over Texas in eighteen years.

Baylor rode the momentum of that win to regular-season victories against Texas Tech, SMU, and Rice on the way to an 8–3 record and the Bears' first Southwest Conference football championship in fifty years. In their first Cotton Bowl game, though, the Bears fell to seventh-ranked Penn State 41–20 on January 1, 1975.

Texas A&M quarterback Johnny Manziel hit wide receiver Malcome Kennedy for a twenty-four-yard touchdown pass, giving the Aggies a 29–17 lead over top-ranked Alabama in the fourth quarter at Bryant-Denny Stadium. Manziel finished the game with 253 passing yards, two touchdowns, and ninety-two rushing yards to lead Texas A&M to a 29–24 victory over the Crimson Tide. The performance vaulted Manziel to front-runner status in the race for the Heisman Trophy, which he claimed after the Aggies finished with a 10–2 record in their first season in the SEC.

"No moment is too big for him," Texas A&M coach Kevin Sumlin said about Manziel in a postgame interview.

NOVEMBER 11, 1978

Baylor sophomore linebacker Mike Singletary seemed to be everywhere on the field as he made thirty-three tackles of Arkansas ball carriers. But the tremendous effort couldn't lift the Bears to victory. The sixteenth-ranked Razorbacks had raced to a 27–0 lead by early in the fourth quarter and held on to a 27–14 victory at Baylor Stadium in Waco.

When Baylor coach Grant Teaff revealed to *Waco Tribune-Herald* sportswriter Keith Randall that Singletary had been officially credited with thirty-three tackles in the game, Teaff pointed out it was the third time that season that Singletary had posted thirty or more stops. Singletary set a Baylor record with 232 tackles that season.

Baylor linebacker Mike Singletary (63) posted 662 tackles during his Baylor career, earning All-America honors twice and All-SWC distinction three times. Photo courtesy of Baylor University Photography.

NOVEMBER 12, 2006

NOVEMBER 13, 1982

Houston Dynamo forward Brian Ching sent the deciding shot past New England Revolution goalkeeper Matt Reis to give the Dynamo a 4–3 edge in penalty kicks and the Major League Soccer Cup at Pizza Hut Park in Frisco. The Dynamo celebrated the MLS title in the franchise's first season in Houston. "I didn't think we were going to get one," Ching said in a postmatch interview, "but we were going to die trying."

Houston goalkeeper Pat Onstad made a crucial save during the fifth round of penalty kicks when he deflected Jay Heaps's shot left of the net. That set up Ching for the winner.

The Dynamo gave a repeat performance, defeating the Revolution 2–1 at RFK Stadium in Washington, DC, to claim the MLS Cup again in 2007.

Southwest Texas State defenders Ken Huewitt, Rod Clark, and Tim Staskus stopped Abilene Christian halfback Steve Gardner at the two-yard line, repelling the Wildcats' fourth-quarter two-point-conversion attempt and preserving the Bobcats' 14–13 victory at Bobcat Stadium in San Marcos. By defeating Abilene Christian, Southwest Texas State clinched its third straight Lone Star Conference championship and kept alive a thirteen-game winning streak.

Bobcat running back Eric Cobble ran twenty-one yards for a touchdown in the first quarter, and Huewitt returned an interception twenty-one yards for another score in the third quarter. Then the Southwest Texas State defense held back a Wildcat surge to give Coach Jim Wacker his 100th career win. "This win belongs to coach Wacker," Huewitt told *San Marcos Record* sports editor Russell Smith after the game. "And it was a tough one too. . . . (ACU) came ready to play."

Southwest Texas State boosted its winning streak to twenty before Northwestern State defeated the Bobcats on October 8, 1983. Along the way, Southwest Texas State claimed the 1981 and 1982 NCAA Division II national championships.

NOVEMBER 14, 1992

NOVEMBER 15, 2014

Rice kicker Darrell Richardson booted a twenty-seven-yard field goal through the uprights with just four seconds remaining on the Rice Stadium clock to give the Owls a monumental 34–31 victory over Baylor. With the win, Rice improved its season record to 5–4. The Owls defeated Navy the next week to secure their first winning season in twenty-nine years.

Moments before Richardson's game-winning field goal, the Rice defense stuffed Baylor running back Robert Strait on fourth-and-one at the Rice thirty-five-yard line. Owl quarterback Bert Emanuel, who passed for 232 yards and two touchdowns in the game, stepped onto the field and quickly assured his teammates that it was their time. "I walked into the huddle and said, 'We're going to win—there's no doubt about it,'" Emanuel said after the game. "Sometimes you just have to step forward and take a leadership role."

Rice running back Trevor Cobb rushed for 128 yards and caught three passes for fifty-seven yards and a touchdown to help Emanuel drive the Owls' offense. Rice traveled fifty-six yards in ten plays on its game-winning drive.

Rice lost its season finale against Houston, finishing 6–5, but didn't receive a bowl bid.

Texas State volleyball coach Karen Chisum guided the Bobcats to a 3–0 sweep of Troy in San Marcos and notched her 800th career victory. Texas State won the opening game of the match 25–17 and kept rolling with 25–17 and 25–19 wins to finish off the Trojans from Troy, Alabama.

Chisum, in her thirty-fourth season at the helm of the Texas State volleyball program, deflected the praise from her milestone win to the hundreds of players she had coached at the school. "I am proud of every one of the kids I have ever coached," Chisum said after the match. "They have all played a big part in my career."

At that point, Chisum had led Texas State to seven regular-season conference championships, nine conference tournament titles, and nine NCAA Tournament appearances. She was the sixth NCAA Division I volleyball coach to reach 800 wins.

NOVEMBER 16, 1957

NOVEMBER 17, 2011

The Rice Owls snapped top-ranked Texas A&M's fourteen-game winning streak, handing the Aggies a 7–6 defeat in front of 72,000 spectators at Rice Stadium in Houston. Rice quarterback King Hill scored the go-ahead touchdown in the second quarter, and he booted the extra point, which proved to be the difference in the game. Texas A&M scored in the fourth quarter, but kicker Loyd Taylor missed the chance to tie the game when the wind gusted and blew his kick off target.

Texas A&M coach Bear Bryant refused to blame the wind for the Aggies' loss. "Rice has a real fine team and they richly deserved the victory," Bryant said after the game. "The difference was in coaching and preparedness."

Rice finished the regular season with shutout wins over TCU and Baylor to win the Southwest Conference championship. Navy, ranked fifth in the nation, defeated eighth-ranked Rice in the Cotton Bowl 20–7.

Highland Park alum Clayton Kershaw, a twenty-three-year-old ace for the Los Angeles Dodgers, won the National League Cy Young Award.

Kershaw posted a 21–5 record and a 2.28 ERA in 2011 as he struck out 284 batters while walking just 54 in 233⅓ innings pitched. Those numbers gave him the pitching triple crown, since he led the National League in wins, strikeouts, and ERA.

He joined the likes of Don Drysdale, Sandy Koufax, Fernando Valenzuela, and Orel Hershiser as a Cy Young winner wearing Dodger blue.

"A lot of things go through my mind," Kershaw said in a press conference announcing him as the award winner. "Just thankful to be a part of it. Undeserving when you see some of the other names up there. I've got a long way to go to have the career that those guys did."

NOVEMBER 18, 1999

NOVEMBER 19, 1938

The support structure of the nearly sixty-foot-high Texas A&M bonfire faltered and soon after collapsed at 2:42 a.m., killing twelve students and injuring dozens more. Students were working around-the-clock shifts for the traditional bonfire celebration, scheduled for November 25, the night before the annual football game against Texas, to be played that year in College Station.

The tragedy drew the attention of the national media and spurred debate about whether to continue the tradition. Texas A&M president Ray Bowen, faced with sorting out the cause of the collapse as well as providing the university's public reaction, said, "Everyone is brokenhearted," and announced the cancellation of the bonfire. The event was discontinued on campus, but was later replaced by a smaller, non-school-sanctioned, off-campus bonfire.

TCU quarterback Davey O'Brien guided the second-ranked Horned Frogs to a 29–7 thumping of the defending Southwest Conference champion Rice Owls at Rice Field in Houston. O'Brien broke an early tie with a touchdown pass to Earl Clark, and the Horned Frogs cruised from there. O'Brien ran one yard for a touchdown, and end Durward Horner came down with a batted ball for a touchdown reception.

TCU's win over Rice boosted the Horned Frogs' season record to 9–0. They kept the winning streak going with a victory over SMU in the season finale at the Cotton Bowl. TCU capped an undefeated campaign with a win over Carnegie Tech in the Sugar Bowl and won the school's second national championship in four years.

NOVEMBER 20, 1999

TCU junior running back LaDainian Tomlinson rushed for 406 yards and six touchdowns, carrying the Horned Frogs to a 52–24 victory over UTEP in Fort Worth. He proved to be an ultraproductive workhorse for TCU, averaging 9.44 yards on forty-three attempts.

"All the credit goes to the offensive line. They've done a great job of creating holes all season," Tomlinson said. "I need to buy them a couple of steaks."

Tomlinson broke the top-level NCAA record for rushing yards in a single game, surpassing Kansas running back Tony Sands's previous record of 396, set in 1991 against Missouri. Tomlinson finished his junior season with 1,974 rushing yards and twenty touchdowns, and posted 5,387 yards and fifty-six touchdowns during his Horned Frog career.

NOVEMBER 21, 1992

Baylor football players lifted Coach Grant Teaff on their shoulders and gave him a victory ride as the clock hit 0:00. After twenty-one years as Baylor's head coach, Teaff won his final home game with a 21–20 triumph over Texas at Floyd Casey Stadium in Waco.

A crowd of almost 40,000 fans braved pouring rain at kickoff to pay tribute to Teaff, and the Bears responded. Baylor quarterback J. J. Joe ran one yard for a touchdown in the first minute of the fourth quarter. Bear kicker Trey Weir added the vital extra point to boost Baylor to a 21–10 lead, which it barely preserved. When it was finally over, fans rushed the field to celebrate with Teaff and the Bears, creating a scene the *Waco Tribune-Herald* described as a fairy-tale ending.

"There was a lot more hullabaloo after the game than I ever expected," Teaff said. "I really thought the stands would be empty and it would be me and the family, but it was a lot of fun."

Baylor added one more win in the Teaff era, defeating Arizona 20–15 in the Sun Bowl in El Paso. Teaff retired with a career record of 170–151–8.

NOVEMBER 22, 2014

The Poth Pirettes claimed their ninth volleyball state championship by sweeping Brock 25–17, 25–18, 25–22 in the Class 3A state final at the Culwell Center in Garland.

Poth senior Alyssa Kruse registered nine kills, ten assists, and seventeen digs to earn MVP honors for the match. She said adding another state-championship trophy to Poth's well-stocked trophy case took season-long focus. "Since August 4, we've had this pretty much set in our mind that we were going to get this (state title), and we weren't going home until we did," Kruse told *San Antonio Express-News* sportswriter Terrence Thomas.

The Pirettes joined Amarillo High, Bellville, Monahans, and Plains in winning their ninth state title. Those elite programs were tied for third place in all-time state volleyball championships behind Windthorst and East Bernard, tied at thirteen. Poth coach Patti Zenner guided the Pirettes to all nine titles, which began with the breakthrough 2A championship in 1995.

NOVEMBER 23, 2002

University of North Texas Mean Green football fans stormed Fouts Field in celebration of UNT's 30–20 victory over Middle Tennessee State, which clinched the Mean Green's second straight Sun Belt Conference championship. After finishing conference play with a 6–0 record and going 8–4 overall, the Mean Green headed to the New Orleans Bowl for the second straight year.

On the field after the game, Mean Green fans donned Mardi Gras beads, and at least one coach chewed on a celebratory cigar. North Texas needed the win over Middle Tennessee to claim the Sun Belt title. Quarterback Andrew Smith threw two touchdown passes, and running back Patrick Cobbs rushed for eighty-two yards and a TD.

"It was what a championship game should be like," North Texas coach Darrell Dickey said. "It's good to see a bunch of kids and a school have something to be excited about. There's a lot of emotion in that dressing room. It's really tough to do what we did."

The Mean Green went on to defeat Cincinnati in the New Orleans Bowl, claiming the program's first bowl victory since 1946 and the second in the history of the school, which had been playing football for eighty-nine years at that point.

NOVEMBER 24, 1986

Texas runners Sandy Blakeslee, Liz Natale, Trina Leopold, and Annie Schweitzer placed in the top twenty to lead the Longhorns to the NCAA Division I cross country national championship at the Canada Hills Country Club in Tucson, Arizona. Blakeslee placed fifth with a time of 17:17.47 over the 5,000-meter course. Natale finished 10th, followed by Leopold in 15th, Schweitzer in 19th, Kelly Champagne in 43rd, Tracy Laughlin in 87th, and Laura McCloy in 122nd. The Longhorns edged second-place Wisconsin by two points in the team standings.

NOVEMBER 25, 1995

The SMU women's soccer team slipped past North Carolina State 4–3 to earn the Mustangs' first trip to the NCAA Women's College Cup, the final four of women's soccer. SMU midfielder Courtney Linex scored the go-ahead goal late in the second half, and fellow midfielder Ryanne Bumps added another goal less than a minute later to put the Mustangs ahead 4–2. Although the Wolf Pack added a late goal, the Mustangs held on and advanced.

Six days later, Portland ended SMU's bid for a national championship by defeating the Ponies 4–2 in the NCAA Tournament semifinals.

SMU forward Danielle Garrett, who led the team with thirty-two goals and nineteen assists, earned first-team All-America honors, and was named Southwest Conference Player of the Year. Linex, who finished with thirty-one goals and fifteen assists, was selected All-SWC and third-team All-America.

NOVEMBER 26, 1994

The Plano East Panthers faced a seemingly insurmountable 41–17 deficit in the closing minutes of the fourth quarter of their third-round playoff game versus Tyler John Tyler.

With 2:36 left before the final whistle, Plano East began digging out of the hole. A twenty-one-yard touchdown pass from Panther QB Jeff Whitley to Terence Green almost escaped the notice of the Tyler sideline. But three onside-kick recoveries later, Plano East had the Lions' full attention. When Whitley threw a twenty-three-yard touchdown pass to Robert Woods, the Panthers had taken a 44–41 lead with twenty-four seconds remaining. It was the greatest comeback in the history of Texas high school football.

Or it would have been.

Instead, it is the greatest redemption story. Roderick Dunn, who mishandled two of the three onside kicks, dropped back deep to receive Plano East's final kick. The Panthers chose to kick deep when Tyler brought nine players up to the line of scrimmage, presumably to recover yet another onside kick. Dunn caught the kick at the three and took off for the other end zone.

"When I was at about the forty-five-yard line, that's when I saw the lane open up," Dunn told the *Tyler Courier-Times-Telegraph*. "I think it was Marc Broyles who threw a great block on the kicker (Terence Green). After that, I was gone."

Dunn's ninety-seven-yard kickoff return for a touchdown put the Lions back in the lead for good, 48–44. Tyler went on to win the Class 5A Division II state championship and post a 16–0 record.

(PHOTO, OPPOSITE PAGE)
Texas running back Ricky Williams (34) breaks away from the Texas A&M defense, November 27, 1998. Williams rumbled sixty yards for a touchdown and into the NCAA record books as he passed former Pitt running back Tony Dorsett as college football's career rushing record holder. Photo courtesy of University of Texas Athletics.

NOVEMBER 27, 1998

On the Friday after Thanksgiving 1998, just about everyone in the stands at Darrell K Royal—Texas Memorial Stadium was a statistician.

The football fans were keeping a running tab of Texas running back Ricky Williams's yardage through most of the first quarter in the annual matchup between the Longhorns and

sixth-ranked rival Texas A&M. Entering the day, Williams needed sixty-three yards to surpass Pittsburgh's Tony Dorsett as the NCAA Division I-A career rushing record holder.

Williams lost a yard on his first attempt and then gained five on his second run. Four yards down, fifty-nine to go. By his fourteenth carry of the first half, Williams was down to eleven yards to break the record. On that tote, he started left through a hole, bounced off an Aggie would-be tackler, and turned on the jets.

The Aggies caught Williams, but not in time to keep him from plowing into the end zone at the end of a sixty-yard touchdown run. "Hello, record book," bellowed Brent Musburger on the *ABC Sports* broadcast. "Ricky Williams runs to the Hall of Fame! Cuts back! Ricky Williams touchdown!"

Williams finished the day with 259 rushing yards on forty-four carries, propelling the Horns to a 26–24 victory. He capped his Longhorn career with 6,279 yards. Less than a month later, he joined Earl Campbell as one of Texas's two Heisman Trophy winners. A year later, the career mark was broken by Wisconsin running back Ron Dayne, who took the lead with a thirty-one-yard run. He didn't score on the play.

Texas A&M running backs Bubba Bean and George Woodard each outpaced Texas star Earl Campbell as the Aggie defense swarmed the Longhorn. That paved the way for second-ranked Texas A&M to defeat fifth-ranked Texas 20–10 at Kyle Field in College Station. Bean rushed for 126 yards, most of which came on a seventy-eight-yard romp that set up the Aggies' final score. Woodard added 84 on the ground, including a one-yard touchdown early in the fourth quarter. Meanwhile, Texas A&M held Campbell to 40 yards on fifteen carries.

In doing so, the Aggies grabbed their first win over archrival Texas in eight years, and their first under head coach Emory Bellard. "The teams I've been associated with have played some great games during my time, but none has meant any more than this one today," Bellard said.

Texas A&M improved to 10–0 with the win and had a shot at the national title. But eighteenth-ranked Arkansas handed the Aggies a 31–6 loss the next week, giving the Razorbacks a share of the Southwest Conference championship with Texas and Texas A&M. Arkansas received the SWC's Cotton Bowl berth. The Aggies fell to USC 20–0 in the Liberty Bowl on December 22.

NOVEMBER 29, 2014

Texas A&M senior forward Allie Bailey scored a pair of goals to lead the Aggies past Penn State 2–1 at Ellis Field in College Station. The victory advanced Texas A&M to the NCAA Women's College Cup for the first time in school history.

Bailey sent a sliding shot into the goal on an assist from Annie Kunz in the fifth minute. After Penn State scored an equalizing goal early in the second half, Texas A&M took the lead for good when forward Bianca Brinson stole an errant pass and deflected the ball into the Nittany Lions' six-yard box. Bailey was in position to punch her second goal into the back of the net, the tenth game-winning goal of her career. The last one meant a dream come true for Texas A&M soccer.

"Obviously, this has been a goal since freshman year," Bailey said in a postmatch interview. "Even the girls that were here before us have carved the path for us to be here. It's just an awesome feeling."

NOVEMBER 30, 1893

The University of Texas played its first football game, defeating the heavily favored Dallas Foot Ball Club 18–16 at the Dallas Fairgrounds.

December

DECEMBER 1, 1993

First-year Texas A&M volleyball coach Laurie Corbelli guided the Lady Aggies to their first NCAA Tournament win. A&M won its first-round match versus George Mason University 15–5, 15–5, 11–15, 15–6 at G. Rollie White Coliseum in College Station.

The Lady Aggies dominated the match by consistently exploiting a weakness in the left side of the Patriots' defense. Texas A&M hitter Dana Santleben posted twenty-five kills, fellow hitter Sheila Morgan added seventeen, and setter Suzy Wente dished out fifty-nine assists. "It was not even in our game plan to get to the left," Corbelli told *Bryan Eagle* sportswriter Olin Buchanan after the match. "Normally we try to be balanced to keep the opposing blockers guessing. We saw the success and did not hesitate to go out there."

Although the Lady Aggies lost to Texas in the next round, they had established their ground. Texas A&M made the NCAA Tournament during the next twelve seasons, and by the end of the 2015 campaign, the Lady Aggies had made nineteen NCAA Tournament appearances in Corbelli's first twenty-three seasons at the helm of the program.

DECEMBER 2, 1989

DECEMBER 3, 1949

Houston Cougar quarterback Andre Ware won the Heisman Trophy, becoming the first African American QB to claim college football's top individual prize. Ware won the Heisman despite unusual and now unfathomable circumstances: Houston was on probation in 1989 and therefore was banned from playing on television, among other sanctions.

Nevertheless, Ware piloted the Cougars' run-and-shoot offense. Behind him, Houston went 9–2 and finished second in the Southwest Conference standings, behind Arkansas. "This just shows that anything is possible," Ware said in his acceptance speech via satellite from Rice Stadium in Houston. "At the beginning of the season, who would believe I would be sitting here today accepting the Heisman Trophy."

As if putting a stamp on his celebrated season, Ware passed for 400 yards and two touchdowns to help the Cougars pound Rice 64–0 on the same day that he accepted the Heisman.

(PHOTO, OPPOSITE PAGE)
Houston Cougar quarterback Andre Ware won the Heisman Trophy after passing for 4,699 yards and forty-six touchdowns in 1989. Photo courtesy of University of Houston Athletics.

SMU offensive back Kyle Rote led a heroic effort as the Mustangs threatened to snap Notre Dame's thirty-seven-game unbeaten streak in front of 75,457 fans at the Cotton Bowl. Rote, carrying a double load since SMU's star running back, Doak Walker, was out of the game with an injury, rushed for 115 yards, passed for 146, and scored three touchdowns. Rote's final score tied the game at twenty in the fourth quarter, but with Walker, also the placekicker, out of the game, the Mustangs failed to convert, remaining tied with the Fighting Irish.

Notre Dame regained the lead late in the fourth quarter when Bill Barrett swept in for a six-yard touchdown, and the Fighting Irish escaped the Cotton Bowl with a 27–20 victory. Notre Dame, which did not play in a bowl game that season, finished a perfect 10–0 campaign with the win over the Ponies, and the Fighting Irish subsequently claimed the national championship.

DECEMBER 4, 1988

Texas Tech matched Billy Joe Tolliver's rocket arm against Oklahoma State running back Barry Sanders's lightning-fast feet in an offensive shootout in the Coca-Cola Classic in Tokyo, Japan. Sanders, who won the Heisman Trophy hours before kickoff, led the twelfth-ranked Cowboys to a narrow 45–42 victory.

Tolliver, who passed for 446 yards and a touchdown, ignited the Red Raiders in the first half, and they surged ahead 21–17 at the break. But Cowboy quarterback Mike Gundy threw a pair of touchdown passes to Hart Lee Dykes in the third quarter to give Oklahoma State a lead it didn't relinquish.

Sanders lived up to his Heisman hype, rushing for 257 yards and touchdowns of one, two, two, and fifty-six yards. Texas Tech running back James Gray also had four touchdowns, though he finished with just twenty-three yards on eleven carries.

DECEMBER 5, 1998

Running back Sirr Parker caught a slant pass from quarterback Branndon Stewart and then turned on the jets and raced thirty-two yards for a touchdown that lifted Texas A&M to a 36–33 double-overtime victory over Kansas State in the Big 12 Championship game at the Trans World Dome in St. Louis, Missouri.

Kansas State safety Lamar Chapman caught up to Parker inside the five-yard line on the deciding play, but it was too late to stop the Aggies' senior speedster. "I saw I had one man to beat," Parker said. "I just ran to the end zone. I'm five-eleven, but on that play I was about six feet stretching for the end zone."

Parker and Stewart connected at the end of the fourth quarter to force overtime. Texas A&M, down 27–12, outscored the second-ranked Wildcats 15–0 in the fourth, culminating when Stewart hit Parker for a nine-yard touchdown and then the two-point conversion with 1:05 left in regulation.

Each team scored a field goal in the first overtime period. By overcoming the Wildcats in the second overtime, the tenth-ranked Aggies squashed Kansas State's hopes of playing in the first BCS National Championship game. Instead, Texas A&M claimed a Sugar Bowl berth, and the Wildcats went to the Alamo Bowl.

Texas A&M running back Sirr Parker races Kansas State safety Lamar Chapman to the goal line during double overtime of the 1998 Big 12 Championship game. Photo courtesy of Texas A&M Athletics.

DECEMBER 6, 1969

Arkansas had Texas all but finished. The second-ranked Razorbacks, riding a fifteen-game winning streak and playing at home, were threatening to break top-ranked Texas's eighteen-game winning streak. Arkansas led 14–0 as the fourth quarter began, and the Razorbacks needed just a few more key plays to seal the deal.

Instead, the Longhorns made all the plays that mattered in the fourth quarter of the "Game of the Century."

Texas quarterback James Street eluded the Razorbacks' defense for a forty-two-yard touchdown run in the first minute of the fourth quarter. Street added a two-point-conversion run to cut Arkansas's lead to 14–8. Although Arkansas answered with a long drive, Texas defender Danny Lester intercepted Hog quarterback Bill Montgomery in the end zone to thwart the march.

Street ignited Texas's go-ahead drive with a forty-four-yard pass to Randy Peschel to move the Longhorns to the Arkansas thirteen-yard line. Two plays later, Jim Bertelsen ran two yards for a touchdown, and Happy Feller kicked the extra point to put Texas in the lead with 3:58 to go. When Arkansas moved into the Horns' territory to possibly take back the lead, Texas's Tom Campbell intercepted a Mont-gomery pass, allowing the Longhorns to run out the clock.

The Longhorns' victory over Arkansas was their most severe test during their 11–0 national championship campaign of 1969. Street sensed the monumental nature of the contest in its immediate aftermath. "Heck, I wish we could play them every week," he said. "They're such a great team. They test your offense and defense and make you play the very best you can."

DECEMBER 7, 1996

The Texas Longhorns lined up in a tight formation on a fourth-and-inches play. Across the line of scrimmage, the third-ranked Nebraska Cornhuskers prepared to beat Texas at the point of attack. ABC's play-by-play announcer Brent Musburger declared, as the teams stepped to the line of scrimmage, "No question what's about to happen."

Musburger, like everyone else watching, anticipated a power running play. That was when the Horns pulled off the play of the year in the first Big 12 Championship game.

Texas, leading the Cornhuskers 30–27 with 2:28 left in the fourth quarter, had the ball at its own twenty-eight-yard line. But instead of punting or plowing ahead for the yard needed for a first down, quarterback James Brown faked a handoff to Priest Holmes. Brown rolled left and threw to wide-open tight end Derek Lewis, who hauled in the pass and scampered to the Nebraska eleven before he was tackled.

"We made the call, no one really tried talking me out of it," Texas coach John Mackovic said in the postgame press conference. "We just made it and said this is what we're doing. The only thing I told James was come ready to run. And then when I saw his arm cock I thought, 'Oh, no.'"

Holmes scored on the next play, and the Longhorns grabbed a 37–27 victory for the first Big 12 title. Texas's win stopped Nebraska's bid for a third straight national title and sent the Longhorns to the Fiesta Bowl.

DECEMBER 8, 1995

Demetria Sance spiked twenty-four kills, and teammate Angie Breitenfield added twenty as Texas slayed its nemesis, the Florida Gators, in an NCAA Volleyball Tournament regional final in Gainesville, Florida. The Gators had ended Texas's season for four straight years in the NCAA Tournament and won the opening game of this series 15–9. But the Longhorns charged back for 15–7 and 15–8 wins, and after Florida took the fourth game 15–10, Texas clinched the match with a 15–13 triumph in the deciding game.

"I just wanted one more shot at them," Texas senior setter Carrie Busch said in a postmatch interview. "To lose to them for so many years and then finally click like this is a great feeling."

Texas, which finished the season with a 28–7 record and went 10–0 in the final year of the Southwest Conference, earned a berth in the Final Four for the first time since the Longhorns' national championship campaign in 1988 with its win over Florida. The Longhorns defeated Stanford in the national semifinal before falling to Nebraska in four games in the national-championship match.

DECEMBER 9, 1938

The Chicago Cardinals selected Temple native and TCU All-American center Ki Aldrich with the first pick of the NFL draft. Aldrich was the first Texan to be picked first overall. The Philadelphia Eagles drafted Horned Frog quarterback Davey O'Brien, from Dallas, with the fourth pick.

Aldrich played seven NFL seasons from 1939 to 1947, leaving Chicago to join the Washington Redskins in 1941. Aldrich helped the Redskins win the 1942 NFL championship and then served in the navy during World War II. He returned from the war to play three more seasons with the Redskins, 1945–1947.

DECEMBER 10, 2011

Robert Griffin III's whirlwind month concluded with a speech at the Downtown Athletic Club in New York. In the span of twenty-eight days, RG3 led Baylor to dramatic victories over Kansas and Oklahoma and a 48–24 demolition of Texas that vaulted him from an also-ran to the favorite to win the Heisman Trophy.

Although it had been a tight race for college football's most coveted individual award between the Bears' quarterback, Stanford QB Andrew Luck, and Alabama running back Trent Richardson, little suspense remained when Griffin III was announced as the winner.

"This moment right here, it's unbelievably believable," Griffin III said in his Heisman acceptance speech. "It's unbelievable because, in the moment, we're all amazed when great things happen. But it's believable because, you know, great things don't happen without hard work. You know, the great coach Art Briles always says great things only come with great effort, and we've certainly worked for this."

Later in December, Griffin III finished his college career by leading the Bears to a 67–56 win over Washington in the Alamo Bowl in San Antonio. RG3's Heisman Trophy and the bowl victory marked huge milestones for a Baylor program that had suffered through fourteen straight losing seasons, including 4–8 records in 2008 and 2009, Briles's first two seasons as head coach.

DECEMBER 11, 1957

Texas A&M two-way star football player John David Crow accepted the Heisman Trophy at the Downtown Athletic Club in New York. Crow, who had already been selected by the Chicago Cardinals with the second overall pick in the NFL draft, ran for 562 yards and six touchdowns, threw five touchdown passes, and made five interceptions on defense in the 1957 regular season. Crow's effort helped Texas A&M win its first eight games and move to the top of the national rankings before falling to Rice and Texas in the last two games of the regular season and to Tennessee in the Gator Bowl. Texas A&M finished the season ranked ninth in the final Associated Press Top 25 poll.

DECEMBER 12, 1937

Sweetwater native and TCU alum Sammy Baugh capped his rookie season in the NFL by passing for 352 yards to lead the Washington Redskins to a 28–21 victory over the Chicago Bears in the NFL Championship game at Wrigley Field.

The Associated Press game story pointed to Baugh's exploits as the catalyst for the victory: "The Washington Redskins with the sensational Sammy Baugh slinging passes with the bow-and-arrow accuracy of the first Americans defeated the Chicago Bears 28 to 21 today to win the National Football League championship," read the first paragraph.

Baugh, a first-round draft pick by the Redskins that year, took to pro football immediately, leading the NFL in passing with 1,127 passing yards in 1937. He saved his best for the biggest stage as he led the Redskins' second-half charge with three touchdown passes.

DECEMBER 13, 1975

The Texas Lutheran College volleyball team rallied for two straight match victories against the University of California, Riverside, to claim the Association for Intercollegiate Athletics for Women national championship in Pocatello, Idaho. Led by future Olympian Laurie Flachmeier, the Bulldogs won five matches on the final day of competition, coming out of the loser's bracket to win the title.

Riverside defeated Texas Lutheran in their initial contest, meaning the Bulldogs had to win twice once they reached the championship round of the double-elimination tournament. It looked bleak early in the match when Riverside won the first game of the champi-onship 15–4. But Texas Lutheran rallied 15–6 and then claimed a thrilling 17–15 third-game victory to take the match and set up a winner-take-all final. Again Riverside won the opening game before the Bulldogs fought back for 15–11 and 14–12 victories to take the national championship trophy home to Seguin.

"We played those last games with guts and desire," Texas Lutheran coach Susan Duke told the *Seguin Gazette*.

The Bulldogs, who were unseeded in their first national championship run, returned to the AIAW national tournament as the top seed in 1976 and won their second straight championship.

The Texas Lutheran College volleyball team won back-to-back AIAW national championships in 1975 and 1976. Photo courtesy of Texas Lutheran Athletics.

DECEMBER 14, 2003

Cody Ohl of Hico and his horse Casino sprang from the gate at the National Finals Rodeo, and less than seven seconds later they had the Thomas and Mack Center crowd in an uproar in Las Vegas, Nevada. Ohl roped his calf, jumped off Casino, dropped the calf, and tied it in 6.5 seconds.

"Listen, that is two records!" exclaimed the arena announcer. "That is not only the fastest calf tied at the national finals, that's the fastest calf tied in the history of rodeo!"

With the record-setting tie-down, Ohl passed fellow Texan Fred Whitfield of Hockley in the standings to claim the NFR championship gold buckle.

"Unbelievable," Ohl told rodeo writer Joe Kusek after the competition. "When I threw my hands up in the air, I knew it was close to an arena record, world record . . . I knew it was fast."

Ohl's record time marked his return to the top after suffering a severe knee injury in the ninth round of the National Finals Rodeo two years earlier.

DECEMBER 15, 1907

Boerne native Adolph Toepperwein fired upon and hit 7,500 2¼-inch wooden cubes without a single miss on his third day of shooting in a marathon attempt to break a world trapshooting record in San Antonio. On December 13, Toepperwein began with 60,000 wooden blocks and shot for ten days, up to seven hours per day, alternating among three Winchester .22s. By the end, he had fired at 72,500 blocks with only nine misses.

In a 2006 *Trap & Field* article entitled "The Fabulous Toepperweins," Toepperwein told trapshooting historian Dick Baldwin that his target throwers resorted to recycling the wooden blocks so he could keep shooting. "As I ran way ahead of my supposed schedule for the first few days, we were running short of blocks toward the end, and the boys selected the blocks that were not mutilated too much for the rest of the score. Some of these blocks toward the end were rather small, but I was lucky, and I don't think I missed any on that account."

Toepperwein and his wife, Elizabeth "Plinky" Toepperwein, who was also a record-setting shooter and a member of the Trapshooting Hall of Fame, entertained audiences at the St. Louis World's Fair in 1904. Plinky shot 967 out of 1,000 clay disks there, setting her first world record.

DECEMBER 16, 1979

Legendary quarterback Roger Staubach of the Dallas Cowboys saved one of his greatest games for one of his last. Playing in his final regular-season contest, Staubach passed for 336 yards and three touchdowns as he led the Cowboys to a dramatic fourth-quarter comeback for a 35–34 victory over the archrival Washington Redskins at Texas Stadium. Dallas's win clinched the NFC East division title and bumped the Redskins from the playoffs.

But Staubach owed the comeback, at least in part, to defensive tackle Randy White. With the Redskins leading 34–21 with less than four minutes remaining in the fourth quarter, White recovered a fumble that stopped Washington's game-sealing drive and gave Dallas the ball at its own forty-one.

Staubach quickly went to work. He hit running back Ron Springs for a twenty-six-yard touchdown with 2:20 left, cutting the Redskins' lead to 34–28.

After a defensive stop, Staubach directed a seventy-five-yard march that began with just more than a minute to go. On the seventh play of the drive, Staubach connected with wide receiver Tony Hill for an eight-yard touchdown with thirty-nine seconds left. Cowboy kicker Rafael Septién booted the extra point to give Dallas the lead for good.

"I've never been in a game like that in my whole life," Staubach said in a postgame interview. "I'm still in shock."

Staubach outdueled Redskin quarterback Joe Theismann, who finished with 200 passing yards and a touchdown. It was Staubach's final triumph, since the Los Angeles Rams eliminated Dallas from the playoffs two weeks later. Staubach announced his retirement in March 1980.

DECEMBER 17, 1988

DECEMBER 18, 2004

Texas swept Hawaii 15–4, 16–4, 15–13 to claim the Longhorns' first national championship in volleyball. In doing so, the Longhorns ended the West Coast's and Hawaii's iron grip on the first seven years of the event. Texas was the first team from east of the Rocky Mountains to win the NCAA Division I volleyball title.

Texas didn't drop a game in its five-match NCAA Tournament run, including victories over top-ranked UCLA and third-ranked Hawaii in the national semifinal and final.

Texas's Dawn Davenport spearheaded the Horns' effort with seventeen kills and fourteen digs against Hawaii. Davenport, Sue Schelfhout, and Stacie Nicols earned spots on the NCAA Final Four All-Tournament team.

President George W. Bush telephoned the field house at Birdville ISD Athletics Complex to congratulate the Crawford Pirates on winning the Class 2A Division II state championship. But the Pirates players, coaches, and fans were too busy celebrating, and the First Fan's call went unanswered.

Crawford quarterback Lee Murphy threw a twenty-four-yard touchdown pass to Jad Tawater in the third quarter to put the Pirates ahead of the Troup Tigers. Then Crawford running back B. J. Christian ran thirteen yards for a touchdown midway through the fourth quarter to help seal the Pirates' 28–14 state championship victory. "I don't even think I was breathing," Christian told the author of this book in a postgame interview. "Adrenaline took over and I had to get there."

President Bush, whose Prairie Chapel Ranch was located less than ten miles from Crawford High School, gave the Pirates a pep talk via telephone and the school's intercom system during the pep rally before the game. Upon traveling to the ranch for Christmas, President Bush and First Lady Laura Bush met with the team to congratulate them in person for winning the state title.

DECEMBER 19, 1997

Granbury girls' basketball coach Leta Andrews notched her 1,000th career victory when her Lady Pirates defeated Waco Midway 53–45 in Waco.

"Now I can enjoy the Christmas holidays," Andrews told reporters after the game. "The pressure is off. I'm so glad it's behind me. I'm comfortable now that the record is history."

Granbury star and future Texas Tech and WNBA guard Jia Perkins scored twenty-two points with ten rebounds and eight steals in the win over Midway. But Andrews failed to build on her milestone victory through the postseason. Graham ousted Granbury from the playoffs in the regional quarterfinal round.

That followed a trend for Andrews. She finished her career with a national-record 1,416 wins, but only one state championship in fifty-one seasons. Andrews led Corpus Christi Calallen to the Class 5A state title in 1990 when the Wildcats defeated Midway 46–39 in the championship game.

DECEMBER 20, 2014

Texas Southern senior Chris Thomas scored twenty-two points, and fellow senior Malcolm Riley came off the bench to add twenty, as the Tigers upended twenty-fifth-ranked Michigan State 71–64 in overtime in East Lansing, Michigan.

Texas Southern's signature win over the Spartans came five days after Gonzaga had routed the Tigers by forty points. But the Texas Southern players remained focused on their season goals after the dramatic two-game stretch.

"It means a lot, but we're not done yet," Thomas said after the win over Michigan State. "We've got to win a lot more games to get to the tournament. It doesn't stop here."

The Tigers went on to win the Southwestern Athletic Conference tournament to earn an automatic bid to the NCAA Tournament. Second-seeded Arizona defeated fifteenth-seeded Texas Southern in the round of sixty-four.

DECEMBER 21, 1963

Baylor quarterback Don Trull threw two fourth-quarter touchdown passes to James Ingram to lift the Bears to a 14–7 victory over LSU in the Bluebonnet Bowl at Rice Stadium in Houston. Trull capped a prolific senior season at Baylor by passing for 255 yards against the Tigers. He connected with Ingram eleven times for 163 yards, including scoring passes of seven and thirteen yards. Trull hit Ingram with the game-winning touchdown pass with 5:20 left.

But another Baylor star still had to make a play to preserve the win. Lawrence Elkins led Baylor and the nation with seventy receptions for 873 yards in 1963. He also handled kickoff duties for the Bears, and came up a hero in that role against LSU. Following Trull's thirteen-yard go-ahead touchdown pass to Ingram, Tiger kickoff returner Joe Labruzzo took a reverse handoff and eluded the Baylor cover team until Elkins caught him and stopped a possible game-tying touchdown.

"They ran that handoff and, man, I was clear over on the other side of the field before I saw that rascal with the ball," Elkins said in a postgame interview. "I'm the safety man on kickoffs. I had to catch him, but I barely made it."

DECEMBER 22, 1996

The Houston Oilers played their final game before owner Bud Adams moved the franchise to Tennessee. The Oilers, who finished their final season in Houston with an 8–8 record, had lost their last game at the Astrodome 21–13 against the Cincinnati Bengals the previous week.

But Houston went out with a victory. Quarterback Steve McNair passed for 238 yards and a touchdown and ran for another score to lead the Oilers to a 24–21 win over the Ravens in Baltimore.

Adams then brought to a close a thirty-seven-year relationship between the Oilers and the city of Houston. The NFL returned to Houston in 2002 with the birth of the expansion Texans.

DECEMBER 23, 1978

Texas took full advantage of a strong wind at its back and splurged for three first-quarter touchdowns on the way to a 42–0 victory over Maryland in the Sun Bowl. The Terrapins chose to receive the opening kickoff and travel into the forty-five-mile-per-hour wind. Texas quickly took the ball away from Maryland and began its domination in El Paso.

Texas flanker Johnny "Lam" Jones ran seven yards on a reverse for the Longhorns' first touchdown, then A. J. "Jam" Jones lunged in for a one-yard touchdown, and Lam Jones caught a twenty-nine-yard touchdown pass from quarterback Mark McBath, all in the first quarter. Johnny "Ham" Jones, the game's MVP with 104 rushing yards on fourteen carries, got into the scoring act with a thirty-two-yard run for the Longhorns' final touchdown late in the third quarter.

Texas's Sun Bowl win over thirteenth-ranked Maryland capped the Longhorns' 9–3 season, and they finished ninth in the nation in the final AP and UPI polls.

DECEMBER 24, 2009

SMU made the most of its first bowl appearance in twenty-five years, defeating the University of Nevada–Reno 45–10 in the Hawaii Bowl in Honolulu.

"It brings back a lot of boosters and a lot of the alumni to know we have a football team again," said SMU quarterback Kyle Padron, who threw for a Mustang-record 460 yards in the win.

Padron, the game's offensive MVP, outdueled Nevada quarterback Colin Kaepernick. The SMU signal caller directed coach June Jones's run-and-shoot offense to perfection, constantly exploiting holes in the Wolf Pack defense. "I was kind of chucking the ball everywhere," Padron said. "Lot of big gaps today and it was fun."

SMU finished the season with an 8–5 record, and the postseason victory ignited a streak of four straight bowl appearances.

DECEMBER 25, 1993

DECEMBER 26, 1955

The Houston Oilers clamped down on San Francisco's offense and dealt the 49ers a 10–7 Christmas Day loss. The Oilers snapped San Francisco's thirteen-game winning streak and kept alive its own chances for home-field advantage throughout the AFC playoffs.

Oiler quarterback Warren Moon threw a seven-yard touchdown pass to Ernest Givens to give Houston a 10–0 lead in the second quarter. The Oilers' defense held on from there, forcing 49er quarterback Steve Young into two interceptions and a fumble in less than three quarters of work. Jerry Rice caught ten passes for San Francisco, but the Houston defense refused to let him get away, holding Rice to 83 receiving yards.

Houston defeated the New York Jets the next week to finish the regular season with a 12–4 record, the Oilers' best-ever mark. But Kansas City eliminated Houston from the playoffs in the divisional round, winning 28–20 in the Astrodome.

Coach Gordon Wood led the Stamford Bulldogs to a convincing 34–7 victory over the Hillsboro Eagles in the Class 2A state football championship at Fair Park Stadium in Abilene. Wood's autobiography *Coach of the Century* reported that the 11,000 fans packed into the stadium watched the Stamford defense control the game, and Bulldog back Mike McClellan rushed for 107 yards to pace the offense as it repeatedly capitalized on Hillsboro turnovers.

Wood added another state championship at Stamford in 1956. Then, after a two-season stint at Victoria High School, he was hired in Brownwood, where he coached from 1960 to 1985. Wood guided the Lions to the 3A state championship in his first season and added six more titles as Brownwood ascended to elite status among Texas high school football dynasties.

Wood retired after the 1985 campaign as the most victorious coach in Texas high school football history, with a career record of 396–91–15, including seven state titles. Multiple sources claim that legendary Alabama coach Bear Bryant, when asked why he left Texas A&M for the Crimson Tide, said, "I had to leave Texas. As long as Gordon Wood was there, I could never be the best coach in the state."

DECEMBER 27, 1995

Texas Tech running back Byron Hanspard rushed for 260 yards and four touchdowns to lead the Red Raiders to a 55–41 victory over Air Force in the Copper Bowl in Tucson, Arizona. Hanspard, a sophomore who led the Southwest Conference in rushing in its final season, scored on runs of two, two, eleven, and twenty-nine yards to pace Texas Tech.

Red Raiders coach Spike Dykes grabbed his second and final bowl win as Texas Tech's head coach. Dykes coached the Red Raiders from the Independence Bowl at the end of the 1986 season through 1999 and took them to eight bowl games in that span, compiling a 2–6 bowl record.

DECEMBER 28, 1946

Hayden Fry's Odessa Bronchos defeated Kyle Rote's San Antonio Jefferson Mustangs 21–14 for the UIL Football State Championship. It was the first football state title won by a school from Odessa.

DECEMBER 29, 1991

DECEMBER 30, 2008

Emmitt Smith rushed for 105 yards and a touchdown, and the Dallas defense clamped down on the Chicago Bears near the goal line to help the Cowboys win their first playoff game in almost nine years. Cowboy backup quarterback Steve Beuerlein adequately filled Troy Aikman's role in directing Dallas to a 17–13 victory over the Bears in an NFC wild card game at Soldier Field in Chicago.

Smith scored on a one-yard run in the first quarter to put Dallas ahead 10–0. Beuerlein hit tight end Jay Novacek for a three-yard touchdown in the third quarter to put the Cowboys up by eleven. The Dallas defense saved the day by stopping the Bears on downs twice from inside the Cowboys' ten-yard line.

Even while deploying the team's second option at quarterback, Cowboys owner Jerry Jones felt bullish after the game. "There's not a person in here today who doesn't believe after this game that we have a great shot at the Super Bowl," Jones crowed in one of his signature postgame interviews.

But Dallas would have to wait. The Detroit Lions throttled the Cowboys 38–6 the next week.

Rice quarterback Chase Clement threw three touchdown passes, ran for a score, and caught a touchdown pass to lead the Owls to a 38–14 victory over Western Michigan in the Texas Bowl. With that, Rice ended a fifty-four-year drought without a bowl win, and reached ten wins in a season for the first time since 1949.

"When you sit down and look back and see how everything has unfolded, it's a special opportunity and just what we've been able to accomplish," Clement said in a postgame interview. "It really sets this program in the right direction."

Clement put Rice in front in the first quarter when he ran twenty-six yards for a touchdown. In the second quarter, he hit Toren Dixon for a six-yard scoring pass and James Casey for a forty-six-yard touchdown to boost the Owls' lead to 24–0 at halftime. Rice wide receiver Jarett Dillard then turned the tables when he tossed an eighteen-yard touchdown pass to Clement midway through the third quarter for a 31–0 lead that iced the win.

Rice, just three years removed from a 1–10 season in 2005, finished the 2008 campaign with a 10–3 mark. The Owls' bowl victory was their first since they won the 1954 Cotton Bowl 28–6 over Alabama.

DECEMBER 31, 1998

TCU claimed its first bowl victory in forty-one years by defeating Southern California 28–19 in the Sun Bowl in El Paso.

Basil Mitchell, who led TCU with 185 rushing yards, helped the Horned Frogs surge to a 21–0 lead as he ran for touchdowns of three and sixty yards in the first quarter. Horned Frog sophomore running back LaDainian Tomlinson caught a pass for a twenty-five-yard gain to the USC twelve-yard line that set up another touchdown early in the second quarter.

By the time TCU quarterback Patrick Batteaux scored on a three-yard run early in the third quarter, the Horned Frogs led 28–3, a margin that let them hold off the Trojans.

By defeating USC, TCU finished the 1998 season with a 7–5 record, an amazing turnaround from 1997, when the Horned Frogs finished 1–10.

"We started the season with very little respect," Horned Frog coach Dennis Franchione said in a postgame interview. "This has not been an unusual situation for us and we responded well. You only earn respect, it isn't given to you."

TCU went on to earn the respect of the entire college football nation after the 1998 season. The Horned Frogs won more than seven games in eleven of the next thirteen years, including a 13–0 campaign in 2010. The Big 12 took notice. Though the conference had excluded TCU from its formation in 1994, it invited the Horned Frogs to join in 2011.

Sources

For those of us who love sports in an over-the-top, obsessive sort of way, part of the thrill includes researching and finding stats and facts that we can later use to prove how awesome our teams really were. In the case of this book, I scratched that itch to the greatest degree I can imagine, since all teams and athletes from Texas became my teams and my players. I used newspaper microfilms, books, magazine articles, and many conversations with other sports lovers to help point me in the direction of days in this book and to verify the accuracy of the accounts.

And, of course, I used the Internet. I wouldn't have tackled this project without the World Wide Web. I can imagine sports editors, whose cluttered offices I have visited, combing through tottering stacks of media guides and old sports sections to write a book like this. While I do have a small stack of media guides somewhere in my house, I didn't crack one open. I didn't need to. By the time I began working on this project in 2015, media guides were readily available to download in seconds from the websites of teams ranging from small college squads to the Dallas Cowboys.

Another fantastic resource was YouTube. I watched highlights from calf roping, diving, track and field, basketball, baseball, and football in order to add colorful and accurate descriptions to many of the days.

Perhaps the most important use of the Internet in this project was the ability to cross-reference facts and stats. I used *Wikipedia* at times to get me started, but I always relied on firsthand accounts for the information that went into each day. Most of the days in this book came at least partly from the Associated Press or from pages of the *Waco Tribune-Herald* (or its Waco predecessors) kept at the West Waco Library and Genealogy Center.

I also want to describe my philosophy on using quotations. In twenty years as a sportswriter, I have had my share of conversations and altercations over the right to conduct one-on-one interviews that produce exclusive comments. Because of that, I did everything I could to ensure that I always attributed excerpts from one-on-one interviews to the sportswriters who gathered them. For the most part, I sought material that seemed to come from press conferences or multiple-reporter situations. That is why many of the quotations in this book contain descriptions like "(subject) said in a postgame press conference."

What follows is specific information on some of the sources I used.

BOOKS

Sometimes I knew where to look for details because I had encountered them in a book. This was the case with *The Match* by Mark Frost (Hyperion, 2007), *Boys Will Be Boys* by Jeff Pearlman (HarperCollins, 2008), *Eating the Dinosaur* by Chuck Klosterman (Simon and Schuster, 2009), *Oh Brother, How They Played the Game* by Carlton Stowers (State House Press, 2007), and *Coach of the Century* by Gordon Wood and John Carver (Hard Times Cattle Company, 2001). I found specific facts in books written about Texas or Texans, including *Rube Foster in His Time* by Larry Lester (McFarland, 2012), *The Texas League Baseball Almanac* by David King and Tom Kayser (History Press, 2014), *Nolan Ryan: The Making of a Pitcher* by Rob Goldman (Triumph Books, 2014), *Junction Boys* by Jim Dent (Thomas Dunne, 2000), and my previous book *The Republic of Football* (University of Texas Press, 2016).

NEWSPAPERS

As mentioned, much of my research took place at the West Waco Library and Genealogy Center, which meant I had access to more than a hundred years of the *Waco Tribune-Herald*. The use of that specific newspaper was especially valuable in one area. Former *Waco Tribune-Herald* sports editor Dave Campbell, who also cocreated the periodical *Dave Campbell's Texas Football*, wrote extensively about the entire Southwest Conference in his time. One account of Campbell's included a reference to Arkansas coach Frank Broyles having sportswriters over to his house for a steak dinner following the "Game of the Century" between Texas and Arkansas in 1969. Though I didn't use this detail in the text about that game, I mention it here in order to illustrate how thoroughly Campbell covered the SWC.

I also found and used material from the *Austin American-Statesman*, *San Antonio Express-News*, *Houston Chronicle*, *Fort Worth*

Star-Telegram, Chicago Tribune, San Marcos Record, Tyler Courier-Times-Telegram, Bryan Eagle, and *Seguin Gazette.*

MAGAZINES

A couple of magazine articles illuminated some obscure corners of Texas sports. "Prizefight on the Rio Grande" by Dick King (*Texas Highways,* October 1974) described the extraordinary effort of Judge Roy Bean to make the 1896 Fitzsimmons-Maher boxing match take place. A compilation of articles by Dick Baldwin, most notably "The Fabulous Toepperweins" (*Trap & Field,* November and December 2006), reprinted at ShowmanShooter .com described the incredible shooting feat of Adolph Toepperwein.

SPORTS WEBSITES AND MEDIA GUIDES

Having worked in sports media relations while in college, and having a close relationship with media relations directors since then, I knew where to look for dates and records involving college and pro teams from Texas. I used sports websites, including media guides published on them, from colleges and universities—Baylor, Houston, Rice, TCU, Texas, Texas A&M, Texas Lutheran, Texas State, Texas

Tech, and Wayland Baptist—and the following professional teams: the Dallas Cowboys, Dallas Mavericks, Dallas Stars, Houston Rockets, Houston Astros, San Antonio Spurs, and Texas Rangers.

OTHER INTERNET REFERENCES

The extraordinary databases at Baseball-Reference.com, Pro-Football-Reference.com, and Basketball-Reference.com were excellent signposts. Other useful websites included those of the National Baseball Hall of Fame (BaseballHall.org), the University Interscholastic League (UILTexas.org), the Houston Astros (AstrosDaily.com), Bassmaster (Bassmaster.com), the Texas Olympic medalist section of the *Texas Almanac* (TexasAlmanac.com), Rodeo Houston (RodeoHouston.com), the track and field archives at NCAA.com, the Houston Gamblers (Houston-Gamblers.com), the International Boxing Hall of Fame (ibhof .com), the Pro Football Hall of Fame (ProFootballHOF.com), the Texas Sports Hall of Fame (TSHOF.org), and USSoccer.com.

YOUTUBE

I mined YouTube for visual proof, details, and snippets of commentary. Clips included the CBS broadcast of Jimmy Johnson's famous

"How 'bout them Cowboys!" postgame speech, posted by Neal Blanchard; the ABC broadcast of the George Foreman match against Joe Frazier, posted by boxingatitsbest; the TBS broadcast of the 1986 NBA Slam Dunk Contest, posted by Ryan Van Dusen; a feature on Shaquille O'Neal posted by Dunkman827; "Ralph Sampson Shocks the Lakers with the Game Winner," posted by the NBA; the ESPN broadcast of the 2008 MLB Home Run Derby, posted by Centepede Soup; the NBC broadcast of Laura Wilkinson's winning dive in the 2000 Olympics, posted by FliPnRip; the ABC broadcast of the 2001 Texas-Oklahoma game, posted by soonerscott2007; "Feliz throws last pitch of 2010 ALCS Rangers Yankees and celebration that follows," posted by dcwildcat97; the ABC broadcast of the 1998 Texas–Texas A&M game, posted by trivinity; the ESPN Classic replay of the 1996 Big 12 Championship football game, posted by BevoCam; and the ESPN broadcast of Cody Ohl's winning time at the 2003 National Finals Rodeo, posted by rwillie22.

PERSONAL EXPERIENCE
Finally, I was a fan or reporter at many of the games and historical events recounted in these pages. One day in particular came directly from an event close to my heart. When I wrote that the families of the Little League Softball World Series champion Midway team drove through the night from Michigan to Texas to meet the players and coaches at the ballpark in Woodway, I knew that detail because I tried to stay awake and keep my dad company as he drove my mom, my sister Calley, and me. My sister Chaney was a member of that team, and we followed them on a wild tour from Texas to Florida, and then to Michigan and back again.

Acknowledgments

I come from a sports family. My dad, John Conine, played basketball and golf in high school, and golf at Texas Tech. He took me to the Astrodome when I was a kid for my first Major League baseball game. Since then, we have been to many ballparks, stadiums, and golf courses together. We had tickets for the Texas Rangers versus the Oakland A's on his thirty-seventh birthday, so we were able to attend the game I wrote about on August 22 of this book. My mom, Shana Conine, might not have been the biggest sports fan when she met my dad, but she is now. We all watch the Red Raiders together. My sisters Chaney Cockrell and Calley Durant were championship softball players. Chaney played in two games mentioned in this book. My brothers, Tim, Cory, and Jeremy Webb, had their moments too. Tim ran on the Waco Midway 4 × 100-meter relay team that made the state meet when we were seniors in 1996. Jeremy once hit a legit inside-the-park home run when he was thirteen, and that was one of the most im-

pressive feats of speed I have ever seen. Cory and I helped First Baptist Woodway claim the city church-league basketball championship in 1995. Their dad, Danny Webb, along with Jeremy's father-in-law, Mickey Johnson, were among my most enthusiastic friends in helping me brainstorm ideas for this book.

That is my way of thanking my extended family, and it makes it easy to see how two of the most important parts of my life fit together.

Thanks to Casey Kittrell and Robert Devens from the University of Texas Press for coming to me with the concept for this book in May 2015. Kittrell continued with me along the way, answering questions and helping me think about important areas of Texas sports to include.

Thanks to my Texas Rangers Opening Day buddies Bob Johns, Tommy Ross, David Deaconsen, Cliff Smith, Ronnie Higgins, and Woody and David Rogers. Baseball is a talking sport, and conversations with those guys came into play here. Smith, in particular, pointed me in the direction of three days in this book. On a trip to a Ranger game in May 2015, we talked about a couple of pole vaulters as well as the quirky brawl between Roger Staubach and Clint Longley at the Cowboys' camp in 1976.

Thank you to Ryan Sprayberry and Jay Black at the Texas Sports Hall of Fame. Sprayberry let me peruse his calendar of Texas sports, and more than once it pointed me toward excellent subjects. He also compiled a stack of photos for me to look through and choose for use in these pages.

Thanks to the people at the West Waco Library and Genealogy Center, in particular Ruben Salazar, Hannah Roquemore, and Bill Buckner (not *that* Bill Buckner) in genealogy. They were friendly faces that I looked forward to seeing as I worked there just about every day in the first half of 2016. The library acquired a new digital microfilm reader during that time, and that made things more efficient after the crew taught me to use it.

Thanks to all my sportswriter friends, especially Brice Cherry, John Werner, Jerry Hill, Jason Orts, Jim Barnes, Kim Gorum, and David G. Campbell. Gorum helped me with valuable insight into Texans in tennis.

Thanks to my friends Chelsea Santos (also my go-to photographer), Jacob Robin-son, Becky Simpson, Zach McFarlen, Shawn Skeen, Jon Davis, Brian Patterson, and everyone else around me that helped me see what it is to diligently pursue your passions.

Index of Sports

auto racing, 101

baseball, college, 33, 90, 102, 107, 109, 113, 121
baseball, pro, 31–32, 33, 34, 68, 69, 73, 76, 78, 83, 86, 105, 110, 115, 119, 122, 123, 125, 129, 130, 131, 132, 133, 135, 137, 138, 139, 140, 145–146, 148, 149, 152, 154, 156, 160, 172, 176, 177, 183, 185, 188, 189, 190, 192, 194, 198, 211
basketball, men's college, 6, 8, 11, 15, 16, 17, 20, 21, 29, 30, 35, 40–41, 43, 44, 45, 46, 48, 50, 51, 52–53, 54, 55, 56, 57, 58, 59, 61, 67, 68, 235
basketball, men's high school, 26, 30, 37, 47
basketball, men's pro, 15, 22, 27, 28–29, 31, 34, 40–41, 79, 84, 86, 90, 92, 94, 97, 100, 110, 114, 119, 120, 146, 188, 197
basketball, women's amateur, 204–205
basketball, women's college, 18–19, 25, 26, 32, 35, 37, 46,

47, 48, 50, 56, 57, 60, 63, 64–65, 66
basketball, women's high school, 43, 44, 45, 235
basketball, women's Olympic, 152
basketball, women's pro, 161
bobsledding, 39
bowling, 69
boxing, pro, 16, 36, 75, 126
bull riding, pro, 204

cross country, women's college, 215
cycling, 137, 191

diving (platform), women's Olympic, 176

equestrian, 76

fishing, 36
football, college, 5, 6, 7, 11, 153, 159, 161, 163–164, 165, 166, 167, 168, 169, 170, 171, 174, 175, 178, 181–182, 183, 184, 185, 186–187, 192, 194–195,

197, 198, 199, 201, 202, 203, 206–207, 208, 209, 210, 211, 212, 213, 214, 217–218, 219, 222–223, 224–225, 226, 227, 228, 229, 230, 236, 237, 239, 240, 241
football, high school, 9, 26, 165, 206, 216, 234, 238, 239
football, pro, 8, 9, 10, 12, 13, 14, 21, 23, 27, 28, 37, 39, 60, 77, 78, 122, 144, 149–150, 155, 158, 165, 167, 171, 172–173, 174, 179, 186, 230, 233, 236, 238, 240

golf, men's college, 77, 106
golf, men's pro, 25, 63, 67, 70–71, 73, 80, 95, 98, 99, 111, 114–115, 116, 117, 118, 128, 130, 131, 133, 134, 135, 136, 158, 193, 196, 203
golf, women's pro, 91, 98, 120, 128, 136, 139, 155, 177, 181
gymnastics, women's Olympic, 144, 153

hockey, pro, 49, 74, 117
horse racing, 87

motor sports, 193

rodeo, 81, 232

soccer, men's pro, 209
soccer, men's World Cup, 112, 129
soccer, women's college, 215, 219
soccer, women's World Cup, 160
softball, Little League, 157
softball, women's college, 38, 72,
    93, 96–97, 99, 100, 103, 105,
    106
swimming, women's Olympic,
    140

taekwondo, women's Olympic,
    159
tennis, men's pro, 80, 81, 126
tennis, women's college, 101
tennis, women's pro, 22, 121, 127,
    176
track and field, 20, 149
track and field, men's college,
    88–89, 95, 108–109, 112–113
track and field, men's high
    school, 91, 94
track and field, men's Olympic,
    20, 138, 141, 143, 147, 148, 149
track and field, women's college,
    85, 107
track and field, women's high
    school, 92
track and field, women's Olym-
    pic, 150–151, 179

trapshooting, 232

volleyball, women's college, 210,
    221, 228, 231, 234
volleyball, women's high school,
    214

General Index

Page numbers in italics indicate photographs.

Aaron, Hank, 129, 138
ABC Sports, 218
Abdallah, Nia, 159
Abdul-Jabbar, Kareem, 31
Abernathy High School, Abernathy, 43
Abilene Christian University, 20, 209
Abrams, A. J., 40
Abreu, Bobby, 132
Adams, Bud, 158, 236
Adams, Valerie, 151
Adcock, Joe, 140
AFC playoffs/championship, 164, 238
Aguirre, Mark, 79
Aikman, Troy, 12, 14, 21, 23, 77, 167, 240
Air Force (football team), 169, 239
Akers, Fred, 6, 194
Alamo Bowl, 224, 229
Alamodome, San Antonio, 68, 198

Alberto, Hanser, 185
Alcott, Amy, 91
Aldrich, Ki, 228
Alexander, Rita, 204–*205*
Algeria (World Cup team), 112
All-America honors, 48, 60, 101, 208, 215, 228
Allen, Terry, 145
Alliss, Peter, 193
All-Star Game (baseball), 130, 135, 138
Alomar, Roberto, 83
Alou, Felipe, 129
Alou, Moises, 86
Alstyne, Van, 206
Alworth, Lance, 13
Amarillo High School, Amarillo, 214
Amateur Athletic Union, 204
Amateur Championship (Britain), 130
American Airlines Center, Dallas, 110
American Basketball Association, 146
American League Championship Series, 194

American League Division Series, 183, 185
Ameriquest Field, Arlington, 123
Anaheim Angels, 123
Andaya, Shawn, 99, *99*
Anders, Benny, 6
Anderson, Matt, 105
Andretti, Mario, 101, 193
Andrews, Leta, 235
Arizona State University, 93, 105, 106
Arlington Stadium, Arlington, 76, 83, 137, 146, 154
Armed Forces Bowl, 169
Armstrong, Lance, 137, 191
Armstrong, Linda, 137
Arrieta, Jake, 175, 192
Artis, Orsten, 52
Ashby, Alan, 160
Association for Intercollegiate Athletics for Women, 37, 231
Astrodome, Houston, 15, 31, 33, 59, 81, 158, 160, 174, 179, 202, 236, 238
AT&T Stadium, Arlington, 11, 31, 67
Ates, Horace, 197

Atlanta Braves, 129, 135
Atlanta Falcons, 164
Atlanta Hawks, 28
Auburn University, 171, 202
Ausmus, Brad, 122
Austin, Miles, 10
Austin High School, Austin, 73
Australian Open, 22
Autry Court, Houston, 21
Aycock, Ryan, 178

Babineaux, Jordan, 8
Backus, LaKeisha, 107
Bagwell, Jeff, 86, 135
Bailey, Allie, 219
Baldwin, Dick, 232
Ballard, Carolyn-Dorin, 69
Ballard, Del, Jr., 69
Ballpark, The, Arlington, 69, 115, 139, 140, 194
Baltimore Colts, 155
Baltimore Ravens, 9, 236
Bank of America Colonial, Fort Worth, 98, 99
Banks, Ernie, 172
Bard, Josh, 90
Barfield, Jesse, 125
Barnett, Tony, 21
Barrett, Bill, 223
Bass, Kevin, 189
Bassmaster Classic, 36
Batteaux, Patrick, 241
Baugh, Sammy, 230
Baylor Stadium, Waco, 197, 208

Baylor University, 153; baseball, 100, 156; basketball, men's, 11, 17, 35, 40, 48, 58, 156; basketball, women's, 18–19, 25, 26, 32, 47, 56, 60, 66; equestrian, 76; football, 91, 161, 164, 169, 170, 186, 197, 206–207, 208, 210, 211, 213, 229, 236; softball, *96–97*, 103, 106; tennis, women's, 101; track and field, men's, 89, 95, 143
BCS National Championship Game, 168, 224
Beall, Bryce, 169
Bean, Bubba, 218
Bean, Roy, 36, 245
Beaumont Exporters, 152
Beavers, Dusty, 182
Behrman, Paul, 203
Bellaire High School, Houston, 37, 59
Bellard, Emory, 170, 218
Bellville High School, Bellville, 214
Beltré, Adrián, 183
Bench, Johnny, 138
Benford, Tony, 20
Berg, Patty, 120
Berkman, Lance, 198
Berman, Chris, 132
Berning, Susie Maxwell, 139
Bertelsen, Jim, 186, 226
Bethea, Larry, 10
Beuerlein, Steve, 240

Big Eight Conference, 153
Biggio, Craig, 122, 188
Big 12 Conference: baseball, 90; basketball, men's, 11, 16, 43, 44, 45, 48; basketball, women's, 32, 37, 47, 50; football, 7, 153, 161, 186, 224, 227, 241; formation of, 153, 161; tennis, women's, 101; track and field, men's, 91
Bird, Larry, 64
Birmingham Stallions, 122
Blackman, Rolando, 79
Blakeslee, Sandy, 215
Blalock, Hank, 123
Bliss, Dave, 17
Blowers, Mike, 125
Bluebonnet Bowl, 236
Bobcat Stadium, San Marcos, 72, 209
Boise State University, 195
Boldon, Ato, 143
Bolling, Frank, 129
Bonk, Thomas, 6
Booth, Calvin, 84
Boros, Julius, 136
Bosh, Chris, 47
Boston Braves, 119
Boston Celtics, 40, 97
Boston Red Sox, 1, 131, 156, 189, 190
Boswell, Ken, 133
Bowen, Ray, 212
Bowl Championship Series

(BCS), 195. *See also* BCS National Championship Game; *and specific bowl games*

Bowling Proprietors' Association of America, 69

Boyce, Andy, 167

Boyd, Patrick, 107

Boykin, Trevone, 186

Boyle, Hugh, 193

Bradley, Shawn, 27

Bradshaw, Terry, 14

Branco, 129

Braumüller, Ellen, 141

Brazil (World Cup team), 129

Brees, Drew, 28

Breitenfield, Angie, 228

Briarwood Country Club, Tyler, 77

Brigham Young University (BYU), 167, 195

Bright, Bum, 39

Briles, Art, 229

Brinson, Bianca, 219

British Open. *See* Open Championship, The

Brock High School, Brock, 214

Brooks, Mark, 117

Brooks, Scott, 94

Brooks, Tonna, 76

Broughton Field, Woodway, 157

Brown, Curtis, 199, 201

Brown, James, 227

Brown, Kevin, 110

Brown, Larry, 21

Brownwood High School, Brownwood, 206, 238

Broyles, Frank, 244

Broyles, Marc, 216

Bryan High School, Bryan, 37

Bryant, Kyle, 198

Bryant, Paul "Bear," 181–182, 211, 238

Bubka, Sergey, 20

Buchanan, Olin, 165, 221

Buck, Jennifer, 46

Buffalo Bills, 23, 122

Buffalo Sabres, 1, 117

Bulkeley, Morgan, 15

Bumps, Ryane, 215

Burke, Chris, 188

Burke, Jack, Jr., 67

Burrell, Leroy, 94, 148

Busch, Carrie, 228

Bush, George W., 234

Bush, Homer, 34

Bush, Laura, 234

Bush, Reggie, 168

Byrd, Sam, 133

BYU. *See* Brigham Young University

Calallen High School, Corpus Christi, 235

California Angels, 76, 110, 139. *See also* Los Angeles Angels

California State University, Fullerton, 107

Cameron, Bert, 109

Campbell, Dave, 153, 170, 244

Campbell, Earl, 164, 185, 218

Campbell, Tom, 226

Canion, Whitney, 106

Canyon High School, New Braunfels, 198

Carleton, Tex, 152

Carlisle, Duke, 5

Carlson, Cody, 197

Carlson, Klint, 54

Carnegie Tech University, 212

Carpenter, Chris, 198

Carter, Khrystal, 112

Carter, Michael, 151

Carter, Michelle, 151

Carter, Tweety, 58

Carter High School, Dallas, 167

Caruso, Alex, 54

Catchings, Tamika, 152

Cedar Crest Country Club, Dallas, 203

Cedeño, César, 125, 160

Celina High School, Celina, 206

Centenary College of Louisiana, 30

Champagne, Kelly, 215

Champions Golf Club, Houston, 111, 193

Chapman, Lamar, *225*

Charles, Bob, 136

Charles, Lorenzo, 61

Chase, Darnell, 197

Chicago American Giants, 31

Chicago Bears, 230, 240

Chicago Blackhawks, 74

Chicago Cardinals, 228, 230

Chicago Cubs, 73, 86, 119, 148, 172, 175, 192

Chicago White Sox, 125, 145–146, 154, 156, 188

Ching, Brian, 209

Chisum, Karen, 210

Christian, B. J., 234

Cincinnati Bengals, 9, 236

Cincinnati Reds, 125, 135, 138

Circuit of the Americas, 193

Clark, Dwight, 10

Clark, Earl, 212

Clark, Rod, 209

Clarke, Darren, 134

Clark Field, Austin, 9

Clarksville High School, Clarksville, 48

Cleburne High School, Cleburne, 9

Clemens, Roger, 34, 86, 131

Clemens High School, Schertz, 169

Clement, Chase, 240

Cleveland Browns, 13

Cleveland Indians, 137

Clopton, Montie, 94

Cobb, Trevor, 210

Cobb, Ty, 15

Cobble, Eric, 209

Cobbs, Patrick, 214

Cockrell, Nikki, 93

Cohen, Audra, 101

Colbert, Nate, 138

Cole High School, San Antonio, 48

College Football Playoff National Championship, 11

College of Charleston, 109

College World Series, 33, 102, 105, 107, 109, 113, 121

Colorado Rockies, 122

Colson, Sydney, 64

Colyer, Alex, 100

Conference USA, 153, 169

Connors, Jimmy, 81

Conradt, Jody, 37, 50, 60, 61, 63

Conroe High School, Conroe, 138

Cooper, Cynthia, 161

Copperas Cove High School, Copperas Cove, 91

Copper Bowl, 239

Corbelli, Laurie, 221

Cornwell, Fred, 179

Corsi, Cristiana, 159

Cosby, Quan, 7

Cosell, Howard, 16

Cotton Bowl, Dallas (stadium), 129, 155, 172, 184, 186, 192, 212, 223

Cotton Bowl Classic, 5, 6, 7, 169, 174, 182, 195, 202, 207, 211, 218, 240

Couples, Fred, 77, 80, 134, 196

Cowboys Stadium, Arlington, 9, 27, 165, 174

Cox, J. B., 121

Crabtree, Michael, 166–167, 166, 201

Craig, Roger, 177

Crawford High School, Crawford, 234

Creed, Clifford Ann, 177

Crenshaw, Ben, 73, 106

Crockrom, Danielle, 19

Crosby, Mason, 27

Crosland, Ben, 198

Crow, John David, 153, 230

Cruz, Enrique, 102

Cruz, Jose, 102, 135, 160

Cruz, Nelson, 198

Csonka, Larry, 12, 13

Culwell Center, Garland, 214

Cummings, Pat, 79

Cunningham, Billy, 188

Curry, Marcus, 163

Cy Young Award, 34, 175, 211

Dallas Athletic Club, 134

Dallas Cowboys: Emmitt Smith signs contract with, 171; and fight during training camp, 149–150; and the "Great Trade Robbery," 187; and induction of Bob Lilly in Hall of Fame, 144; losses in the regular season by, 155, 158, 199; in new stadium, in Arlington, 174; in NFC Championship game, 12, 14; in playoffs, 8, 10, 172, 240; and removal of Jimmy Johnson as head coach, 60; and removal of Tom Landry as head coach, 39; and selection of Troy Aikman in the draft, 77; in Super Bowl, 13, 21, 23; victories in the regular season by, 167, 172–173, 179, 224, 233

Dallas Fairgrounds, 219

Dallas Foot Ball Club, 219

Dallas Mavericks, 27, 79, 84, 94, 100, 110, 188, 197

Dallas Stars, 1, 49, 74, 117

Dalton, Andy, 165, 195

Daniel-Meyer Coliseum, Texas Christian University, 30

Darrell K Royal–Texas Memorial Stadium, Austin, 94, 109, 171, 174, 194, 203, 217

Darvish, Yu, 78

Davenport, Dawn, 234

Davey O'Brien Award, 167

Davis, Chili, 110

Davis, Clarissa, 26, 60, *61*

Davis, Danny, 169

Davis, Glenn, 189

Day, Jason, 98

Dayne, Ron, 218

Dean, Dizzy, 130, 152

Deer Park High School, Deer Park, 34

Deike brothers, 154

de la Hoz, Mike, 129

Dellucci, David, 123

Demaret, Jimmy, 25, 67

Dempsey, Clint, 112

Dennehy, Patrick, 17

Dent, Jim, 181

Denver Broncos, 13, 14

Denver Nuggets, 146

Deshaies, Jim, 177

DeShields, Delino, 185

Detmer, Ty, 167

Detroit Lions, 240

Detroit Pistons, 34

Detroit Red Wings, 74

Detroit Tigers, 105

Dickerson, Eric, 194

Dickey, Darrell, 214

Dickinson, Gardner, 193

Didrikson, Babe. *See* Zaharias, Babe Didrikson

Diegel, Leo, 203

Dierker, Larry, 86

Dillard, Jarett, 240

Dillon, Joe, 90

DiMaggio, Joe, 140

Disarcina, Gary, 139

Disneyland Pigskin Classic, 159

Disney/National Car Rental Classic, 196

Ditka, Mike, 13

Dixon, Toren, 240

Dodds, DeLoss, 153

Dodge, Todd, 171

Don Coleman Coliseum, Houston, 37

Dorsett, Tony, 13, 179, 216, 218

Dotel, Octavio, 198

Dotson, Carlton, 17

Dotson, Santana, 170

Douglas, Leland, 197

Dowell's Dolls, 204

Drew, Scott, 17, 58

Drexler, Clyde, 6, 86

Drysdale, Don, 211

Duhon, Brent, 171

Duke, Susan, 231

Duke University, 50, 57, 67

Dunbar High School, Fort Worth, 30

Dunbar High School, Temple, 14

Duncan, Dominique, 112

Duncan, Tim, 90, 114, 120

Duncanville High School, Duncanville, 44

Dunn, LaceDarius, 48, 58

Dunn, Roderick, 216

Durant, Kevin, 40, 94

Duval, David, 116

Dykes, Hart Lee, 224

Dykes, Spike, 239

Dykhuizen, Kyle, 112

Dykstra, Lenny, 189

East Bernard High School, East Bernard, 214

East Carolina University, 169

Eastern Washington University, 167

Elkins, Lawrence, 236

Elliott, Lin, 23, 203

Ellis Field, College Station, 219
Ellisor, John, 182
Emanuel, Bert, 210
England (World Cup team), 112
Engle, Clyde, 190
Erving, Julius "Dr. J," 84
ESPN's *College GameDay*, 201
Everett, Adam, 188
Ewing, Daniel, 37

Fairfield High School, Fairfield, 92
Fair Park Stadium, Abilene, 238
Falk, Bibb, 113, 121
Favre, Brett, 12
Fazio, George, 111
Felix, Allyson, 151
Feliz, Neftalí, 194, 198, 246
Feller, Happy, 186, 226
Ferguson, Lisa, 100
Ferguson, Vagas, 6
Fernández, Gigi, 121
Ferrell Center, Waco, 11, 19, 25, 32
Fielder, Prince, 183
Fields, Jitter, 194
Fiesta Bowl, 7, 195, 227
FIFA Confederations Cup, 112
Final Four, 30, 37, 40, 50, 52, 57, 59, 61, 63, 64, 68. *See also* NCAA Tournament (basketball)
Finley, Michael, 27, 84, 100
Fisher, Derek, 90

Fisk, Carlton, 115
Fitzpatrick, Tim, 164
Fitzsimmons, Bob, 36
Flachmeier, Laurie, 231
Flanigan, Ramon, 198
Florida State University, 107, 112
Flournoy, Harry, 52
Floyd Casey Stadium, Waco, 213
Football Bowl Subdivision, 163
Ford, T. J., 29, 37, 59
Foreman, George, 16, 75, 246
Formula One US Grand Prix, 193
Fort Worth Cats, 130
Fossum, Casey, 107
Foster, Andrew "Rube," 31–32, *31*
Foster, Arian, 9
Fouts Field, Denton, 214
Foyt, A. J., 101
Franchione, Dennis, 241
Francis, Carlos, 178
Frank Erwin Center, Austin, 29, 37, 40, 45, 47, 48
Frank G. Anderson Track and Field Complex, College Station, 95
Franklin, Eric, 202
Franklin, Michael, 94
Frazier, Joe, 16, 246
Freeman, Roger, 178
Freese, David, 198
French Open, 22
Frittelli, Dylan, 106
Fry, Hayden, 239
Furyk, Jim, 134

Gardner, Larry, 190
Gardner, Steve, 209
Garms, Kay, 204–*205*
Garrett, Danielle, 215
Garrido, Augie, 121
Garrison, Zina (also Garrison-Jackson), 121, 127, *127*
Gator Bowl, 230
Georgantas, Ginny, 93
Georgetown High School, Georgetown, 27
Georgetown University, 20, 40, 51, 61
Georgia Tech University, 47
Gervin, George "the Iceman," 84
Getterman Stadium, Waco, 97
Gettys, Reid, 6
Gibson, Bob, 175
Gibson, Megan, 105
Gideon, Blake, 201
Gilchrist, Brent, 74
Gilder, Admon, 54
Gill, Jamie, 203
Gillispie, Billy, 43, 50
Gimenez, Chris, 185
Ginobili, Manu, 22
Ginter, Keith, 90
Givens, Ernest, 238
Glen Garden Country Club, Fort Worth, 70, 111
Globe Life Park, Arlington, 78
Glory Road (2006), 52
Glover, Nehemiah, 183
Goldman, Rob, 146

Gonzaga University, 235
Gonzalez, Juan, 131, 140
Gordon, Jason, 72
Gorum, Kim, 101
Grace, Branden, 118
Graf, Steffi, 121, 127
Graham High School, Graham, 235
Gramática, Martin, 8
Granbury High School, Granbury, 235
Granderson, Curtis, 78
Grand Prairie High School, Grand Prairie, 86
Granger, Jeff, 159, 182
Grant, Marcus, 202
Gratny, Maggie, 76
Graves, Danny, 135
Gray, James, 224
Gray, Jerry, 171
Green, A. C., 27
Green, Caroline, 76
Green, Mike, 84
Green, Pat, 194
Green, Robert, 112
Green, Terence, 216
Green Bay Packers, 12, 27
Greenberg, Hank, 140
Greene, Joe, 14
Greene, Johnny, 206
Greer, Rusty, 139
Gregson, Malcolm, 193
Gribble, Cody, 106
Griese, Bob, 13, 144

Griffin, Robert, III, 91, 229
Griner, Brittney, 25, 32, 45
G. Rollie White Coliseum, College Station, 221
GTE Byron Nelson Classic, 95
Guillén, Ozzie, 125
Guldahl, Ralph, 25, 63, 67
Gundy, Mike, 224
Gustafson, Cliff, 113
Gutierrez, Eric, 33
Gutierrez, Ricky, 86
Gwynn, Tony, 135

Haddad, Aminah, 107
Hagen, Walter, 203
Haley, Charles, 167
Haley, Jack, 34
Halliburton, Suzanne, 137
Ham, Darvin, 51
Hamels, Cole, 183
Hamilton, Josh, 132, 183
Hamilton, Lewis, 193
Hanna, Steve, 109
Hanspard, Byron, 239
Harper, Alvin, 23, 167, 187
Harper, Jim, 170
Harrah, Toby, 154
Harrell, Graham, 166, 168, 201
Harris, Phil, 5
Hart, Dick, 134
Hašek, Dominik, 117
Haskins, Don, 52
Hassey, Ron, 156
Hawaii Bowl, 237

Hawkins, Andy, 125
Hawkins, Ari, 103
Hayes, "Bullet Bob," 172
Hayes, Elvin, 15, 30, 52, 188, *189*
Haymon, Desmond, 55
Haynie, Sandra, 155, 177
Hays, Todd, 39
Heaps, Jay, 209
Heard, Jerrod, 186
Heart O' Texas Coliseum, Waco, 35; Fair Complex, 76
Heck, Chris, 107
Heisman Trophy, 5, 168, 171, 224; Earl Campbell wins, 185, 218; John David Crow wins, 230; Ty Detmer wins, 167; Robert Griffin III wins, 229; Johnny Manziel wins, 7, 207; Andre Ware wins, 223
Henderson, Rickey, 156
Hershiser, Orel, 211
Hicks, David, 206
Higgins, Johnnie Lee, 168
Highland Park High School, Dallas, 211
Hill, Bobby Joe, 52
Hill, Calvin, 67
Hill, Grant, 67
Hill, Jerry, 170
Hill, King, 211
Hill, Thomas, 67
Hill, Tony, 233
Hillsboro Hill School, 238
Hofheinz Pavilion, Houston, 188

Hogan, Ben, 67, 70, *111*, 118,
128, 130, 158; in automobile
accident, 25; wins the Open
Championship, 130; wins
the PGA Championship, 158;
wins the Ryder Cup as part
of US team, 193; wins the US
Open, 111
Hogan, Valerie, 25
Hokkaido Nippon-Ham Fighters,
78
Holcomb, Steven, 39
Holl, Holly, 106
Holmes, Jonathan, 16
Holmes, Priest, 227
Holyfield, Evander, 75
Honey, Gary, 147
Hooton, Burt, 73
Horner, Durward, 212
Hornsby, Rogers, 119, 130
House, Danuel, 54
Houston Astros, *3*, 86, 115, 123,
125, 129, 133, 135, 160, 177,
189; Craig Biggio gets 3,000th
hit of his career for, 122;
first game of, in Astrodome,
68; first triple play in team
history by, 133; selection of
Lance Berkman by, 105; team
name changed to, 33; as wild
card team, 183; in the World
Series, 188
Houston Buffaloes, 152
Houston Colt .45s, 33

Houston Comets, 161
Houston Cougars, 15, 169, 188
Houston Dynamos, 209
Houston Fat Stock Show (now
Houston Livestock Show and
Rodeo), 81
Houston Gamblers, 122
Houston Heights High School,
Houston, 9
Houston Livestock Show and
Rodeo, 81
Houston Oilers, 158, 164, 179,
236, 238
Houston Open (golf), 80
Houston Rockets, 40, 86, 97, 119,
146, 188, 197
Houston Texans, 9, 158, 236
Howard, Frank, 76
Howard, Juwan, 67
Howell, Jack, 86
Howell, Lenzie, 57
Howell, Tran, 112
HP Byron Nelson Champion-
ship, 98
Hudler, Rex, 139
Huewitt, Ken, 209
Hughes, Robert, 30
Hull, Brett, 1, 117
Humber, Philip, 102
Hurst L. D. Bell High School,
Hurst, 44
Hutcherson, Claude, 204

IAAF World Championships, 149

Independence Bowl, 239
Indiana Pacers, 146
Indiana University, 56
Indianapolis Colts, 28
Indianapolis 500, 101
International Cycling Union,
191
Iowa State University, 19, 186
Ireland, Jeff, 170
Irvin, Michael, 12, 21, 77, 167
Italy (World Cup team), 129
Iverson, Allen, 51
Ivey, Royal, 29

Jacklin, Tony, 131
Jackson, Bo, 171
Jackson, Ray, 67
James, Craig, 194
James, LeBron, 110
Jameson, Betty, 120
Jang Ji-won, 159
Jarrett, Tanya, 107
Jeffrey, Neal, 206
Jeffries, Jim, 126
Jennings, Bubba, 20
Jerrells, Curtis, 17, 48
Jesperson, Paul, 54
Jeter, Derek, 1
Joe, J. J., 213
Johnson, Andre, 9
Johnson, Avery, 92
Johnson, Ban, 15
Johnson, Butch, 13
Johnson, Dustin, 118

Johnson, Jack "the Galveston Giant," 126
Johnson, Jimmy, 14, 39, 60, 245–246
Johnson, Lady Bird, 68
Johnson, Lance, 125
Johnson, Lyndon B., 68
Johnson, Magic, 31
Johnson, Michael, 95, 143, 149
Johnson, Randy, 156
Johnson, Shawn, 153
Johnson, Vinnie "the Microwave," 35
Johnson, Walter, 15
John Tyler High School, Tyler, 216
Jones, A. J. "Jam," 237
Jones, Alton, 36
Jones, Bobby, 130
Jones, Cleon, 133
Jones, Ed "Too Tall," 10
Jones, Felix, 10
Jones, Jalen, 45
Jones, Jerry, 10, 39, 60, 174, 240
Jones, Johnny "Ham," 237
Jones, Johnny "Lam," 237
Jones, Julius, 8
Jones, June, 237
Jones, Rosie, 136
Jones Stadium, Lubbock, 201

Kaepernick, Colin, 166, 237
Kalliomäki, Antti, 138
Kansas City Chiefs, 238
Kansas City Royals, 154, 183, 192

Kansas State University, 16, 161, 186, 224
Karolyi, Bela, 144
Karolyi, Marta, 144
Keenum, Case, 169
Kelly, Jim, 122
Kennedy, Malcome, 207
Kenon, Larry, 84
Kent, Phillip, 206
Kentucky Derby, 87
Kershaw, Clayton, 211
Kettler, Elwood, 181–182
Kidd, Jason, 110
Kimbrough, Rick, 170
King, Jimmy, 67
King High School, Corpus Christi, 73
Kingsbury, Kliff, 183
Kinsler, Ian, 115
Kipyego, Sally, 84–85, *85*
Kirk, Peggy, 120
Kirkland, Krista, 46, 57, 64
Kirsch, Adam, 109
Kite, Tom, 106, 117
Klingler, David, 202
Knight, Bob, 56
Kostadinova, Stefka, 179
Koufax, Sandy, 211
Kruse, Alyssa, 214
Kuehne, Hank, 80
Kunz, Annie, 219
Kusek, Joe, 232
Kyle Field, College Station, 170, 182, 183, 218

Labat, Florencia, 121
Labruzzo, Joe, 236
Ladies Professional Golf Association (LPGA), 91, 98, 139
LaFrentz, Raef, 11
Lajoie, Nap, 15
Lamar University, 46
Lancaster, Jim, 89
Lancaster High School, Lancaster, 67
Landreth, Jason, 90
Landrith, Robin, 103
Landry, Tom, 10, 13, 39, *173*
Langenbrunner, Jamie, 74
Lanier, Hal, 189
Lanier High School, San Antonio, 47
Lantz, Stu, 188
Lattin, David, 52
Laughlin, Tracy, 215
Laver, Rod, 126
Law, Acie, 43, 50
LBJ High School, Austin, 165
Leach, Bobby, 194
Leavell, Allen, 97
Lehman, Teddy, 184
Lehtinen, Jere, 74
Leonard, Justin, 99, 134
Leopold, Trina, 215
Leslie, Lisa, 57
Lester, Danny, 226
Levelland High School, Levelland, 43
Lewis, Carl, 147, *147*

Lewis, Derek, 227
Lewis, Duffy, 190
Lewis, Guy, 15
Lewis, Ira, 32
Lewis, JaQuan, 55
Leyritz, Jim, 125
Liberty Bowl, 170, 197, 218
Lidge, Brad, 188
Lilly, Bob "Mr. Cowboy," 144
Li Na, 176
Lincoln High School, Dallas, 47
Lincoln High School, Port
    Arthur, 8
Linex, Courtney, 215
Little League Softball World
    Series, 157, 246
Liukin, Nastia, 153
Liukin, Valeri, 153
Livestrong Foundation, 191
Lloyd, Graeme, 34
Lone Star Conference, 209
Long, Dustin, 183
Longley, Clint, 149–150
Los Angeles Angels, 183. *See also*
    California Angels
Los Angeles Dodgers, 160, 175,
    211
Los Angeles Lakers, 31, 79, 90,
    92, 97
Los Angeles Open, 111
Los Angeles Rams, 233
Louisiana State University
    (LSU), 63, 97, 197, 236
Love, Davis, III, 73

LPGA. *See* Ladies Professional
    Golf Association
LPGA Championship, 139, 177
LSU. *See* Louisiana State
    University
Lubbock Municipal Coliseum, 20
Lucas, Porscha, 112
Luck, Andrew, 229
Lu Liang-Huan, 128
Lunke, Hilary, 128
Lynn, Lance, 198
Lyons, Ted, 156

Mack, Connie, 15
Mackovic, John, 227
Maddon, Joe, 175
Maddux, Greg, 148
Maher, Peter, 36
Mahomes, Patrick, 186
Major League Baseball (MLB):
    and definition of no-hitter,
    125; draft, 105; Home Run
    Derby, 132, 246. *See also*
    All-Star Game (baseball);
    Cy Young Award; National
    Baseball Hall of Fame; World
    Series (baseball); *and specific
    teams*
Major League Soccer Cup, 209
Maleeva, Manuela, 176
Maler, Melissa, 97
Malone, Karl, 31
Mangrum, Lloyd, 25, 111
Mann, Carol, 139

Manning, Eli, 178
Mansfield Legacy High School,
    Mansfield, 192
Mansfield Summit High School,
    Arlington, 45
Mantle, Mickey, 68
Manyweather, Anthony, 203
Manziel, Johnny, 7, 207
Marino, Dan, 195
Maroul, David, 121
Marsh, Michael, 148
Martin, Harvey, 13
Martin, Kelvin, 167
Martinez, Conchita, 121
Masters Tournament, 63, 67, 70,
    73, 77, 116, 130, 131, 133, 158
Mathewson, Christy, 15, 190
Matson, Randy, *88*, 89
Matulich, Joe, 178
Mayberry, Lee, 57
Mayo, Gabby, 112
Mays, Travis, 57
Mays, Willie, 138
McBath, Mark, 237
McBride, Justin, 204
McClain, John, 169
McClellan, Mike, 238
McCloy, Laura, 215
McCoy, Colt, 7, 199
McCray, Rodney, 97
McCulloch, Kyle, 121
McDowell, Oddibe, 137
McEnroe, John, 81
McGee, Vondrell, 201

McGraw, John, 15
McGruder, Kim, 107
McIlhenny, Lance, 194
McKinley, Chuck, 126
McNair, Steve, 236
McNeese State University, 102
McNeil, Lori, 121
Meadows, Sandra, 44
Medwick, Joe "Ducky," 152
Memorial Stadium. *See* Darrell
    K Royal–Texas Memorial
    Stadium, Austin
Memphis Grizzlies, 47
Mench, Kevin, 123
Mendez, Carlos, 206
Menke, Denis, 133
Meredith, "Dandy" Don, 172–173
Merkle, Fred, 190
Mesler, Steve, 39
Metzger, Roger, 133
Meyers, Chief, 190
Miami Dolphins, 12, 13, 144, 158
Miami Heat, 110
Micheaux, Larry, 6
Michigan State University, 59,
    66, 235
Mickelson, Phil, 70, 116
Middle Tennessee State Univer-
    sity, 214
Midway All-Stars, 157, *157*, 246
Midway High School, Waco, 125,
    235
Mike A. Myers Stadium, Austin,
    91

Miller, Bryan, 112
Miller, Cheryl, 60
Miller, Harry, 11
Milwaukee Brewers, 69, 175
Minnesota North Stars, 74
Minnesota Timberwolves, 92
Minnesota Twins, 132, 154
Minnesota Vikings, 10, 187
Mitchell, Basil, 241
Mitchell, Dennis, 148
Mkrtchyan, Margarita, 159
MLB. *See* Major League Baseball
Moceanu, Dominique, 144
Modano, Mike, 49
Monahans High School,
    Monahans, 214
Monceaux, Ashley, 100
Monday Night Football, 167
Montana, Joe, 6, 10
Montreal Expos, 135
Moody Coliseum, University
    Park, 79, 176
Moon, Warren, 179, 238
Moore, G. A., 206
Moore, Glenn, 97, 103
Moore, Lenny, 155
Moorer, Michael, 75
Moreland, Mitch, 183
Morgan, Gil, 117
Morgan, Jeremy, 54
Morgan, Joe, 129, 132, 138
Morgan, Sheila, 221
Morneau, Justin, 132
Morris, Bam, 21

Morris, Eric, 166
Morrow, Macie, 105
Muecke, Tom, 197
Mulkey, Kim, *18*, 19, 32, 56, 66
Murphy, Dale, 135
Murphy, Daniel, 192
Murphy, David, 115
Murphy, Lee, 234
Musburger, Brent, 218, 227
Myers, Gerald, 20

Napier, Shabazz, 68
NASCAR, 101
Nash, Steve, 27, 84, 100
Nashville Business College, 204
Natale, Liz, 215
National Baseball Congress
    World Series, 154
National Baseball Hall of Fame,
    15, 156, 172, 190
National Basketball Associa-
    tion (NBA): All-Star Game,
    31; championship title, 40,
    86, 92; draft, 30, 40, 47, 120;
    expansion of, 188; Finals,
    97, 110, 114, 119; lockout, 27;
    merger of, with American
    Basketball Association, 146;
    scoring leader, 84; Slam Dunk
    Contest, 28. *See also specific
    teams*
National Collegiate Athletic
    Association (NCAA):
    records, 38, 84–85, 99, 199,

202, 213, 216, 218; sanctions by, 17, 163, 198. *See also specific tournaments and championships*
National Finals Rodeo, 232, 246
National Football League (NFL): Championship game, 172, 230; draft, 9, 77, 78, 228, 230; welcomes USFL players, 122. *See also* AFC playoffs/championship; NFC playoffs/championship; Super Bowl; *and specific teams*
National Hockey League (NHL), 49. *See also specific teams*
National Invitational Tournament, 43, 48
National League Championship Series, 177, 188, 192
National League Division Series, 160
National Soccer Hall of Fame, 160
Navratilova, Martina, 127, 176
Navy (football team), 5, 210, 211
NBA. *See* National Basketball Association
NCAA. *See* National Collegiate Athletic Association
NCAA Division I cross country national championship, 215
NCAA Men's Outdoor Track & Field Championship, 109, 112–113, 138

NCAA national championship (golf), 106
NCAA national championship (tennis), 101
NCAA Tournament (baseball), 102, 107. *See also* College World Series
NCAA Tournament (basketball): men's, 16, 40, 43, 44, 46, 48, 50, 51, 52, 54, 55, 56, 57, 58, 59, 64, 67, 68, 235; women's, 25, 37, 46, 47, 50, 56, 57, 60, 63, 64, 66. *See also* Final Four
NCAA Tournament (softball), 72, 93, 96–97. *See also* Women's College World Series
NCAA Tournament (volleyball), 221, 228, 234
NCAA Women's College Cup (soccer), 215, 219
NCAA Women's Outdoor Track & Field Championship, 107, 112–113
Negro National League, 31–32
Neiland, Larisa, 121
Nelson, Byron, 67, 70, *71*, 133
Nelson, Dave, 76
Nelson Field, Austin, 165
Neslony, Tyler, 109
Netherlands (World Cup team), 129
Neuerburg, Nicole, 72
New England Revolution, 209
Newhouse, Robert, 13

New Jersey Devils, 74
New Jersey Nets, 100, 114
New Orleans Bowl, 214
New Orleans Saints, 28
New York Giants (baseball), 119, 190
New York Giants (football), 78, 172, 174, 177
New York Jets, 238
New York Knicks, 92, 119
New York Liberty, 161
New York Mets, 33, 133, 135, 177, 189, 192
New York Nets, 146
New York Yankees, 1, 34, 68, 78, 125, 140, 183, 194
NFC playoffs/championship, 8, 10, 12, 14, 233, 240
NFL. *See* National Football League
NHL. *See* National Hockey League
Nicklaus, Jack, 67, 115, 118, 131, 134, 196
Nicols, Stacie, 234
Nieuwendyk, Joe, 74
Niittymaki, Antero, 49
Nike, 191
Nimitz High School, Houston, 45
Nimphius, Kurt, 79
Norman, Greg, 134
North Carolina State University, 61, 215
Northern Illinois University, 33

North Texas State University, 14, 164
Northwestern State University, 209
Northwestern University, 101
Norton, Ken, 14
Novacek, Jay, 21, 240
Nowitzki, Dirk, 27, 84, 94, 100, 110
NRG Stadium, Houston, 59, 81
Nyambui, Suleiman, *108*–109

Oakland Athletics, 156
Oana, Hank, 130
Oates, Johnny, 140
O'Brien, Davey, 212, 228
O'Brien, Larry, 119
Odessa High School, Odessa, 239
O'Donnell, Neil, 21
Odor, Rougned, 185
O. D. Wyatt High School, Fort Worth, 94
Ohio State University, 6, 7, 11, 64, 168
Ohl, Cody, 232, 246
Ohlendorf, Ross, 185
Okafor, Emeka, 37, 59
Oklahoma City Thunder, 90, 94
Oklahoma State University, 169, 178, 199, 224
Olajuwon, Hakeem, 6, 34, 40, *41*, 61, 86, 119, 197
Olazábal, José María, 116
Oliver, Ed, 158

Oliver, Justin, 112–113
Olsen, Justin, 39
Olsen, Pat, 107
Olson, Billy, 20
Olympics, 127; 1932 (Los Angeles), 141; 1964 (Tokyo), 89; 1968 (Mexico City), 89; 1976 (Montreal), 138; 1980 (Moscow), 20, 138; 1984 (Los Angeles), 20, 144, 147, 151; 1988 (Calgary), 20; 1988 (Seoul), 127, 179; 1992 (Barcelona), 148; 1996 (Atlanta), 143, 148, 160; 2000 (Sydney), 92, 176; 2002 (Salt Lake City), 39; 2004 (Athens), 140, 152, 159; 2008 (Beijing), 151, 152; 2010 (Vancouver), 39; 2012 (London), 85, 140, 150, 151; 2016 (Rio de Janeiro), 149, 151
O'Neal, Shaquille, 48, 246
Onstad, Pat, 209
Open Championship, The, 73, 118, 128, 130, 131, 133, 134, 158
Orange Bowl, 6
Oregon State University, 165
Orlando Magic, 48, 86
Ormsby, Serena, 72
Orosco, Jesse, 189
Osterman, Cat, 38, *38*
Oswalt, Roy, 188
Overbeck, Carla, 160
Owens, Terrell, 8

Ownby Stadium, Dallas, 164
Ozen High School, Beaumont, 30, 47

Pacific-10 Conference, 153
Padron, Kyle, 237
Pagliarulo, Mike, 131
Palmeiro, Rafael, 83
Palmer, Arnold, 67, 118, 136, 193
Palmer, Jordan, 168
Parcells, Bill, 8
Pardee, Jack, 181–182
Parker, Jacob, 55
Parker, Sirr, 224, *225*
Parnevik, Jesper, 134
Pat Olsen Field, College Station, 107
Patterson, Angel, 107
Patterson, Gary, 165, 195
Patterson, Steve, 59
Pearson, Drew, 14, 149–150
Pecan Valley Golf Club, San Antonio, 136
Penick, Harvey, 73, 181
Pennsylvania State University, 48, 207, 219
Pepperdine University, 109
Perkins, Jia, 235
Perkins, Kendrick, 47
Perry, Charles, 197
Perry, Kenny, 99
Perry, Nanceen, 2, 92, 107
Peschel, Randy, 226
Pettitte, Andy, 34

Pflugerville High School, Pflugerville, 45
PGA. *See* Professional Golf Association
PGA Championship, 70, 73, 95, 118, 133, 134, 136, 158, 177, 196, 203
Philadelphia 76ers, 84, 188
Philadelphia Eagles, 10, 228
Philadelphia Flyers, 49
Philadelphia Phillies, 73, 160, 172
Phillips, Eddie, 174
Phillips, Gene, 35
Phillips, John, 10
Phillips, Wade, 10, 174
Phoenix Mercury, 161
Phoenix Suns, 22
Pierson, John, 183
Pierson, Plenette, 35
Pillar, Kevin, 185
Pilot Point High School, Pilot Point, 206
Pittsburgh Pirates, 119, 175
Pittsburgh Steelers, 14, 21, 27, 164, 195
Pizza Hut Park, Frisco, 209
Plains High School, Plains, 214
Plano East Senior High School, Plano, 175, 192, 216
Pole Vault Hall of Fame, 138
Polonia, Luis, 110
Polytechnic High School, Fort Worth, 30
Portland Trail Blazers, 92

Poth High School, Poth, 214
Presidents' Trophy (hockey), 74
Price, David, 1
Price, Duane, 90
Professional Bull Riders, 204
Professional Golf Association (PGA), 73, 77, 80, 95, 111, 114–115, 130, 196. *See also* PGA Championship
Professional Women's Bowling Association, 69
Pro Football Hall of Fame, 28, 78, 144
Pujols, Albert, 198
Pullig, Corey, 184
Punto, Nick, 198
Purdue University, 57

Rader, Doug, 133
Radinsky, Scott, 125
Randall, Keith, 208
Randle, Len, 76
Rawls, Betsy, 120, 139, 181
Rawson, Tana, 76
Reckling Park, Houston, 102
Redin, Harley, 204
Red Oak High School, Red Oak, 151
Red River Showdown, 184, 192
Redstone Golf Club, Houston (now Golf Club of Houston), 80
Reed Arena, College Station, 45
Reeves, Dan, 149, 172

Reichenbach, Mickey, 113
Reid, Suziann, 107
Reis, Matt, 209
Reliant Stadium, Houston, 12, 58, 68, 158
Retton, Mary Lou, 144
Reunion Arena, Dallas, 28, 46, 50, 57, 74, 79, 81, 117
Reynolds, Butch, 149
Rhodes, Arthur, 198
Rice, Jerry, 238
Rice Field, Houston, 212
Rice Stadium, Houston, 12, 210, 211, 223, 236
Rice University, 153; baseball, 102, 105; basketball, men's, 21; football, 164, 206, 210, 211, 212, 223, 230, 240; track and field, men's, 138
Richards, Golden, 13
Richardson, Darrell, 210
Richardson, Nolan, 57
Richardson, Trent, 229
Richardson High School, Richardson, 160
Richards-Ross, Sanya, *150*, 151
Richey, Nancy, 22
Ritchie, Natalie, 35
Ritter, Louise, 179
Robbins, Kelly, 128
Roberts, Dave, 138
Robertson, Alvin, 34
Robertson Stadium, Houston, 163

Robin, Brett, 184
Robinson, David, 34, 92, 114, 120
Robinson, Frank, 138
Robinson, Jamal, 169
Robinson, Zac, 169, 199
Rochester International, 136
Roddick, Andy, 80
Rodgers, Aaron, 27
Rodriguez, Alex, 78, 194
Rodríguez, Iván "Pudge," 115, 131
Rogers, Kenny, 139
Rogers, Kevin, 17
Romo, Tony, 8, 10
Rose, Jalen, 67
Rose, Justin, 70
Rose Bowl, 6, 165
Ross, Aaron, 151
Rote, Kyle, 199, 223, 239
Royal, Darrell, 5, 175, 186
Russell, Bill, 29
Russell, Jeff, 131
Russell, Seth, 186
Ruth, Babe, 15
Ryan, Amanda, 76
Ryan, Nolan, 2, *2–3*, 83, 86, 133, 145–146, *145*, 156, 177
Ryder Cup, 111, 193, 196

Sabbatini, Rory, 99
Saint Mary's University, 57
Salido, Mike, 167
Sam Houston Hall, Houston, 81
Sam Houston State University, 57

Sampras, Pete, 80
Sampson, Ralph, 97, 197
San Antonio Spurs, 22; draft Tim Duncan, 120; join the NBA, 146; as NBA champions, 114, 188; in the playoffs, 84, 90, 92, 100
Sance, Demetria, 228
Sanchez Vicario, Arantxa, 121
Sanders, Barry, 224
San Diego Chargers, 150
San Diego Padres, 135, 138
San Diego Rockets, 30
Sands, Tony, 213
San Francisco 49ers, 10, 14, 151, 238
San Francisco Giants, 148, 177, 194
Sangster, Mike, 126
San Jacinto College, 34
Santleben, Dana, 221
Sarazen, Gene, 130
Sasser, Jason, 51
Scarborough, Steve, 107
Schelfhout, Sue, 234
Schorp, Greg, 159
Schramm, Tex, 39
Schreiber, Heather, 50, 63
Schweitzer, Annie, 215
Scott, Byron, 97
Scott, Mike, 177
Seattle Seahawks, 8
Seattle SuperSonics, 27, 40, 79
Seay, Alicia, 45

SEC. *See* Southeastern Conference
Seles, Monica, 127
Self, Bill, 44
Septién, Rafael, 233
Sharp, Marsha, 35, 49
Sherman, Ed, 167
Sherrill, Jackie, 202
Shipman, David, 170
Shoemaker, Willie, 87, *87*
Shortridge, Kirsten, 100
Shula, Don, 12
Sierra, Ruben, 83, 110
Sims, Odyssey, 25, 32, 47
Simms, Chris, 184
Singletary, Mike, 208, *208*
Skinner, Brian, 11
Sloan, Jerry, 86
Sluman, Jeff, 117
Slusarski, Tadeusz, 138
Smith, Andrew, 214
Smith, Anne, 176
Smith, Billy, 160
Smith, Emmitt, 12, 14, 21, 77, 167, 171, 187, 240
Smith, Kevin, 14
Smith, Russell, 209
Smith, Sarah, 103
Smoak, Justin, 185
SMU. *See* Southern Methodist University
Snead, Sam, 63, 111, 136
Sneva, Tom, 101
Songer, Don, 119

Sörenstam, Annika, 98, 128
Soriano, Alfonso, 123
Sosa, Sammy, 125
Southeastern Conference (SEC), 7, 45, 153
Southern Methodist University (SMU): basketball, men's, 20, 35, 46, 52; football, 151, 153, 163–164, 194–195, 198, 199, 201, 206, 212, 223, 237; golf, men's, 80, 116; soccer, women's, 215
Southland Conference, 163
Southwest Conference (SWC), 244; basketball, men's, 20, 40, 45, 49, 52, 57, 64; basketball, women's, 26, 35, 37, 46, 49; disbanding of, 153; football, 5, 169, 170, 182, 197, 198, 199, 202, 207, 211, 212, 218, 223, 228, 239; golf, men's, 77, 196; soccer, women's, 215; track and field, men's, 89, 95; volleyball, 228
Southwestern Athletic Conference (SWAC), 235
Southwest High School, San Antonio, 167
Southwest Texas State University. See Texas State University
Speaker, Tris, 15, 190, *190*
Speyrer, Charles "Cotton," 186
Spieth, Jordan, 70, 98, 106, 118

Spittler, Kelsey, 105
Springs, Ron, 233
Spring Woods High School, Houston, 34
Stallings, Gene, 182
Stamford High School, Stamford, 238
Stanczak brothers, 154
Stanford, Angela, 128
Stanford University, 64, 102, 159, 228, 229
Stanley Cup Finals, 1, 49, 74, 117
Stargell, Willie, 138
Staskus, Tim, 209
state championship, Texas high school football, 9, 239; Class 2A, 234, 238; Class 4A, 30, 47; Class 5A, 37, 216
state championship, Texas high school men's basketball: Class 3A, 38
state championship, Texas high school women's basketball: Class 1A, 43; Class 2A, 43; Class 3A, 43; Class 4A, 43; Class 5A, 43, 44, 45
Staubach, Roger, 5, 13, 149, 233
Stearns, Heather, 103
Stephen F. Austin State University, 55
Stephens, Stacy, 50, 63
Stewart, Branndon, 224
Stewart, Payne, 77, 116, 196
St. John's University, 20

St. Louis Blues, 74
St. Louis Browns, 119
St. Louis Cardinals, 119, 152, 175, 188, 198
Stockton, John, 31
Stolle, Fred, 126
Stowers, Carlton, 154
Strait, Robert, 210
Strawberry, Darryl, 135, 189
Street, James, 174, 178, 186, 226
Strug, Kerri, 144
Sugar Bowl, 6, 175, 212, 224
Sukkhongdumnoen, Nootcharin, 159
Sumlin, Kevin, 169, 207
Sun Belt Conference, 214
Sun Bowl, 213, 237, 240
Sundberg, Jim, 154
Super Bowl, 10, 60, 77, 122, 144, 167, 171, 172, 187, 240; Drew Brees plays in, 28; Dallas Cowboys lose, 14; Dallas Cowboys win, 13, 21, 23; played in Texas, 12, 27. *See also* AFC playoffs/championship; NFC playoffs/championship
Swann, Lynn, 14
SWC. *See* Southwest Conference
Sweed, Limas, 168
Switzer, Barry, 60, 185
Swoopes, Sheryl, 49, 57, 64, *65*, 152
Swoopes, Tyrone, 186
Symons, B. J., 178

Syndergaard, Noah, 192
Syracuse University, 50, 59, 63
Szabo, Ecaterina, 144

Tadlock, Tim, 33
Tascosa High School, Amarillo, 43
Taveras, Willy, 122
Tawater, Jad, 234
Taylor, Isaiah, 16
Taylor, Loyd, 211
TCU. *See* Texas Christian University
Teaff, Grant, 170, 197, 208, 213
Team USA (men's World Cup team), 112
Team USA (women's World Cup team), 160
Teixeira, Mark, 123
Terry, Jason, 110
Texas A&M University, 153; baseball, 90, 107; basketball, men's, 17, 40, 43, 45, 46, 50, 54, 64, 89; basketball, women's, 32, 47, 60; bonfire, 212; equestrian, 76; football, 7, 159, 161, 170, 181–182, 183, 184, 198, 202, 207, 211, 217–218, 219, 224–225, 230, 238, 246; softball, 99, 105; track and field, men's, 89, 112–113; track and field, women's, 112–113; volleyball, 221
Texas Bowl, 240

Texas Christian University (TCU), 212, 213; baseball, 109, 175, 192; basketball, men's, 30, 35; football, 21, 153, 165, 186, 195, 197, 202, 211, 212, 213, 228, 230, 241; golf, women's, 128
Texas Cowboy Hall of Fame, 204
Texas Football magazine, 153
Texas League, 130, 152
Texas Lutheran College, 231, *231*
Texas Rangers, 78, 110, 131, 132, 140, 154; in the American League Division Series, 185; clinch the American League West, 183; and the famous brawl, 145–146; and first home game at Arlington Stadium, 76; hit eight home runs in a game, 123; Oddibe McDowell hits for the cycle for, 137; and opening of The Ballpark, Arlington, 69; Iván Rodríguez sets catching record for, 115; Kenny Rogers throws a perfect game for, 139; and Nolan Ryan's 5,000th strikeout, 156; Nolan Ryan throws no-hitter for, 83; in the World Series, 194, 198
Texas Southern University, 78, 235
Texas Sports Hall of Fame, 44, 144

Texas Stadium, Irving, 12, 149, 167
Texas State University, 72, 163, 209, 210
Texas Tech University, 153; baseball, 33, 90, 109; basketball, men's, 20, 44, 46, 51, 56; basketball, women's, 35, 37, 46, 49, 50, 57, 60, 64–65, 152, 235; football, 11, 21, 23, 161, 163, 166–167, 168, 169, 178, 181, 183, 184, 186, 201, 203, 206, 224, 239; track and field, women's, 85
Texas Western College, 52–53
Texas Woman's University, 179
Theismann, Joe, 233
Thomas, Chris, 235
Thomas, Dave, 193
Thomas, Dyral, 169
Thomas, Earl, 199
Thomas, James, 29
Thomas, Pat, 170
Thomas, Terrence, 214
Thomas, Zach, 184
Thomas Jefferson High School, Dallas, 151
Thomas Jefferson High School, San Antonio, 239
Thompson, Ricky, 206
Thorp, Greg, 182
Thumann, Kaitlyn, 103
Thurmond, Nate, 34
Toepperwein, Adolph, 232, 245

Toepperwein, Elizabeth "Plinky,"
232
Tomasevicz, Curtis, 39
Tomjanovich, Rudy, 188
Tomlinson, LaDainian, 165, 213,
241
Tomme, Jennie, 72
Toronto Blue Jays, 34, 83, 154,
183, 185
Toronto Raptors, 47
Torre, Joe, 129
Tour de France, 137, 191
TPC (Tournament Players
Course) Las Colinas, 98
Treece, Robert, 183
Trevino, Lee, 114–115, 128, 131
Trinity University, 126
Triple Crown, 87
Trlica, Alex, 168
Trotter, DeeDee, 151
Troy University, 210
Truitt, Steven, 107
Trull, Don, 236
Tulia High School, Tulia, 43
Tulowitzki, Troy, 185
Turner, Lesley, 22
Turnesa, Joe, 203
Tynes, Lawrence, 174

UCLA. See University of
California, Los Angeles
Udoh, Ekpe, 58
UIL. See University
Interscholastic League

UIL Football State Champion-
ship, 239
UIL Track & Field Champion-
ships, 91, 92, 94
Unitas, Johnny, 155
United Spirit Arena, Lubbock,
44, 56
United States Bowling Congress
Hall of Fame, 69
United States Football League
(USFL), 122
United Virginia Bank Classic, 91
University High School, Waco,
165
University Interscholastic
League (UIL), 9, 26
University of Alabama, 6, 106,
207, 229, 240
University of Arizona, 72, 213, 235
University of Arkansas, 21, 26,
46, 49, 57, 121, 153, 170, 174,
195, 197, 201, 208, 218, 223,
226, 244
University of California,
Berkeley, 174
University of California, Los
Angeles (UCLA), 15, 30, 52,
55, 59, 77, 99, 107, 109, 174
University of California,
Riverside, 231
University of Cincinnati, 214
University of Colorado, 29, 170
University of Connecticut, 47, 50,
59, 63, 68, 164

University of Florida, 56, 103,
112, 121, 228
University of Georgia, 57, 175,
181–182
University of Hawaii, 234
University of Houston: baseball,
109; basketball, men's, 6,
30, 40, 46, 52, 57, 61, 86, 102;
conference membership of,
153; football, 163, 169, 174,
202, 210, 223; golf, men's,
80; track and field, men's, 95,
147, 148
University of Illinois, 97
University of Kansas, 11, 44, 48,
186, 213, 229
University of Kentucky, 45, 50,
52, 68, 103
University of Maryland, 169, 237
University of Memphis, 50
University of Miami, 109, 167
University of Michigan, 6, 67,
93, 100
University of Mississippi, 121,
170, 175, 178
University of Missouri, 48, 106,
161
University of Nebraska, 93, 227,
228
University of Nevada–Las Vegas,
38
University of Nevada–Reno, 166,
237
University of New Mexico, 198

University of North Carolina, 51, 59, 97
University of Northern Iowa, 54
University of North Texas (UNT), 214
University of Notre Dame, 6, 25, 47, 64, 174, 182, 223
University of Oklahoma, 6, 7, 35, 184, 185, 186–187, 192, 229, 246
University of Oregon, 11, 112
University of Portland, 215
University of South Carolina, 76, 113
University of Southern California (USC), 57, 60, 168, 170, 240
University of South Florida, 93
University of Tennessee, 230
University of Texas, 153; baseball, 34, 73, 109, 113, 121; basketball, men's, 16, 29, 35, 40, 43, 57, 59, 94; basketball, women's, 26, 37, 46, 49, 50, 60, 63, 64; cross country, women's, 215; football, 5, 6, 7, 161, 168, 170, 171, 174, 175, 178, 184, 185, 186–187, 192, 194–195, 199, 201, 202, 203, 206, 213, 217–218, 219, 226, 227, 230, 237, 246; golf, men's, 73, 106, 117, 134; golf, women's, 181; softball, 38, 93; track and field, women's, 92,

107, 150–151; volleyball, 221, 228, 234
University of Texas at El Paso (UTEP), 109, 168, 213
University of Texas at San Antonio, 72
University of the Incarnate Word, 93
University of Virginia, 61
University of Washington, 229
University of Wisconsin, 165, 215, 218
US Amateur Championship, 130
USC. *See* University of Southern California
USFL. *See* United States Football League
US Men's Clay Court Championship, 80
US Open (bowling), 69
US Open (men's golf), 63, 73, 133; absence of, from Texas, 95; Ben Hogan wins, 111, 130, 158; Tom Kite wins, 117; Jordan Spieth wins, 118; Payne Stewart wins, 116, 196; Lee Trevino wins, 114–115, 128, 131
US Open (tennis), 22
US Women's Open (golf), 128, 177, 181
Utah Jazz, 31, 84, 86, 90
UTEP. *See* University of Texas at El Paso

Valentine, Bobby, 83
Valenzuela, Fernando, 211
Valparaiso University, 30
Vancouver Canucks, 74
Vanderbilt University, 45
Van Exel, Nick, 100
van Niekerk, Wayde, 149
Varsity Equestrian National Championships, 76
Venetoulias, Terry, 159, 182
Ventura, Robin, 2, 125, 145–146, *145*
Victoria High School, Victoria, 44, 238
Villanova University, 59
Virginia Commonwealth University, 55
Virginia Slims of Dallas, 176
Vitek, Cristin, *96*, 97
Vogler, Matt, 202
Vollmer, Dana, 140
Vosberg, Ed, 131
Voskuil, Alan, 44

Wacker, Jim, 209
Waddell, Tom, 137
Wade, Dwyane, 110
Wagner, Honus, 15
Wakaluk, Darcy, 74
Wake Forest University, 164
Walker, Doak, 199, 223
Walker, Herschel, 187
Walkup, Thomas, 55
Walling, Denny, 160, 189

Walls, Everson, 10
Walsh, Bill, 64, 159
Wangrin, Mark, 93
Ware, Andre, 202, *222*, 223
Wariner, Jeremy, 149
Washington, James, 14
Washington, Tyrone, 21
Washington Bullets, 84
Washington Redskins, 149, 228, 230, 233
Watson, Tom, 73
Watt, J. J., 9
Wayland Baptist University, 204
Weatherspoon, Chuck, 202
Webb, Anthony "Spud," 28
Webber, Chris, 67
Weber, Brianté, 55
Weir, Trey, 213
Welker, Wes, 183
Wells, David, 34
Wente, Suzy, 221
Wersching, Ray, 10
Wesley, DeMario, 94
Wesley, Milton, 94
Westbury High School, Houston, 78
Western Athletic Conference, 153, 163
Western Conference, 90, 92, 94, 97, 100
Western Michigan University, 240
Westlake High School, Austin, 28

Westside Tennis Club, Houston, 80
West Texas A&M University, 69
West Texas State University. *See* West Texas A&M University
Wheeless, Chance, 121
White, Danny, 179
White, Lakeesha, 107
White, Randy, 10, 13, 233
White, Tyra, 64
Whitesell, Amanda, 93
Whitfield, Fred, 232
Whitley, Jeff, 216
Whitley, Wilson, 169
Whitsett, Cory, 106
Whitworth, Kathy, 91, 136, 139, 155, *155*
Wilkins, Dominique, 28
Wilkinson, Laura, 176, 246
Willard, Jess, 126
Williams, Christa, 93
Williams, Maddi, 76
Williams, Malcolm, 199
Williams, Ricky, 216–218, *217*
Williams, Roy, 184
Williams, Ted, 76
Williams, Walter Ray, Jr., 69
Willowridge High School (Fort Bend ISD), Houston, 37, 59
Wilmer-Hutchins High School, Dallas, 29
Wilmoth, Kim, 97
Wilson, Bobby, 126
Wilson High School, Dallas, 63

Wimbledon, 22, 121, 126, 127
Windthorst High School, Windsthorst, 214
Winfield, Dave, 110
Winslow, Ricky, 6
Wissel, Liz, 72
Witten, Jason, 8
WNBA. *See* Women's National Basketball Association
Women's College World Series, 38, 93, 99, 100, 103, 105, 106
Women's National Basketball Association (WNBA), 161, 235
Women's Western Open, 120, 155
Women's World Cup (soccer), 160
Wood, Craig, 118
Wood, Gordon, 206, 238
Wood, Kerry, 86
Woodard, George, 218
Woodard, Ricci, 72
Wooden, John, 15, 52, 59
Woods, Robert, 216
Woods, Tiger, 67, 70, 95, 118, 196
Woodson, Darren, 187
Woosnam, Ian, 117
Wootten, Morgan, 30
World Championships in Athletics. *See* IAAF World Championships
World Championship Tennis final, 81
World Cup (soccer), 112

World Series (baseball), 34, 160,
188, 189, 190, 192, 194, 198.
See also American League
Championship Series; American League Division Series;
National League Championship Series; National League
Division Series
Worsley, Willie, 52
Worster, Steve, 186
Wortham, Richard, 113
Wright, George, 15
Wright, Joey, 57
Wylie High School, Abilene, 169

Xavier University, 57

Yancey, Bert, 115
Yates High School, Houston, 44
Yerkes, Steve, 190
Young, Cy, 15
Young, Jimmy, 195
Young, Michael, 6, 40, 61, 194
Young, Sophia, 66, *66*
Young, Steve, 14, 238
Young, Vince, 168

Zachry, Pat, 125
Zaharias, Babe Didrikson, 120,
141, *141*, 181
Zemenova, Zuzana, 101
Zenner, Patti, 214
Zmeskal, Kim, 144